EARLY CHILDHOOD EDUCATION SERIES

Sharon Ryan, *Editor*

Teaching and Learning in a Diverse World, 4th Ed.
PATRICIA G. RAMSEY

In the Spirit of the Studio
Learning from the *Atelier* of Reggio Emilia, 2nd Ed.
LELLA GANDINI, LYNN HILL, LOUISE CADWELL,
AND CHARLES SCHWALL, EDS.

Leading Anti-Bias Early Childhood Programs
A Guide for Change
LOUISE DERMAN-SPARKS, DEBBIE LEEKEENAN,
& JOHN NIMMO

Exploring Mathematics Through Play in the Early
Childhood Classroom
AMY NOELLE PARKS

Becoming Young Thinkers:
Deep Project Work in the Classroom
JUDY HARRIS HELM

The Early Years Matter: Education, Care, and the
Well-Being of Children, Birth to 8
MARILOU HYSON AND HEATHER BIGGAR TOMLINSON

Thinking Critically About Environments for Young
Children: Bridging Theory and Practice
LISA P. KUH, ED.

Standing Up for Something Every Day:
Ethics and Justice in Early Childhood Classrooms
BEATRICE S. FENNIMORE

FirstSchool: Transforming PreK–3rd Grade for African
American, Latino, and Low-Income Children
SHARON RITCHIE & LAURA GUTMANN, EDS.

The States of Child Care: Building a Better System
SARA GABLE

Early Childhood Education for a New Era:
Leading for Our Profession
STACIE G. GOFFIN

Everyday Artists: Inquiry and Creativity in the
Early Childhood Classroom
DANA FRANTZ BENTLEY

Multicultural Teaching in the Early Childhood
Classroom: Approaches, Strategies, and Tools,
Preschool–2nd Grade
MARIANA SOUTO-MANNING

Inclusion in the Early Childhood Classroom:
What Makes a Difference?
SUSAN L. RECCHIA & YOON-JOO LEE

Language Building Blocks:
Essential Linguistics for Early Childhood Educators
ANITA PANDEY

Understanding the Language Development and Early
Education of Hispanic Children
EUGENE E. GARCÍA & ERMINDA H. GARCÍA

Moral Classrooms, Moral Children: Creating a
Constructivist Atmosphere in Early Education, 2nd Ed.
RHETA DEVRIES & BETTY ZAN

Defending Childhood:
Keeping the Promise of Early Education
BEVERLY FALK, ED.

Don't Leave the Story in the Book: Using Literature to
Guide Inquiry in Early Childhood Classrooms
MARY HYNES-BERRY

Starting with Their Strengths: Using the Project
Approach in Early Childhood Special Education
DEBORAH C. LICKEY & DENISE J. POWERS

The Play's the Thing:
Teachers' Roles in Children's Play, 2nd Ed.
ELIZABETH JONES & GRETCHEN REYNOLDS

Twelve Best Practices for Early Childhood Education:
Integrating Reggio and Other Inspired Approaches
ANN LEWIN-BENHAM

Big Science for Growing Minds:
Constructivist Classrooms for Young Thinkers
JACQUELINE GRENNON BROOKS

What If All the Kids Are White? Anti-Bias Multicultural
Education with Young Children and Families, 2nd Ed.
LOUISE DERMAN-SPARKS & PATRICIA G. RAMSEY

Seen and Heard:
Children's Rights in Early Childhood Education
ELLEN LYNN HALL & JENNIFER KOFKIN RUDKIN

Young Investigators: The Project Approach in the
Early Years, 2nd Ed.
JUDY HARRIS HELM & LILIAN G. KATZ

Supporting Boys' Learning: Strategies for Teacher
Practice, PreK–Grade 3
BARBARA SPRUNG, MERLE FROSCHL, & NANCY GROPPER

To look for other titles in this series, visit www.tcpress.com

(continued)

Early Childhood Education Series, *continued*

Young English Language Learners: Current Research and Emerging Directions for Practice and Policy
EUGENE E. GARCÍA & ELLEN C. FREDE, EDS.

Connecting Emergent Curriculum and Standards in the Early Childhood Classroom:
Strengthening Content and Teacher Practice
SYDNEY L. SCHWARTZ & SHERRY M. COPELAND

Infants and Toddlers at Work: Using Reggio-Inspired Materials to Support Brain Development
ANN LEWIN-BENHAM

The View from the Little Chair in the Corner:
Improving Teacher Practice and Early Childhood Learning (Wisdom from an Experienced Classroom Observer)
CINDY RZASA BESS

Culture and Child Development in Early Childhood Programs: Practices for Quality Education and Care
CAROLLEE HOWES

The Early Intervention Guidebook for Families and Professionals: Partnering for Success
BONNIE KEILTY

The Story in the Picture:
Inquiry and Artmaking with Young Children
CHRISTINE MULCAHEY

Educating and Caring for Very Young Children:
The Infant/Toddler Curriculum, 2nd Ed.
DORIS BERGEN, REBECCA REID, & LOUIS TORELLI

Beginning School:
U.S. Policies in International Perspective
RICHARD M. CLIFFORD & GISELE M. CRAWFORD, EDS.

Emergent Curriculum in the Primary Classroom
CAROL ANNE WIEN, ED.

Enthusiastic and Engaged Learners
MARILOU HYSON

Powerful Children: Understanding How to Teach and Learn Using the Reggio Approach
ANN LEWIN-BENHAM

The Early Care and Education Teaching Workforce at the Fulcrum: An Agenda for Reform
SHARON LYNN KAGAN, KRISTIE KAUERZ, & KATE TARRANT

Windows on Learning:
Documenting Young Children's Work, 2nd Ed.
JUDY HARRIS HELM, SALLEE BENEKE, & KATHY STEINHEIMER

Ready or Not:
Leadership Choices in Early Care and Education
STACIE G. GOFFIN & VALORA WASHINGTON

Supervision in Early Childhood Education, 3rd Ed.
JOSEPH J. CARUSO WITH M. TEMPLE FAWCETT

Guiding Children's Behavior
EILEEN S. FLICKER & JANET ANDRON HOFFMAN

The War Play Dilemma, 2nd Ed.
DIANE E. LEVIN & NANCY CARLSSON-PAIGE

Possible Schools
ANN LEWIN-BENHAM

Everyday Goodbyes
NANCY BALABAN

Playing to Get Smart
ELIZABETH JONES & RENATTA M. COOPER

How to Work with Standards in the Early Childhood Classroom
CAROL SEEFELDT

Understanding Assessment and Evaluation in Early Childhood Education, 2nd Ed.
DOMINIC F. GULLO

The Emotional Development of Young Children, 2nd Ed.
MARILOU HYSON

Effective Partnering for School Change
JIE-QI CHEN ET AL.

Young Children Continue to Reinvent Arithmetic—2nd Grade, 2nd Ed.
CONSTANCE KAMII

Bringing Learning to Life
LOUISE BOYD CADWELL

The Colors of Learning
ROSEMARY ALTHOUSE, MARGARET H. JOHNSON, & SHARON T. MITCHELL

A Matter of Trust
CAROLLEE HOWES & SHARON RITCHIE

Embracing Identities in Early Childhood Education
SUSAN GRIESHABER & GAILE S. CANNELLA, EDS.

Bambini: The Italian Approach to Infant/Toddler Care
LELLA GANDINI & CAROLYN POPE EDWARDS, EDS.

Serious Players in the Primary Classroom, 2nd Ed.
SELMA WASSERMANN

Young Children Reinvent Arithmetic, 2nd Ed.
CONSTANCE KAMII

Bringing Reggio Emilia Home
LOUISE BOYD CADWELL

Teaching and Learning in a Diverse World

Multicultural Education for Young Children

FOURTH EDITION

Patricia G. Ramsey

Foreword by
Sonia Nieto

TEACHERS COLLEGE PRESS

TEACHERS COLLEGE | COLUMBIA UNIVERSITY
NEW YORK AND LONDON

Published by Teachers College Press, 1234 Amsterdam Avenue,
New York, NY 10027

Library of Congress Cataloging-in-Publication Data

Ramsey, Patricia G.
Teaching and learning in a diverse world : multicultural education for young
children / Patricia G. Ramsey ; foreword by Sonia Nieto. — Fourth edition.
    pages cm. — (Early childhood education series)
  Includes bibliographical references and index.
  ISBN 978-0-8077-5625-6 (pbk. : alk. paper)
  ISBN 978-0-8077-7362-8 (ebook)
    1. Multicultural education—United States. 2. Multiculturalism—Study and
  teaching (Early childhood)—United States. 3. Early childhood education—
  United States. 4. Educational sociology—United States. 5. Teaching—United
  States. I. Title.
LC1099.3.R36 2015
370.117--dc23   2014050015

ISBN 978-0-8077-5625-6 (paperback)
ISBN 978-0-8077-7362-8 (ebook)

Printed on acid-free paper
Manufactured in the United States of America

In memory of my father
Norman F. Ramsey, Jr.
1915–2011

Contents

Foreword *by Sonia Nieto*   ix
Preface   xiii
Acknowledgments   xv

PART I: MULTICULTURAL SCHOOLS AND CLASSROOMS   1

1. **Growing Up in a World of Contradictions and Injustices:**
   A Multicultural Response   3
   Purpose, Trends, and Scope of Multicultural Education   6
   Multicultural Goals for Children   9
   Families and Schools Working Together   12
   The Language of Multicultural Education   12

2. **We Are All Learning**   15
   How Adults Can Identify and Challenge Their Assumptions   18
   How Children Learn About Their Worlds   20

3. **Creating Caring and Critical Communities**   38
   Creating Caring and Critical Communities Among Adults   40
   Creating Caring and Critical Classroom Communities   50

PART II: CONTEXTS OF LEARNING   63

4. **The Context of Race**   65
   Reflections on Race   65
   Growing Up in a Racially Divided Society   66
   Children's Responses to Race   73
   Learning and Challenging What Children Know,
      Think, and Feel About Race   79

5. **The Context of Economic Class and Consumerism**   84
   Reflections on Economic Class   84
   Socioeconomic Divisions in the United States   86
   Children's Awareness and Feelings About Economic Class   94
   Reflections on Consumerism   97
   Living in a Consumerist Society   98
   Children's Understanding and Experience of Consumerism   99
   Learning and Challenging What Children Know,
      Think, and Feel About Economic Class and Consumerism   102

6. **The Context of Culture and the Natural Environment**   **107**
    Reflections on Culture   107
    Children and Culture   109
    Learning About and Challenging What Children Know,
        Think, and Feel About Culture   118
    Reflections on Culture and the Natural Environment   120
    Children's Knowledge, Attitudes, and Feelings About
        the Natural Environment and Sustainability   122
    Learning and Challenging What Children Know,
        Think, and Feel About the Natural Environment   126

7. **The Context of Gender and Heteronormativity**   **132**
    Reflections on Gender Identification and Roles   132
    Growing Up in a Gendered and Heteronormative World   134
    Children's Responses to Gender   136
    Reflections on Sexual Orientations and Identities   139
    Growing Up in a Heterosexist World   141
    Children's Understanding of Sexual Orientation and Identity   144
    Learning and Challenging What Children Know,
        Think, and Feel About Gender and Sexual Orientation   145

8. **The Context of Abilities and Disabilities**   **152**
    Reflections on Abilities and Disabilities   152
    Growing Up in an "Abled" World   154
    Social Participation of Children with Disabilities   157
    Children's Knowledge and Feelings
        Related to Abilities and Disabilities   162
    Learning and Challenging What Children Know,
        Think, and Feel About Abilities and Disabilities   164

Conclusion   **169**

References   **171**
Index   **195**
About the Author   **208**

Foreword

Multicultural education has been through many changes since Patricia Ramsey and I first met as doctoral students in 1975. That autumn, a course taught by Professor Bob Suzuki was a magnet for us both. It was the first course on multicultural education that had ever been taught on our campus and, as it turned out, it changed our lives, both personally and professionally. Patty (as she is known to her friends and family) and I were electrified by the ideas, questions, and challenges at the core of that and subsequent courses. Bob Suzuki became a valued mentor to us both, always impressing upon us that multicultural education was far more than adding ethnic content to the curriculum. In those invigorating days when multicultural education was in its infancy, Patty and I spent many hours talking about and puzzling through issues concerning diversity, racism, social justice, and many others we studied and lived with daily. A central question for us concerned what our roles might be in helping to move education in a direction that would be more just, equitable, and affirming.

Consequently, when Patricia Ramsey's *Teaching and Learning in a Diverse World* was first published in 1988, I welcomed it both as the first book of a dear friend and colleague, and as a significant contribution to the field we both loved. Before this, few books had considered what it meant to include a multicultural perspective in the places where our very youngest children are educated, preschools and daycare centers. Some early childhood educators and parents went so far as to suggest that a multicultural approach was too "serious," too "solemn," too "dangerous" for very young children. Others limited their concerns to what has come to be called a "holidays and heroes approach": that is, that it was fine to celebrate Chinese New Year, Chanukah, and Cinco de Mayo, and it was acceptable to invite parents to school to cook spaghetti or to teach the polka, but racism and sexism, or institutional and structural barriers to equal education and other concerns about social justice were not deemed suitable for early childhood education. These matters were thought to be best left for older students. Patricia Ramsey's book became one of the first to fill a conspicuous void by directly addressing these issues, and doing so in appropriate and developmentally sensitive ways in early childhood settings.

It was also true at the time that traditional human development texts rarely examined race, ethnicity, social class, gender, or other aspects of diversity. Most human development theories were presented as universal in spite of the fact that they consistently drew their examples primarily from the lives of middle-class European American children. Even the covers of most human development texts at the time featured White children exclusively, as if they were representative of all children in our schools and early childhood centers. Consequently, there was a wide divide between those few educators who advocated using a multicultural approach with young children and most developmentalists, who seldom ventured into discussions of diversity.

Fortunately, Patricia Ramsey came along and wrote her now-classic text to address both of these crucial issues. She honestly and directly confronted racism, sexism, and other institutional forms of discrimination as they might affect the education of young children, and she critically analyzed theories of child development that paid little attention to the cultural, social, and political contexts of children's lives. Hers was also one of the first multicultural education texts to take language differences seriously by including a substantial discussion on language development and bilingual education. In subsequent editions, she introduced other themes to the multicultural conversation, issues such as moral development, economic diversity, environmental concerns, and consumerism. In doing so, she challenged us to recognize that multicultural education is not just about racial and ethnic diversity, but about diversity in its many manifestations. On the other hand, she has not lost sight of the original goal of multicultural education: to make education equitable for those children who have historically been most miseducated by our schools, specifically poor children and children of color. The synthesis of issues of diversity, with concerns about the economy, the environment, and consumerism, makes *Teaching and Learning in a Diverse World* a unique contribution to the field.

In this 4th edition, Patty has made more important changes. Visiting numerous schools and early childhood centers here and around the globe, she has retained the theoretical rigor of her approach while combining it with even more practical applications, an approach certain to be appreciated by the many practitioners who find this book so instrumental to their work. The numerous vignettes and activities she has woven throughout the text also helps define what multicultural education means in concrete settings of all kinds, from rural to urban, from multicultural to more homogeneous settings. In this edition, Patty has also confronted the current context of accountability, standardization, and the privatization of public education, issues that have further eroded the efforts of teachers and others to provide an antiracist, bias-free, and equitable education for all students. She has not retreated from her commitment to prepare teachers to work for a more socially just society, but she understands that the issues of equity, diversity, and social justice are more complex than she and I once thought at the dawn of the field. Nevertheless, as in previous editions, she has taken on the most daunting of tasks: guiding teachers to help our very youngest children make sense of this complex world by becoming curious, critical, and compassionate learners.

Patricia Ramsey has written a text to which there are no easy answers. Instead, in these pages she questions, coaxes, and inspires readers to be reflective and critical teachers so that education can become liberating, fulfilling, and meaningful for even our youngest children. She reminds us that teaching is not a technical activity, but rather that it is fundamentally a decisionmaking and political process that can forever change the lives of all those who experience it, be they children, educators, or parents.

Sonia Nieto

Preface

The four editions of *Teaching and Learning in a Diverse World* mirror my life and the times in which we live. The first edition, written in the 1980s, reflected the optimism of the early days of the multicultural movement that we believed would transform education so that it would realize the hopes and goals of the Civil Rights Movement.

The second edition was written in the mid-1990s, when my children, Daniel and Alejandro, both adopted from Chile, were in preschool and primary grades in a small town in Mexico, where we lived for 2 years. My joy at watching them grow and learn was tempered by the realization that, despite 2 decades of multicultural education and many other reforms, discrimination and economic inequities still divided our society and the larger world.

When I wrote the third edition in the early 2000s, Daniel and Alejandro were young teens and valiantly trying to weave together their adolescent identities from the many strands of their lives. The fissures that tear the fabric of our society became even clearer to me as I saw my sons struggling to bridge the gap between their White middle-class parents' expectations and the pervasive stereotypes of Latino males.

As I write this fourth edition, my sons are in their 20s and continuing to negotiate these tensions as well as trying to make their way in a devastated economy with diminished opportunities for young adults. They and their friends, all of whom work in minimum wage service jobs, are living examples of the economic inequities and downward mobility that are affecting millions of people around the world.

As international and transracial adoptees, my sons face particular challenges, but their struggles are not unique. The prospects of many college graduates, and even those with professional degrees, are undermined by shrinking opportunities. Young people also are struggling to define their values in a world where caring and social justice are often overwhelmed by the media that glorify racism, sexism, homophobia, violence, and greed. In the face of these challenges and contradictions, it is tempting to yield to cynicism and self-destructive behaviors. Yet, as the true effects of our inequitable economic and political systems are unmasked, more people, young people in particular, are recognizing the need for a profound reorientation of our society.

For the past 4 decades multicultural education has been a constant yet flexible force for raising questions and generating ideas to transform our schools and society. However, the path has not been smooth. The current push for accountability has resulted in an emphasis on testable academic skills that often crowds out curricula geared toward exploring and challenging societal divides and inequities. Increasingly, these pressures are affecting early childhood education. Moreover, endemic lack of funding means that many young children are denied access to programs, and underpaid and overworked teachers have little time to do the planning and reflection that multicultural education requires.

Yet many brave, wise, and compassionate educators are boldly moving forward, challenging inequities and transforming classrooms. To prepare for writing this fourth edition, I visited schools, met with teachers, and read many articles and books about current research and practice in multicultural education. I was humbled, challenged, and stretched by the insights and innovations of colleagues from all over the world and how they are using the social media to share ideas and support.

The book is divided into two parts. Part I, "Multicultural Schools and Classrooms," contains three chapters that review various dimensions of multicultural education and guidelines for their implementation. Part II, "Contexts of Learning," has five chapters. Each one explores how specific lines of division and their associated inequities in our society (race, economics, culture, gender/sexual identities and orientation, and abilities/disabilities) affect children's lives and worldviews and how we can encourage children to challenge inequities related to them.

While writing this edition, I was inspired by the wealth of ideas, programs, and practices across many communities and countries. However due to space limitations in the printed book, some material has been moved to the Teachers College Press website. Throughout the book you will see references to supplemental resources at www.tcpress.com (click on "Free Downloads," scroll down to this book). I encourage you to explore these online materials and to use them along with the book itself to reflect on your practice; to initiate conversations with colleagues, parents, and children; and to collectively work toward creating truly multicultural classrooms.

Acknowledgments

Many people have made it possible for me to write this edition of *Teaching and Learning in a Diverse World*. First, many thanks to my colleagues at Mount Holyoke College, especially those in the Department of Psychology and Education, for supporting me in ways too numerous to count. Many members of the current and past staff at Gorse Children's Center, including Janna Aldrich, Jean Guarda, Susannah Heard, Helen Johnson, Mary Ellen Marion, Candace Ribiero-Gagnon, Valerie Sawka, Leela Sundquist, and Barbara Sweeney, have been a source of inspiration; a number of the ideas in this book are based on their insights about children and their creative curricula.

In preparation for writing this edition, I visited the Eliot-Pearson School at Tufts University and had the privilege of observing several inspiring classrooms and talking with Debbie LeeKeenan, who was the director at that time, and the following teachers: Maggie Beneke, Chris Bucco, Heidi Given, Maryann O'Brien, and David Robinson. Thank you also to John Nimmo, former director of the Child Study and Development Center at the University of New Hampshire, for inviting me to come and observe there. I had wonderful conversations with the following teachers: EJ Albin, Sandy Cormier, Karen DuBois-Garofalo, Beth Gachowski, Jamie Gleason, Beth Hallett, Shannon Johanson, Sarah Jones, Sarah Leonard, Pam Battin-Sacks, and Harlee Tuttle.

Over the past decades many friends and colleagues have had the patience to hear me talk through the ideas and issues in this book, and the compassion and integrity to push me to see some of my blind spots and contradictions. Thank you especially to Andrea Ayvezian, Sherryl Graves, Louise Derman-Sparks, Sandra Lawrence, Sonia Nieto, Sherri Oden, Beverly Tatum, Angela Taylor, Edwina Battle Vold, and Leslie Williams.

Many ideas for this fourth edition were stimulated by working for the past 4 years with colleagues in Una, an international network of researchers and practitioners committed to reducing racial and ethnic divisions by promoting effective early childhood programs. I am particularly grateful for the chance to work closely with the members of my learning group: Deevia Bhana (South Africa), Audrey D'Souza Juma (Pakistan), Anke van Keulenthe (the Netherlands), Sumalee Kumchaiskul (Thailand), Glenda

MacNaughton (Australia), Rohaty Mohd Majzub (Malaysia), and Sri Marpinjun (Indonesia).

I am very grateful to all the people at Teachers College Press who encouraged me to do this project and expedited its completion. A special thanks to Susan Liddicoat who skillfully and patiently supported me through several drafts. Marie Ellen Larcada has provided wonderful support and guidance on a number of writing projects over the years. Thank you so much, Marie Ellen, and best wishes as you start your retirement.

As always, my sons Daniel and Alejandro are my primary teachers—shaking me from my complacency, challenging my expectations, and inspiring me to push myself because I want them to live in a better world. My husband, Fred Moseley, continues to be my main supporter and best friend and my truest colleague in every way.

PART I

MULTICULTURAL SCHOOLS AND CLASSROOMS

This section of the book provides an overview of different aspects of multicultural learning. Chapter 1 describes the dilemmas of raising and teaching children in a world of contradictions and inequities and discusses how different approaches and goals of multicultural education potentially address these issues. Chapter 2 illustrates how all of us—adults and children—learn concepts and attitudes about the world and how we can challenge our assumptions and broaden our perspectives through discussions and classroom activities and materials. Chapter 3 makes a case for creating caring, cooperative, and critical communities and the roles that adults and children play in this process.

CHAPTER 1

Growing Up in a World of Contradictions and Injustices: A Multicultural Response

Alison and Stephanie (both European American 3-year-olds) are busily feeding their (light-skinned) baby dolls and bustling about the kitchen of the housekeeping corner, chatting about how their babies won't sleep. Sofia (a Mexican American 3-year-old) bounces up, holding a darker skinned baby doll. She grins broadly at Alison and Stephanie and announces, "We came to visit!" Alison and Stephanie stop what they are doing and stare at Sofia. Then Stephanie says (in an adult-like voice), "I'm sorry; we *have* to go shopping." Alison and Stephanie toss their babies into a stroller and head out of the area. They walk across the classroom, talking about what they are going to buy. Sofia stares after them, a small frown on her face. Then she enters the area, plops her doll in a high chair and lifts a spoon to her baby's mouth a few times, all the while looking after Alison and Stephanie as they stroll around the classroom.

Terrance (a biracial child adopted by a European American family), Jeremy, and Sam (both European American) are building a highway in the block corner of their K–1 classroom. All three boys are 6 years old; Terrance and Jeremy live in a relatively affluent neighborhood; Sam lives with his mother in a subsidized apartment complex. As they begin to move cars along their highway, Terrance says, "When we drove to see my grandma, we got to watch three DVDs— that's how long it took to get there!" Jeremy says, "When we watch DVDs in our car, my sister and I fight over what to watch so my parents are going to get another DVD player so we can each have our own." As this conversation goes on, Sam looks down, his shoulders slumped. He starts sorting through the blocks on the floor and picks up a triangle piece. "Look," he says, "We can use this to keep the robbers off of the highway!" As he goes to put the piece on the highway, he (accidentally) knocks off a few pieces already in place. Both Jeremy and Terrance yell, "Hey! Stop that!" Jeremy then hisses to Sam, "You stupid retard!" Sam frowns and hisses back, "You faggot!" A teacher approaches the area and asks if there is anything wrong. All three boys look down and silently and industriously start adding blocks to their construction.

3

These events that I observed in a preschool and a K–1 classroom are similar to ones that occur dozens of times a day in early childhood settings. Each lasted less than 3 minutes and neither was particularly dramatic or remarkable: two close friends "politely" rejected the entry of a third child; two boys expressed annoyance at a peer who knocked down part of their construction. The overt disputes were fleeting, and the children did not request adult help. In fact, the boys pointedly ignored the teacher. To be honest, had I been a teacher rather than an observer, I would probably not have noticed these momentary conflicts. I would have been too busy—replenishing paint cups, attending to a crying child, helping a child record her story, or working with a reading group.

Yet these short episodes reveal how young children are constructing their views of the world and interpreting the attitudes and values that pervade our society. As I reflect on these observations, many questions come to mind. Was it coincidence that the children I observed were playing in gender-segregated groups, or is that a common pattern in these classrooms? Were Stephanie and Alison simply protecting their time together? Or were they reacting to Sofia's darker skin? Or did the manner of her arrival make them uncomfortable—possibly reflecting cultural differences? Is Sofia, who is the only Latina in the classroom, rejected by other European American classmates? If so, what is she learning and feeling about herself and her family? What gender roles are all three girls enacting? What early economic views are children expressing when they go "shopping"?

How does Sam, whose mother does not own a car, feel when his friends talk about watching DVDs in their cars? How conscious are these three children of the economic disparities among them? What role does competitive consumerism play in their relationships? What are children learning when conflicts are resolved by purchasing additional equipment? What values about the environment and land use are all three boys expressing as they build a bigger and better highway, filled with cars and trucks? Do the boys know what "retard" and "faggot" mean? How do these insults reflect and influence their developing attitudes about people with disabilities or about gender roles and sexual orientation?

Our children are growing up in a world of contradictions. On one hand, they are learning that all people are "created equal" (Declaration of Independence) and that we as a nation are united to provide for the common good (Constitution). Yet, as these observations illustrate, children are learning that some groups are valued more than others, that it is acceptable to exclude classmates, and that material wealth is a source of individual status and control.

One simple but useful way of thinking about these issues is to consider the two meanings of the word *race*. In one sense we are running in a race, whether it is to get the newest toys, the best grades, the biggest house, or the latest electronics. Even collaborative activities such as sports teams or cooperative work groups function in a competitive context that can undermine teamwork.

As competitors in this race, we can only win as much as others lose. To ensure that there will always be someone behind us, we divide humanity by *race* (among many attributes) and accord some groups more power than others. In biological terms, race is a meaningless concept. There are more genetic differences within "racial groups" (a slippery concept that has been defined and disputed repeatedly) than across them. However, for much of human history and throughout the world people have created "racial" divisions (often based on little or no visible physical differences) to justify exclusion, slavery, and genocide (e.g., the Romans enslaved the Britons; the British subjugated the Irish; the Europeans and European Americans enslaved the Africans; the Nazis killed millions of Jewish people).

Race has been an intractable division in our country since the arrival of the European settlers in the 17th century. Many of the men who wrote and signed the Declaration of Independence and the Constitution, which extol liberty and the equality of all people, took for granted their right to kill and cheat the American Indians in order to obtain their lands; and few questioned the practice of buying, owning, and selling slaves. By accepting and codifying these contradictions, our forebears established the precedent that private ownership, material wealth, and profits take precedence over the ideals of liberty and equality.

As immigrants arrived, those who could quickly learned to identify themselves as White in order to distinguish themselves from the lower-status African Americans and Indian, Mexican, or Chinese Americans. The racism that lies at the core of our national identity has established a pattern of exploitation and marginalization that has been played out with varying levels of intensity against immigrants, women, poor people, the elderly, children, gay men and lesbian women, and people with disabilities.

At the same time, many of the fixed divisions that we have taken for granted (e.g., race, culture, gender) are becoming increasingly blurred and inconsistent with the current social reality. Borders among groups are fluid and complex and are spaces that foster creativity, new ideas, and more in-depth understanding (Atkinson, 2009, Skott-Myhre, 2012).

The intersections among divisions emerge in many aspects of our lives. First, all of us have a number of identities and are often caught in the complicated cross-currents of advantage and disadvantage. For example, a poor White woman is racially privileged but may resent the economic advantage of the middle-class Black woman next to her in the supermarket checkout line. Generally in our society, men enjoy more power and privilege than women, but African American men are more vulnerable than African American women to unemployment and incarceration. Some gay men have more buying power than their heterosexual peers because their households include two highly paid male professionals. At the same time, they live with the threat of harassment and violence. A child born with cerebral palsy is clearly at a disadvantage in many respects. However, if she is from an affluent family, her access to services may mean that her prospects for a good education and gainful employment are better than those of a child with no identified disabilities raised in a poor family.

Second, we are also living in a time of rapid social change and are seeing shifts in what it means to belong to particular groups. For example, gender roles and sexual identities have expanded and changed over the past few decades. Furthermore, as groups come into contact, more children have multicultural and multiracial backgrounds that embrace many traditions and values.

Rapid globalization has blurred international boundaries. Through social media, news about disasters and injustices is quickly disseminated, and people all over the world can join together to pressure officials or corporations to stop mistreating vulnerable groups and destroying fragile environments. However, globalization has also meant that the exploitation of human and natural resources has increased in scale and intensity. Governments and corporations can more easily collude to destroy natural habitats and build unsafe factories in poor countries to provide cheap goods for wealthier markets. Likewise the wide-ranging migrations of many groups have resulted in more diverse communities and potential cross-cultural connections. Yet these demographic shifts have also caused many intergroup tensions.

Thus, it is necessary to critically question long-held assumptions about national, racial, gender, and cultural divisions. At the same time many individuals and institutions still hold expectations and stereotypes based on these distinctions that, in turn, profoundly affect the life prospects of individuals and groups.

PURPOSE, TRENDS, AND SCOPE OF MULTICULTURAL EDUCATION

The purpose of multicultural education is to engage children in understanding and challenging the injustices that divide and diminish their world. Goals include the development of stable yet flexible identities, solidarity with others, critical thinking, and liberatory action (Banks, 1999; Derman-Sparks & Edwards, 2010; Gay, 2000; Gollnick & Chinn 1998; Kendall, 1996; Nieto & Bode, 2012; Sleeter & Grant, 1988).

Over the past 4 decades multicultural education has shifted from surface portrayals and celebrations of cultural diversity to deeper analyses of power and oppression and the need for radical social and economic change. The scope has also broadened since the movement began in the 1970s, when the focus was primarily on race and culture. However, it quickly became apparent that the effects of social class and economic discrimination also

needed to be included. Then the feminist movement demonst
der inequities cut across race, culture, and class, and they b
the conversation. As people with disabilities and their famil
their educational and occupational marginalization, these issu
woven into the multicultural conversation. In the 1980s and 19
orientation and identities became another theme in multicultural   ucation
in recognition of the harassment and discrimination targeting gay men, lesbian women, and bisexual and transgendered individuals.

Over the past few decades the connections between the exploitation of
people and the destruction of the natural environment have become clearer
(Bowers, 2001; Running-Grass, 1994). Because this dimension of multicultural education is often overlooked, I will discuss in more detail how it is an
essential part of social justice work.

First, poor communities and countries suffer the effects of environmental degradation far more than affluent ones do. Toxic waste dumps, unregu-
lated factories, unsafe water, and smog are far more common in areas where
poor people of color who have less political clout live (Bullard, 2005, 2014;
Center on Race, Poverty, and the Environment, 2011). In 1982 the people of
Afton, North Carolina, a poor Black rural community, resisted the dumping
of toxic PCBs in their community landfill. This protest and the subsequent
investigations revealed a clear pattern of siting hazardous waste sites in
communities of color throughout the South, and the Environmental Justice
Movement (EJM) was born (Skelton & Miller, 2006). In the 1990s leaders
of the EJM pressured traditional White environmental groups (e.g., Sierra
Club) to address these issues, and many of these organizations became allies
in the struggle. Together they gained some political clout. In 1994 President
Clinton signed an order directing federal agencies to "identify and address
disproportionately high adverse health or environmental effects of their policies or programs on low-income people and people of color" (Skelton &
Miller, 2006, p. 2). Many low-income communities have taken up the cause
and are reclaiming land, making riverside parks, and growing gardens in
abandoned lots in cities; and the EJM has grown from 400 groups in 1994
to 3,000 in 2013. Unfortunately, however, efforts to clean up sites and protect poor communities from further environmental degradation are woe-
fully underfunded, so there is still much to do (Bullard, 2014). These issues
are not unique to the United States as indicated by the recent protests of
indigenous groups in Bolivia, Colombia, and Ecuador (among many other
places) against their governments and international companies over plans to
extract resources from indigenous lands.

Poor people also are disproportionally affected by climate change. They
often live in areas that are more prone to floods or landslides; their houses
are less likely to withstand the effects of hurricanes; and the rise in food
prices that results from climate change–related droughts, freezes, and infes-
tations has more impact on their budgets.

In addition to the environmental inequities that clearly are relevant to multicultural education, an ecological perspective enables us to see the world and our similarities and differences in a more holistic way. We all live on the same planet, breathe the same air, and drink the same water; ultimately it is in everyone's interest to conserve and protect our natural resources. As we learn more about the interconnections among ecological systems, we know that polluting in one area or squandering resources in another eventually has an impact on all of us.

Moreover, the multicultural focus on learning about diverse values and ways of life open up new ways of perceiving and enacting alternatives to the "conquering nature" mentality that has created widespread environmental degradation. For example, Rigoberta Menchu (1983), Nobel Peace Prize winner in 1992, describes how her people, the Quiche (Mayan) Indians of Guatamala, respect and love all living things and pray to the Earth asking permission to cultivate the soil before planting their seeds. These practices are stark contrasts to large agribusinesses that maximize profits by raising animals in inhumane settings and harming consumers and the environment by using pesticides, hormones, and antibiotics. Menchu's perspective also provides a good counternarrative to the popular assumption that "progress" and the "good life" mean bigger cars and houses and more malls, roads, and parking lots. The integration of multicultural and ecological goals can lead to a more comprehensive critique of the privilege, power, and exploitation and open our minds to new possibilities.

In sum, I use the term *multiculturalism* in a broad sense and include in this book issues related to race, economic class, consumerism, culture, language, gender, sexual identities and orientation, abilities and disabilities, and our relationship to the natural world. To me, the term implies personal awareness and strength; critical analysis of the existing social, political, and economic structures; and participation in social justice movements. Throughout its history, multicultural education has been interpreted in many different ways and has been the site of many controversies both from within the field and from outside of it (for a review, see Ramsey & Williams, 2003). However, it continues to offer a comprehensive approach for encouraging children to understand their world and to work toward social justice. At the same time, multicultural education alone will not change the basic inequities of our society. Rather, it is a tool to prepare ourselves and our children to participate in that effort. (To learn about research on the outcomes of multicultural curriculum, see Supplemental Resource 1.1 for Chapter 1, at www.tcpress.com)

Multicultural education does not occur in a vacuum, and, before discussing specific goals and approaches, I want to acknowledge the vast inequities in our educational system at every level. All of us who care about children *must* do everything in our power to ensure that all children gain the academic skills that will give them access to the knowledge of our society and the power to make a difference. In particular, excellent schools in all communities, especially those with high rates of poverty, are a must, as are teaching practices that encourage all children to see that school and academic skills are relevant to their lives and can support rather than contradict their identities and critical perspectives.

Ironically, legislation geared to closing the gap in educational outcomes between affluent and poor children (No Child Left Behind Act of 2002 [NCLB]) has resulted in rigid high-stakes testing programs that are pushing many children out of school. Moreover, the emphasis on test preparation, resulting in scripted curriculum, has meant that teachers have little flexibility to create their own curriculum, build on children's interests, and engage them in complex discussions and activities that are at the heart of multicultural education.

Even though testing does not start until the primary grades, the anticipation of upcoming tests has meant that narrowly defined "school readiness" (or maybe it should be "test readiness") is now driving many early childhood programs. Moreover, state and national early childhood accreditation programs, designed to ensure quality programs for all groups, have become increasingly complex and require more and more documentation that impinges on the time teachers have to plan and work directly with children. As one well-known early childhood educator put it, "These days teachers are drowning in accountability. They spend more time documenting than teaching" (Mary Pat Martin, personal communication, June 2013).

On the positive side, I have seen many teachers creatively work within the constraints of the testing and accreditation—finding openings in even the most rigid curriculum to raise meaningful questions about the testing itself and to encourage children's interests. Also, these constraints are inspiring many students, teachers, and families to become activists as they pressure local and state education boards to ensure that the system is equitable and responsive to a wider range of backgrounds and learning and teaching styles.

MULTICULTURAL GOALS FOR CHILDREN

The heavy and controversial issues of oppression, exploitation, and social justice may seem to be a world away from young children. However, as evident in the observations that opened this chapter, young children are already constructing their ideas about power, privilege, and exploitation. Rather than let them come to misinformed conclusions (Pelo, 2008b), we can use a multicultural approach to encourage them to critically investigate and, when appropriate, challenge assumptions and inequities.

The following working goals provide a framework for this book. I use the term *working goals* for two reasons. First, as I learn more about the world, my goals and priorities change, and I expect that they will continue to evolve in years to come. The second reason is to encourage readers not to adopt these goals per se but to use them as a base to develop goals that are most appropriate to the priorities and experiences of their particular children, families, and communities.

Multicultural teaching requires critically analyzing our own knowledge and biases, our society, and the history of inequities from many perspectives, and closely observing and getting to know children and families (DiAngelo & Sensoy, 2010). Above all, multicultural work requires taking risks. Although the word *risk* is commonly associated with impulsive and irresponsible actions, taking risks can "be a thoughtful process involving individual agency and community responsibility in the pursuit of a different, but positive future for ourselves . . . and future generations (Robinson, 2005, p. 186). Multicultural education is not safe and predictable; it varies across situation, evolves over time, and is filled with surprises. The following goals are suggestive rather than prescriptive as we continually explore and debate what insights and skills children will need to navigate and challenge the contradictions and inequities of our society.

Strong Flexible Identities

Strong yet flexible and multifaceted identities—as individuals, as members of communities, and as living beings on this planet—provide children with a secure base for interacting with the world. Rather than learn about "how I am special" (a common theme in some self-esteem curricula), or "I am what I own" (the message from commercially driven media), children can explore and develop their interests and gain a confident yet realistic awareness of how they can contribute to their immediate and larger communities. Strong attachments to family, friends, and whatever groups and combinations of groups they belong to enable children to feel a sense of belonging to the society as a whole. Through deep connections to the natural world—to the rhythms of days and seasons that define our lives—children may begin to see themselves as inhabitants and sustainers, rather than conquerors, of their environment. Strong identities are neither static nor defined by a particular group or activity. They develop as children experiment with a range of roles and possible physical attributes (e.g., enacting a puppy or a firefighter, portraying themselves with purple skin) in their play and art work. These explorations lead to flexible, multifaceted identities that change over time.

Sense of Connection

A strong sense of solidarity with all people and the natural world enables children to broaden their range of connection and caring. By learning that human similarities and differences are continua, not polarities, they will be more comfortable meeting and working with people who at first glance may seem "different" and possibly threatening. As they learn how to recognize and manage their own feelings, they build their capacity to understand and empathize with others, and to care for all beings in their social and natural worlds.

Critical-Thinking Skills

By becoming critical thinkers, children gain the skills to challenge the status quo and to ask good, hard questions. Adults often assume that understanding broad issues of exploitation and inequality are beyond the capacity of most young children. However, when peers and adults ask meaningful questions and listen respectfully, children can be very astute and insightful. Often they recognize stereotyped messages in books, materials, and electronic media; and identify and challenge classroom, school, and community policies and practices that seem unfair and/or environmentally destructive.

Confidence and Persistence

By becoming confident and persistent-problem solvers, children will be able to take action rather than feel overwhelmed by the challenges of their immediate and broader worlds. Children's confidence will grow as they work with different materials and media, brainstorm solutions to problems, and see projects through to completion. As they engage in these activities, they gain skills in collaborating with others and developing creative and eclectic strategies. Learning about beliefs, tools, and technologies from many cultures potentially expands their ideas about how to conserve cultural diversity and natural resources and improve the quality of life for everyone. Stories of people who have fought for social justice, through working with people, animals, plants, words, paints, music, or machines, may inspire children to see possibilities for their own activism.

Optimism and Activism

Teachers can create spaces for children to imagine and work toward hopeful futures. With activities such as storytelling and role playing, children can explore and express their visions of a world in which people share resources and power rather than dominate one another. When teachers and children become aware of injustices in the classroom, school, or community, they can challenge and attempt to rectify these situations through conversations and community engagement. As Pelo (2008b) says,

> This is early childhood education at its best: teachers, children, and families opening themselves to each other and to the earth in ways that invite joyful play, collaborative inquiry, thoughtful observation, and deep caring that gives rise to action. (p. x)

FAMILIES AND SCHOOLS WORKING TOGETHER

Multicultural and environmental issues are wide-ranging and complex and can only be adequately addressed if families and schools work together. Throughout this book I use the word *parents* to signify the adults who care for children in their homes—be they biological, adoptive, step or foster mothers or fathers; grandparents, aunts, uncles, older siblings, or close family friends. Likewise, children have many teachers—parents, relatives, neighbors, and other children. However, for clarity's sake, I use the term *teachers* to refer to professionals employed in early childhood settings.

Although often constrained by economic realities such as job locations and available affordable housing, parents define the physical parameters of children's lives. Parents and children spend decades learning from each other. Children construct their basic social orientations in the context of observing how their parents interact with people inside and outside the family. They learn about power and values by participating in conversations and activities that reflect their parents' relationships with individuals and institutions and their attitudes toward material goods and the natural environment.

Teachers, in contrast, have short-term but intense relationships with children. They provide stimulation with activities, materials, books, and conversations and facilitate interactions among the children in the classroom. At school children may hear and see things that surprise, intrigue, and even trouble them because they may not mesh with messages and experiences at home.

Children often become very attached to teachers, but teacher–child relationships do not have the long-term intimacy of parent–child ones. Instead, children and teachers form working partnerships, in which they together discover, absorb, and challenge new information and perspectives. Teachers enjoy and support individual children, but usually they focus more on fostering positive group dynamics than on developing intense one-on-one relationships. Unlike parents, who may have long, open-ended conversations with their children that can go on for years, teachers are more likely to start discussions and create spaces where children can compare their views with those of their peers.

Thus, teachers and parents, and homes and schools, have complementary roles. Conflicts sometimes arise, but these can create opportunities for all parties to reconsider their own views and assumptions, stretch their perspectives, and deepen their understanding of life experiences. Even though they may go through some periods of tension, children, parents, and teachers can mutually support each other to grow and change.

THE LANGUAGE OF MULTICULTURAL EDUCATION

The ambiguities and contradictions in our society echo in the imprecise and clumsy way we talk about different groups and dynamics. As discussed

earlier in this chapter, boundaries and distinctions among groups are fluid and complex, yet the words used to identify specific attributes imply
permanent and rigid boundaries (e.g., Black/White, male/female, afflu-
ent/poor). Moreover, the terms themselves are full of contradictions and
misinformation.

The confusing labels used to designate racial groups reflect the difficulty
of defining categories that do not exist in reality but play an enormous role
in people's lives. Color labels—black, brown, red, yellow, and white—are
the most succinct but do not accurately describe the range of physical attributes of individuals from different groups. Moreover, because color terms
distinguish groups on the basis of a single physical dimension, they also
objectify and polarize the groups and are associated with evaluative and
stereotyped images.

Current usage favors names that refer to the continent of origin, such
as African American, European American, and Asian American. Although
these terms are more precise and neutral, they exclude many groups whose
immigration history does not fit these categories. There also are not adequate terms to describe people native to this land. While clearly "Indian" is
a misnomer, is "Native American" an accurate description of people whose
residence here long predated the arrival of the explorer Amerigo Vespucius?
In short, terms for different groups reflect the confusion that characterizes
efforts to make distinctions among people.

In this book I have used primarily names that refer to the continent of
origin, but I have also used color labels when the former seemed inaccurate
or too cumbersome. One exception is that I consistently use the term *White*
to reflect the power and privilege accorded people who are identified as
White, regardless of their continent of origin.

I have also tried to be as precise as possible and avoid describing groups
by what they are *not*, such as "non-English-speaking" or "non-White," and
as much as possible have used specific group names (e.g., "Puerto Rican"
instead of "Latino," or "Algonquin" rather than "Native American").
However, much of the literature on diversity lumps groups together, resulting in overly broad terms.

The relationships between people and nature, discussed in Chapter 6,
also pose problems with terminology. I have used *ecology, nature, natural
world,* and *environment* because those are the most commonly used terms.
However, none of them conveys the sense of unity and harmony between the
human and "natural" world that I am trying to express.

I have struggled with how to refer to people's sexual identities and orientations. In many contemporary writings, gay, lesbian, bisexual, and transgendered people are collectively referred to as "queer." However, I have too
many vivid memories of hearing that word hurled across playgrounds and
hissed in school corridors to use it comfortably at this point. For this reason, I have used the more cumbersome phrase "gay, bisexual, lesbian, and

transgendered people" and its acronym GBLT. Referring to heterosexual people is also a dilemma. The term *straight* is often used, but as one of my lesbian friends said, "So does that make the rest of us crooked?" For these reasons, I have primarily used the term *heterosexual,* even though it seems awkward because I do not use the equivalent term *homosexual.*

Terms for people with disabilities are also confusing and inaccurate. First, the terms *ability* and *disability* represent a polarized way of categorizing people—all of whom have some abilities and disabilities. In the early 1990s the term *differently abled* was used. It was a useful term because it implied a continuum that is closer to reality, but many people felt that it was just a euphemism for "disabled," and that it was too cumbersome and "politically correct," and it is rarely used now. In this book, I use "individuals (or children) with disabilities" rather than "disabled people (or children)" to avoid making the disability the first and only definition of a person. However, the term is awkward and still incorrectly implies that people with and without disabilities are fundamentally different.

Another dilemma is how to characterize the status and power differentials among particular groups. Terms such as *oppressed, excluded,* or *marginalized* are all in the passive voice and overemphasize the victimization of people and fail to convey their resilience and resistance. How can the power and abuses of one group be acknowledged without presenting others as passive and powerless? In this book, I have tried to point out how groups have resisted oppression as well as suffered from it. However, the results are imperfect, and the phrases are often awkward and cumbersome.

As social values and the relationships among groups change, names and descriptions continue to evolve. The terms used in this book probably will become obsolete at some point. Readers are encouraged to continue to be sensitive to the messages implied by specific labels and to modify their language to reflect changing identities and relationships and in particular the names favored by groups themselves.

These complex issues of terminology illustrate the challenges of multicultural teaching. At the same time, they underscore the necessity; even as children learn to speak, they are bombarded by the misinformation, questions, and contradictions that swirl around them in their homes, communities, classrooms, and on the media. Multicultural education has the potential to engage young children in exploring, critiquing, and challenging these complex and troubling issues and envisioning a more just world.

CHAPTER 2

We Are All Learning

All of us—children *and* adults—are continually constructing our ideas about the world as we observe and participate in a range of social, political, and economic contexts. Our evolving beliefs and expectations, in turn, guide our decisions and behaviors.

Bronfenbrenner's ecological framework is a useful tool for analyzing how different contexts may influence children's experiences and prospects as adults (Bronfenbrenner, 1979, 1986; Bronfenbrenner & Morris, 1998). Consider how the following systems identified by Bronfenbrenner influence your life and the children and families you serve:

1. The *microsystems* of the family, school, and neighborhood
2. The *mesosystems* that include the relationships among elements in the microsystem, such as those between the family and school, home and neighborhood
3. The *exosystems* that are institutions that affect children's lives but exclude children from participating (e.g., parent workplaces, school boards, and social service agencies, to name just a few)
4. The *macrosystems* that include evolving cultural values and ideologies of both immediate and broader social groups; religious and national "norms"
5. The *chronosystems* that reflect the cumulative experiences individuals have over the course of their lifetimes, including external events (e.g., recession, war) and major life transitions (e.g., getting married, having children)

A comparison of the after-school activities of two children living in the same city illustrates how Bronfenbrenner's systems influence the details of children's lives and provide the contexts for constructing their attitudes and expectations and prospects as adults.

Elisa, age 7, lives in a low-income, primarily African American and Latino community in a large city. Each day her mother comes to pick her up from school. As they walk home, they make a brief stop at a small corner store to buy milk, where it costs twice as much as at the supermarket. (Lacking a car, they take the hour-long bus ride to go there only once every 2–3 weeks.) Then they walk quickly back to their apartment in a large housing project. Elisa and her 13-year-old sister Lani spend the afternoon in the apartment, doing their homework, calling and texting friends, watching TV, and helping their mother with the housework. The community center in the housing project has fallen into disrepair, and funding for recreation programs has long since disappeared, as has the playground equipment. The church half a mile away has weekly art and dance classes, but Elisa's mother, who has to catch a 5:00 P.M. bus to her job as a night custodian, does not want her daughters walking home alone.

After their mother leaves for work, the girls eat the dinner that she has prepared for them. Lani ties to helps Elisa with her homework, but there are a few questions that neither of them can quite figure out. Lani herself is struggling with her homework because she does not have a computer to look up some of the material that she needs for her project. She hopes that she can get on one of the school computers first thing in the morning but is worried because there are usually long lines. During the evening their mother calls them a couple of times, and their aunt who lives downstairs comes by to check on them. The two girls go to bed long before their mother returns from work.

Katie, also age 7, who lives 3 miles away in a leafy, primarily White residential neighborhood, is dropped off at her corner by the school bus. She runs home, where her mother urges her to change quickly into her leotard so that she will not be late to her dance class. Katie grabs a snack to eat in the car and also takes her soccer clothes, because she does not have time to go home between her dance class and soccer practice. As Katie gets ready, her mother contacts another parent to confirm arrangements to transport Katie's older sister from her after-school science enrichment class to a play rehearsal later that afternoon. Both girls will arrive back home about 7:00 P.M. when their father, a corporate lawyer, comes home from work, if he is not traveling for business. The family then eats together, and the girls work on their homework, often getting help and advice from their parents as they do it. They each have their own laptop computer as well as an i-Pad so they can quickly get answers to questions they have, as well as easily type up assignments.

For Elisa, a member of a group disadvantaged by discrimination and political and economic priorities (macrosystem), the poverty of her community and lack of funding for activities and transportation (exosystem) limit the ability of the school and community to provide services (mesosystem) and therefore determine how she spends her time and what skills she is learning (microsystem).

In contrast, Katie is a member of an advantaged group (macrosystem) that is reaping benefits of political and economic policies (exosystem). She has lots of extracurricular opportunities (mesosystem), but she may feel pressured to "keep up" with her classmates (microsystem) by taking part in multiple activities. She is also being groomed to get into the "best" colleges that will ensure her future financial success. Both Elisa and Katie are developing skills and ideas about how the world works and expectations about their future roles. What they are learning, however, is profoundly affected by their backgrounds and position in society.

Projecting forward, we can speculate how these two girls might grow up and respond to the challenges of social and economic inequities as parents or as teachers. As an adult (chronosystem), Elisa is likely to have many practical skills and a pretty clear understanding of the effects of discrimination and poverty and how the lines of advantage and disadvantage are drawn. Potentially these insights prepare her to assume leadership positions in educational and social services and in social justice movements. However, the poor quality of her schools and lack of extracurricular activities may limit her educational, employment, and leadership opportunities. Moreover, she may feel disenfranchised and/or overwhelmed by the daily demands of making ends meet and the stress of living in a poor community. She may need a lot of encouragement and support to further her education and gain the confidence to participate in social justice work.

Katie, on the other hand, is likely to attend a good college and graduate school and be well positioned for a successful professional career and positions of community leadership (chronosystem). Although she may go through her life with only a peripheral awareness of the racial discrimination and the economic disparities that barely touch her world, it is possible that she might begin to see these inequities and become an advocate for social change. However, her depth and range of understanding may be limited by her privileged status in society. She will have to critically examine her history, beliefs, and expectations in order to collaborate with people from less-advantaged backgrounds and to participate fully in social justice movements.

When engaging children and adults in multicultural work, we need to recognize that each individual's response to these initiatives reflects his or her unique experiences, knowledge, and patterns of behavior. As illustrated above, some will need to work through their privilege, others their disenfranchisement; and most will have to critically analyze their histories that embody a complex mix of advantage and disadvantage.

Regardless of their starting points, adults and children can all learn to scrutinize their assumptions and expand their awareness and knowledge about the world. In this process we all learn from each other. For example, one day, when my son Daniel was 4 years old, he asked if an elderly visitor (fortunately after she had left!) was a "mean old witch." His comment, which of course horrified me, made me aware of one of my blind spots. I realized that, despite our efforts to raise him in a diverse community, we as a family did not have much direct contact with elderly people.

In this chapter I will first describe how adults can use personal reflections and group discussions to identify and challenge their attitudes and blind spots. The second part of the chapter will focus on how children construct their ideas about themselves and their worlds and how teachers can provide activities and materials to challenge the stereotypes and misinformation that surround children during this process. Although adults and children will be discussed separately, we need to keep in mind that there is constant interaction among them.

HOW ADULTS CAN IDENTIFY AND CHALLENGE THEIR ASSUMPTIONS

To encourage children to be aware of their world, we, as adults, need to develop a critical consciousness, "an ability to step back from the world as we are accustomed to perceiving it and to see the ways our perception is constructed through linguistic codes, cultural signs, and embedded power . . . [to] ask penetrating questions" (Kincheloe, 1993, p. 109). We each have our unique history of experiences, and throughout our lives we construct lenses through which we view the world. These lenses have many different facets; some are clear, others are blurred, and still others are completely opaque. Yet we often assume that we are seeing absolute truths. Thus the task of stepping back and asking "penetrating questions" requires a great deal of emotional and cognitive effort.

Personal Reflections and Inquiry

We need to honestly see our reactions to other individuals and the larger world and to analyze the sources and effects of our underlying assumptions. None of us is free of bias; even those who are deeply committed to social justice work often admit with dismay how often stereotypes flash into their minds (Devine, Plant, & Buswell, 2000; Dovidio, Kawakami, & Gaertner, 2000; Lin, 2005). We may feel ashamed and tempted to deny them. However, we grow stronger and clearer if we acknowledge and confront them and analyze how we learned them and how they influence our current perceptions and relationships (Irving, 2014). Clarifying our goals, moral values, and cultural identities enable us to broaden our perspectives and discern the complex contexts in which we are teaching (Schussler, Stooksberry, & Bercaw, 2010). In one study teachers reported that these types of reflection played a crucial role in developing their professional identities, their critical self-awareness, and their practice (Dewar, Servos, Bosacki, & Coplan, 2013). In short, practicing reflection and inquiry "enable lifelong learning and resilience on the part of teachers" (Kroll, 2013, p. 63).

One way to engage in this process is to keep journals where we record reactions to other people and incidents that we might be afraid or embarrassed to voice in front of others. Because they are a record of our thoughts over time, they also show how our views and assumptions are changing. Reading books, articles, websites, and blogs by authors from a wide range of life experiences and perspectives is another way to recognize and stretch our limited worldviews and to broaden our understanding of how societal inequities affect specific groups and individuals. (For examples of how reflection and inquiry is developed in college classes, see Supplemental Resource 2.1 for Chapter 2, at www.tcpress.com)

To engage in these reflections, we need to be open to others' perceptions of us and be prepared to challenge even our most cherished beliefs and self-images. Although conflict and criticism are often painful, we need to hear and respond openly to what others have to say and recognize that even our best intentions are limited by our own perspectives and experiences.

Group Discussions

Personal reflection should be balanced by conversations in which people can compare experiences, point out each other's misperceptions, and give and receive support for confronting assumptions, making changes, and taking risks. These discussions can occur among school staff, among parents, and in parent–teacher meetings, college classes, and religious or community groups.

Guidelines for Supportive Group Discussions. Hearing and understanding each other's point of view is a monumentally challenging process, especially when discussing sensitive issues related to race, culture, class, gender, sexual orientation, and abilities. Most people approach these discussions with considerable apprehension and anxiety (Tatum, 1997). It is crucial to provide a mutually honest and supportive environment, in which participants can share life stories and examples to generate discussion (Chang, Muckelroy, Pulido-Tobiassen, & Dowell, 2000). Clear ground rules and trained facilitators can help create safe environments so that people can speak freely (for specific guidelines and procedures, see Supplemental Resource 2.2 for Chapter 2, at www.tcpress.com).

Regardless of how well planned and facilitated these discussions are, participants will at times feel uncomfortable and resistant. In fact if everyone is comfortable, then the group is not functioning well. Some participants may resist these discussions covertly by being silent or by outwardly appearing to support multicultural work but inwardly hardening their opposition. Others might be more open about their disagreements, which may cause tension within the group but also lead to more honest discussions. Strategies for working with and through overt and covert resistance include promoting relationships between high- and low-prejudice participants; fostering interpersonal empathy for individuals who are targets of their prejudice;

and pointing out how discrimination contradicts values that participants *do* espouse, such as a belief in equal opportunity (Devine et al., 2000).

Topics and Questions for Identifying and Challenging Assumptions.

Topics and questions that follow a sequence from relatively safe disclosures to more risky confrontations can be used for journal-writing assignments or to stimulate group discussions. Many antiracism and diversity workshops and college courses follow a similar sequence (e.g., Derman-Sparks & Phillips, 1997). (For specific topics and questions to generate discussions, see Supplemental Resource 2.3 for Chapter 2, at www.tcpress.com)

To be effective, the group should meet over a period of time so that members can support each other through the slow process of uncovering and challenging their assumptions. Obviously there are many logistical problems with this kind of commitment, but often groups can meet online to continue the process through list serves or Facebook. Some individuals who are uncomfortable speaking in a group situation find it easier to be honest in the online environment because they are not constantly worrying about others' reactions.

Uncovering and challenging our biases is a lifelong process, and no book, writing assignment, workshop, or conversation can provide the magic "cure." Yet if we are open, we can use each conversation to learn something new and push ourselves to critically examine our assumptions. Andrea Ayvazian (1997), a long-time antiracist educator, says it well:

> None of us have reached the promised land where we are free of stereotypes and prejudices. . . . For me it has been more useful to pledge continually to move forward on this journey rather than to be crippled with shame or to be tied in knots with defensiveness or denial. . . . We are not required to be perfect in our efforts, but we do need to try new behaviors and be prepared to stumble and then to continue (pp. 15, 17).

HOW CHILDREN LEARN ABOUT THEIR WORLDS

Like adults, children's current lives, future prospects, and attitudes about the world are influenced by their environments. This part of this chapter will explore how children construct their worldviews as they interact with a range of social, economic, and cultural contexts.

As children grow up, they expand their knowledge and change how they process information, as the following example illustrates:

My son Daniel, then 4 years old, had chosen a biography of Martin Luther King for his bedtime story. (He has the same birthday as Dr. King and, from a very young age, felt a strong attachment to stories and pictures of Dr. King's life). When we got to the part about the assassination, Daniel said in a voice full of bravado, "I'd get my sword and kill James Earl Ray!" I smiled, thinking how simple things can be when all the "bad guys" can be killed by indomitable 4-year-old "good guys."

Another night about a year and a half later, we were reading the same story, and afterwards we talked for a while about good laws and bad laws and how today African Americans and many other people in this country often are still treated unfairly and how we need to be strong like Martin Luther King to change things in our country that are unfair. It was a familiar conversation, and as usual Daniel repeatedly asked why people were still mean and why the police did not arrest them. We talked about how people who are in charge often don't want to change the way things are. Later, as I was rubbing his back while he fell asleep, Daniel started to cry. I asked what was wrong and he said, "I am scared; I don't want to go to jail."

I was surprised because we had had this conversation and similar ones many times, but this time it had touched his sense of vulnerability. At first I felt guilty—had I been pushing my agenda onto my child too forcefully? Was I being a heartless, "politically correct" mom? Then I realized that Daniel had turned a cognitive corner; he was now able to imagine himself as an adult—to project himself into the future, so that the story of Martin Luther King was no longer about a distant hero but potentially about himself. He was listening to an old story, but developmentally he was hearing a new one. This incident also made me appreciate yet again how in our discussions with children about some of the harsh realities of their world, we are always walking a tightrope balancing honesty with hope, reality with reassurance—with the fulcrum shifting as children develop more insights and connections.

All of our children are growing up in a world full of contradictions. We teach them about equality, but every day they see and experience inequality. We tell them that they should share, but then they are bombarded with messages on the media telling them they need more possessions. We urge them to work hard for a better future, but many see their parents lose their jobs and even the family home; others are surrounded by poverty and despair. How do we support children to become confident idealists and activists, yet able to live in and negotiate our very imperfect world?

Early childhood teachers in particular face the challenge, of making complex issues meaningful to young children without oversimplifying or trivializing them and of raising issues and concerns without making children feel fearful and hopeless. Understanding how children are learning about the world around them enables teachers to develop effective strategies to encourage curiosity, investigation, and activism.

Child Development Theories and Research: A Critique

Which aspects of development are universal? Which ones are individual? And which ones are environmental? According to Bowman and Stott (1994) children from all backgrounds establish mutually satisfying social relationships and ways of organizing and integrating their perceptions and categorizing new information. They also learn how to speak—and perhaps to write—a particular language (or languages) and how to think, imagine, and create. Individual physical differences, such as sensitivity to pain, timing of onset of puberty, and body build, also play a formative role in children's development. However, Bowman and Stott point out that all developmental phases and individual traits become meaningful *only* in the context of the child's social life. Children learn how to express their emerging needs and skills in response to the values and expectations of their group—whether they conform or resist. What information they learn, how and to whom they express their emotions, and what languages they use are influenced by their immediate and distal material and social worlds.

Most studies about how children learn have been done by researchers trained in traditional child development theories and methodologies. These theories and methods are derived from the work of early psychologists, most of whom were European or North American men (e.g., Erikson, Freud, Piaget, Hall, Skinner) and conducted their research and wrote from positions of racial, economic, and gender privilege. Moreover, and perhaps because of their status, developmental theorists and researchers have tended to ignore the context of children's lives and have assumed that developmental goals, stages, and trajectories are universal—the same for all children in all situations. Because these "norms" are based on research largely done on European and European American middle-class families, children from other backgrounds have often been judged "deficient."

Over the past 4 decades educators and researchers have increasingly challenged the universalistic assumptions underlying child development theories and research (e.g., Cannella, 1997; MacNaughton, 2000; MacNaughton & Davis, 2009; Skattebol, 2003). The 1980s and 1990s saw the publication of several books and research reviews that interpreted children's development and behaviors within their own contexts instead of measuring them with the norms, paradigms, and methods based on studies of White children (e.g., "Minority children," 1990; McAdoo, 1993; Spencer, Brookins, & Allen, 1985). Cynthia Garcia Coll and colleagues (1996) urged researchers and educators to view children's development within the larger context of social stratification, including racism, prejudice, oppression, and segregation; and to be aware of local manifestations of discrimination, such as quality of schools, access to health care, and resources available in neighborhoods. While they did not dispute the deleterious effects of political and economic disadvantage, Garcia Coll et al. argued against pathologizing groups of people. They noted that many communities, families, and individuals develop adaptive cultures, competencies, and strategies to overcome and resist the effects of discrimination. Extended families, fictive kinships (groups of nonrelated people who function as an extended family), churches, social and service organizations, and neighborhood groups have all served and continue to serve as buffers between individuals and the devastating effects of poverty and oppression. When thinking and talking about groups that face many disadvantages, teachers and researchers should monitor their assumptions to avoid falling into the trap of seeing families as passive victims of the system, images that further demean people. The history of every group is filled with stories about people who have resisted oppression in small and large ways, and these stories should be included in discussions. Furthermore, Garcia Coll et al. argue that definitions of developmental competencies need to be expanded to include abilities such as resilience in the face of discrimination, functioning in more than one culture, and coping with discrimination and segregation.

Developmental theories and educational practices also reflect the European American ideal of independence. Thus children (and adults) are often judged on their individual achievements that, in turn, may stimulate competition, another American ideal. Children are expected to grow up to become autonomous and self-sufficient adults who go off on their own and start their "own families" often hundreds of miles away from their original family and community. These goals are not shared by communities that value family loyalty and cooperative living above individual achievement. As a result, developmentally based educational policies may be in conflict with family and local community values. These tensions are not unique to the United States. Ritchie (2001) describes a time-honored early childhood practice in New Zealand called "fruit time" that reflects Maori community values and practices. All the children in a class gather together, choose a piece of fruit from a supply that children have brought from home, and eat it while listening to a story. However, new government policies that reflect more individualistic goals now require that children each bring their own snack, which they eat themselves rather than having a shared snack time.

In the past 3 decades the reconceptualizing early childhood movement has gone a step farther from pointing out the cultural limitations of developmental theories; it has raised questions about the whole notion of childhood and the idea of "developmentally appropriate" programs (Grieshaber & Cannella, 2001). Silin (1995) likewise has challenged the attachment to developmental stages and the tendency to protect children's innocence and asks whether we are simply trying to distance children from the "disquieting material realities in which they live" (p. 104).

Instead of foregrounding children's developmental limitations, reconceptualists urge teachers and researchers to recognize the complexities and biases in society and the enactment of power differentials in the classroom;

genuinely collaborate with families, children, and communities to design programs; and constantly re-examine values and practices for their impact on who is being served, excluded, or disqualified (Grieshaber & Cannella, 2001). Teachers should recognize that their work and identities are inherently political (Boutte, 2000) and situated within historical, political, and economic contexts (Ryan, Ochsner, & Genishi, 2001). Kroll (2013) describes children as "strong and capable participant[s] in the culture" and notes that "learning and development are cultural and constructivist . . . there is no generic child and no ideal developmental path" (p. 64). The reconceptualist perspective highlights children' agency and strengths rather than their limitations and opens up possibilities for engaging children in new and exciting ways. (For a brief description of a toddler program taking this approach, see Supplemental Resource 2.4 for Chapter 2, at www.tcpress.com)

One might argue that, with all the flaws and limitations, we, as educators, should simply dismiss all child development theory and research. However, this work has provided much valuable information about how children think and change as they mature. As Stott & Bowman (1996) say:

> What makes theories worth reading and discussing is not the assumption that they mirror reality but that they serve as suggestions or estimations—they help us to arrange our minds. Theories are helpful in that they organize and give meaning to facts, and they guide further observation and research. (p. 170)

In short, rather than "throwing the baby out with the bath water," we can use developmental theories and research to help us pay closer attention to nuances in children's thinking and how their ideas evolve over time. However, we must read this information critically; apply it cautiously; and develop new theories, research methods, and educational practices that reflect broader perspectives and challenge us to see the world in new ways.

Developmental Trends and Processes

Many principles of early childhood education are based on the theories of Jean Piaget (e.g., Piaget, 1951; Piaget & Inhelder, 1968), who provided compelling insights into how children interpret the world and construct their ideas. However, as discussed above, child developmentalists and early childhood educators—certainly including myself—have traditionally focused on children's cognitive limitations at each stage. I am not suggesting here that children do not change over time. I firmly believe that they do. However, we can shift our focus away from identifying children's stages of development to looking more closely at *how* they construct their ideas.

Constructing Ideas. One useful framework for understanding children's construction of ideas is Piaget's (Piaget & Inhelder, 1968) concepts of *assimilation* and *accommodation*—the continuous cycle in which children's expectations about the world are formed, confirmed, challenged, and changed (e.g., a child shifts from assuming that all four-legged creatures are dogs [assimilation], to experiencing uncertainty as she notices differences in names, sizes, shapes, and sounds; to developing more refined categories, such as horses and cats [accommodation]). As children go through this process, they experience *disequilibrium* when new questions and ideas emerge and take shape. This phase offers many possibilities for cognitive growth. Daniel experienced disequilibrium when he realized that being a good guy did not mean simply killing the bad guys with a sword, but meant that he himself might have to take risks and get hurt. A familiar story converged with his growing understanding of himself as a vulnerable person with a future and precipitated new insights and discomforts.

Vygotsky (1978), like Piaget, viewed children as actively constructing their own knowledge. However, unlike Piaget, who focused on children's interactions with the physical world, Vygotsky believed that children's learning is a social process that occurs in a particular space and time that reflects the beliefs, politics, and practices of the adults around them. He also reversed Piaget's assumption that development must precede learning and proposed that learning makes development possible (Silin, 1995). These differences are reflected in Vygotsky's concept of the *zone of proximal development,* which refers to the difference between a child's level of *independent* problem solving and his *potential* level of problem solving that is evident when an adult or more knowledgeable peer provides assistance or guidance (often referred to as *scaffolding*). I recall watching a young child and her mother weaving in a small town in Chiapas, Mexico. As the girl worked on her small hand-held loom, her mother glanced over frequently and occasionally pointed to the child's work and made a comment or demonstrated an action on her own loom. A few times the child nudged her mother and asked her a question pointing to her work. Through demonstration and a few verbal instructions, the mother was scaffolding her daughter's efforts to refine her weaving skills.

Disequilibrium and the zone of proximal development work hand in hand. As children experience disequilibrium, they are approaching new insights, and often, with the support of an adult or older child, they move to the next level of understanding. Although teachers and parents may rarely think in terms of disequilibrium and the zone of proximal development, they often apply these principles in their day-to-day interactions with their children. When a child comes storming in from a fight with a friend declaring that she will *never* again play with that child, an adult may try to help her rethink that assumption. By asking about what happened or reading or telling related stories, he can help the child come to some new understandings about why fights start and how friends can get mad at each other and still be friends.

When Daniel was crying about being put in jail, I have to say that the terms *disequilibrium* and *zone of proximal development* did not enter my head. I only thought about what information would be useful in getting him to see beyond the scary part of being a social activist. I talked to him about the fact that people work together to change things and that they help each other out and that every time Martin Luther King was in jail people all over the country made sure that the police let him out right away. We talked about all the people who might work with Daniel to stop the "mean people." As together we listed friends, teachers, family members, and neighbors, Daniel seemed comforted and reassured. We shifted to talking about things in our town and his school that are unfair and should be changed and how he and his family and friends might go about that. At this point what had been a story about a distant historical hero had become a discussion about local issues and possible responses. I did wonder at the time whether or not to mention all the people who were in jail and did *not* have people all over the country trying to get them out. I decided not to—I felt at that moment that I needed to shift the balance toward the hope and reassurance end of the continuum. There would be many more conversations.

When we talk with children about complicated events and issues, we need to listen for how they are interpreting information, what they understand and feel at the moment, where they are trying to go, and what they are ready to learn. As young children grapple with new information, unfamiliar experiences, and disequilibrium, they often draw erroneous conclusions. One teacher introduced her kindergartners, all of whom spoke only English, to the idea that theirs is only one of many languages by teaching them some songs and words in a few other languages and talking about the countries where they originate. Later she overheard two children arguing about whether or not the children who lived in the next town spoke English. The children were beginning to make connections between locale and languages, but the specific nature of that relationship eluded them. The children also may have heard people in their own family or community speaking other languages and then fused the concepts of town and nationality. The activity was not a failure—the children were clearly thinking about language in new ways. Moreover, this argument gave the teacher insights into how they were interpreting her explanations and generated new ideas for future discussions. She asked the children about people in their lives who spoke different languages; organized a project in which the children interviewed children and teachers in other classes about which languages they spoke and where they were from; and invited bi- and multilingual people to come into the classroom to talk about how and where they learned their different languages. She and the children found many ways to continue the discussion of the relationship between language and place—a complicated issue for any of us but one filled with fascination for young children who are just learning the power of language.

Forming and Applying Categories. As children learn new information, they organize it into categories to make their thinking more efficient. If they have a category for a "fork," then they do not have to "rediscover" its use each time they see a new one. The downside of forming categories is the likelihood of overgeneralizing and making unwarranted assumptions. This tendency is clearly a problem when it occurs—as it often does—in judgments about people. Where do useful generalizations end and prejudices begin?

Developmental intergroup theory (Bigler & Liben, 2007) provides some answers to this question by analyzing how children develop and apply categories. According to this theory, children notice particular attributes and use them to categorize people into groups. They then embellish these categories with images and information that may embody stereotypes and lead to prejudice.

In terms of what attributes children notice and use for forming categories, Bigler and Liben posit that children use ones that are perceptually salient. Thus, instead of categorizing classmates by their favorite foods, children use more obvious and relevant dimensions such as gender and size. However, what is most salient is not universal. Bigler and Liben point out that specific cultural and political environments make some dimensions more salient than others (e.g., Jews became very "visible" in Nazi Germany, as did Muslims in the United States after 9/11). The following conditions and actions may make particular attributes more salient to children:

- Perceptual discriminability of particular groups (e.g., differences in appearance, language, and clothing)
- Proportional group size (equal or unequal numbers of particular group members in a classroom or neighborhood)
- Exposure to explicit labeling and mention of groups (e.g., teachers referring to students as "boys and girls"; parents talking about immigrants)
- Exposure to implicit categorization of people (e.g., observing racially segregated housing)

As children develop categories, they attach meanings to them. In this process they often engaged in essentialist thinking, assumptions that all group members share the same attributes, even when there is no evidence of that (e.g., "All mothers like to cook"). These assumptions often reflect power differentials in the society and serve to justify and preserve the status quo (Mahalingam, 2007). For example, rather than talk about structural causes of unemployment, individuals use essentialist thinking and say that poor people are lazy and do not want to work. These assumptions often lead to generalized positive or negative feelings about all members of a group based on little information or contact. Not surprisingly, children often engage in essentialist thinking and usually feel more positive about their own groups and more negative about those that they perceive as out-groups (e.g., "I'm a girl, and I hate boys because they are mean").

Whether children become more or less biased may depend in large part on their environment, including the attitudes of the family and community and the amount and type of contact with people from other groups. In a review of 121 studies on the development of prejudice, Raabe and Beelman (2011) concluded that across all ages, children growing up in more racially diverse schools developed lower levels of prejudice toward out-group members than their peers in racially homogeneous settings. (See also Crystal, Killen, & Ruck, 2008; Rutland, Cameron, Bennett, & Ferrell, 2005.) The nature of the contact is also critical. According to Tropp and Prenovost (2008), several decades of research suggest that children are more likely to develop positive intergroup attitudes when they attend schools where they have ongoing interactions with members of other groups, and the school structure and atmosphere exemplify the principles of Allport's (1954) contact hypothesis. Those principles include: equal status between groups, which implies equal numbers and equal access to resources; support of institutional authorities for intergroup contact; common goals; and opportunities to work cooperatively. Unfortunately, very few schools meet these criteria. Many are racially and economically segregated due to funding sources and neighborhood composition. Even in integrated settings, the disparities and inequities in society are often reflected in children's peer groups, their status within the school, and academic tracking.

Developmental intergroup theory and related research suggest that, when differences are psychologically salient, the potential for out-group stereotyping and in-group bias increases (Bigler & Liben, 2007; Patterson & Bigler, 2006). These findings imply that minimizing or blurring distinctions among groups might be a better strategy than exposing children to them. In fact, many educators uphold the ideal of "colorblindness" and deny the significance of racial, economic, and cultural backgrounds. However, as discussed earlier, children's lives are affected by the perceptions of others, and young children notice and act on differences, so pretending they do not exist only silences children and implies that these differences are negative. These two perspectives—exploring versus minimizing differences—are not irreconcilable. Teachers can include images and talk about a wide range of people but also emphasize that similarities and differences are continua, not polarities, and that we all have a combination of common and unique traits and experiences. For example, children can learn that most people have the ability to speak, but how they talk and when and how they express their views depends on cultural and individual differences. By being aware of the assumptions that children are learning from their immediate and larger environments, teachers can engage them in conversations and activities to challenge bias and misinformation. (For more details on how children at various ages in several countries construct biased images of others, see Supplemental Resource 2.5 for Chapter 2, at www.tcpress.com)

All children have unique experiences and perspectives. To work effectively with them, teachers need to learn what specific children do and do not know, how they are interpreting information, what puzzles them, and how they react to both familiar and unfamiliar people and situations. Each chapter in Part II of this book includes suggestions for observing and talking with children to learn how they think and feel about the issue specific to that chapter.

Challenging Children's Assumptions and Expanding Their Perspectives

To counteract children's limited and/or biased views about the social and natural worlds, teachers need to provide them with experiences and information that will expand their views and encourage them to reconsider their assumptions. At the same time, early childhood education "must reflect, accept, and celebrate the cultural particularities of individual contexts and include the parents, families, and communities as partners in education" (Kroll, 2013, p. 64). Thus teachers face the challenge of finding a balance between solidifying children's connections to their own families and communities and encouraging them to expand their ideas about the world. These efforts need to be ongoing and integrated into all curriculum because one-time add-on activities can inadvertently reinforce stereotypes (Boutte, López-Robertson, & Powers-Costello, 2011; Earick, 2009). Furthermore, there is no formula for this work; activities and discussions should be meaningful and relevant to the children who are in a particular classroom.

This section contains general guidelines for how to assess and modify physical settings and materials to support children to expand their awareness and understanding of the world. Suggestions and examples related to particular issues will be discussed in Chapters 4–8; Chapter 3 will focus on creating strong social justice communities.

Physical Settings. Where children live and go to school profoundly affects what they learn about the social and natural worlds. All settings have their assets and drawbacks, and teachers need to find ways to work around the limitations, while taking advantage of the possibilities to create multicultural environments.

One of the first things to consider is the relationship between the physical setting and the social world:

- Do the children at the school represent the diversity in the community? If not, why not? Are transportation, admissions, or financial aid policies discouraging some families from sending their children to the school? How might these be changed?

- How diverse is the staff? If it is not diverse, what employment criteria and practices might be instituted to attract staff from a wider range of backgrounds?
- Does the staffing hierarchy replicate typical dominance patterns? Are Whites, especially White males, in charge, with members of other groups as subordinates? What jobs, if any, are held by people with disabilities?
- What are nearby potential learning sites outside the school (e.g., stores, parks, small factories, farms, homeless shelters, museums)? What can children learn from these resources? What ethnic, age, and occupational groups are present in these spaces? Are there places where children can see a range of jobs (not just the usual glamorous firefighters and doctors)?
- How can staff members develop closer relationships with the community? Are there senior citizens who might volunteer? local business people or artists who could visit the classroom and/or sponsor field trips to their workplace? community activists who could share information and perhaps get children and families involved in addressing local issues?

The second area to question is how the physical setting relates with the natural world:

- Do children have easy access to the outdoors? If so, what spaces are available (e.g., community gardens, woods, parks, farms)?
- In places where access to the outdoors is limited, how can the natural world be "brought in" with plants, seedbeds, aquaria, terraria, and small pets?
- How is the natural world portrayed in classroom images? How well do they stimulate children's awareness and appreciation of the natural world with its many climates and landforms? Do they illustrate how people and animals adapt to different environments?

Photographs. Photographs potentially expand children's awareness by visually representing both familiar and unfamiliar people and settings. However, like any other materials, they need to be critically analyzed for the messages that are conveyed.

Why do I recommend photographs instead of drawings or paintings? Commercial drawings on school posters often depict static and stereotyped images and do not add meaningful information. Paintings, especially those that convey social justice themes (e.g., the works of Diego Rivera and Fasanella), often convey powerful messages and can provoke compelling discussions. However, to recognize unfamiliar people as individuals, children need images of real people in the context of their daily lives.

Generally photographs capture the range of human variety and the depth of feelings better than most available drawings and paintings. (For an activity using photographs to heighten awareness of individual differences, see Supplemental Resource 2.6 for Chapter 2, at www.tcpress.com)

Ideally collections of photographs, whether in print or digital format, consist of individuals with many varieties of skin color, hair texture, facial features, dress, and adornment. They should also include people with and without disabilities and in scenes that show a range of occupations, homes, and family constellations. People should be shown in situations and expressing feelings that young children can recognize in order to convey the message that people look, dress, and live differently but have similar feelings and activities. Photographs that challenge common stereotypes should also be available (e.g., Black male executives and doctors, White males sweeping streets, women doing construction work, and people with disabilities participating in sports). Photographs of protest marches and strikes and other acts of resistance provide concrete evidence that people can and do participate in making changes as well as introduce children to social justice movements.

Photographs of the natural world and of people living in different types of landscapes expand children's ideas of how people live their lives. They also illustrate how all beings, including people, share common experiences and needs and are connected because we all live on the same planet.

Calendars, magazines, catalogues, and websites are all potential sources of photographs. To ensure that the images are reasonably authentic and representative, potential photographs for a school collection should be reviewed by several knowledgeable adults, including, if at all possible, members of the groups that are being portrayed. Teachers and parents can collaborate to build up a large collection of digital and printed photographs and organize them in either digital or physical folders so that teachers can easily find relevant images as they are developing curriculum themes or challenging particular stereotypes that their children express.

Electronic Media. As they are growing up in this age of electronic media, children hear, watch, and absorb millions of visual and verbal messages about people and how they relate to each other and to the natural environment. They are bombarded with information that can both undermine and support multicultural views. There is much heated debate about the advantages and disadvantages of electronic media, the optimal amount of screen time for young children, and the role, if any, that electronic media should play in the classroom (Ernest et al., 2014). As educators, we need to understand the many points of view, keep an open mind, and use electronic media judiciously and strategically.

Teachers, preferably in consultation with parents, need to decide whether or not to allow media-based play (derived from television, movies, or electronic games) in their classrooms. Some people believe that, as an integral part of peer culture, popular cartoons, movies, and electronic games are a way to connect with children, especially those who may feel uncomfortable in school. Moreover, children's interpretations of media story lines and images are opportunities to explore feelings, inequities, and worldviews (Souto-Manning & Price-Dennis, 2012). Others see school as the one place where children can explore other aspects of the world and believe that media-based play should be excluded (for more detailed discussions of these debates, see Campaign for a Commercial-Free Childhood et al., 2012; Ernest et al., 2014; Souto-Manning & Price-Dennis, 2012).

When teachers notice that particular children are exclusively enacting media-based characters and story lines, they might talk with parents about ways to expand their children's interests and to counteract their dependence on media. Some schools have a week during the year when all the families (children and parents) are encouraged to turn off all nonessential media (e.g., televisions, computer, video, and cellphone games). Teachers and parents can plan activities to generate all-school commitment to follow through and make this "media-free" week a fun and growing time for everyone. (See Campaign for a Commercial-Free Childhood et al., 2012, for more details on how to organize this project.) In some cases, parents can collaborate to reduce the amount of children's screen time by cooperating to get children involved in other activities (e.g., trips to local parks and recreational activities).

On the other hand, electronic media can be useful tools for teaching children critical thinking skills because many electronic media images reflect biases (for more details, see Souto-Manning & Price-Dennis, 2012). Teachers can talk to children about the programs and advertisements that they have seen and encourage them to identify stereotypes and misinformation. Children also can discuss the underlying messages of stories and figure out why certain shows are so appealing. When children discover that a show is biased or an advertisement is misleading, they might write letters to the producers and advertisers. Elementary school children can make film clips using cellphones or small handheld cameras and learn how decisions about what to include and how to film it (e.g., distance and angle) affect the viewer's interpretation of the image (e.g., how advertisers make toys look bigger than they are).

Despite the many drawbacks, electronic media are not all negative. The social media has the potential to create meaningful connections. Increasingly children of all ages are exchanging information and forming relationships with peers at other schools, often in different communities and countries through Facebook, email, digital exchanges of photos and film clips, and by Skyping (see Terry, 2009, for ways teachers are using Skype). Teachers also can download images from programs about different cultures, social injustices, environmental issues, and movements for social change. These examples can potentially enhance discussions of different issues with the children. However, even the most careful documentaries reflect particular points of view, so teachers always need to watch with a critical eye as to what is *not* shown (e.g., effects of bringing in tourists and photographers on the animals and habitat being portrayed). Moule (2012) points out that often in our efforts to portray groups in a positive light we end up romanticizing them (e.g., the popular "Disneyfied" [p. 16] images of Indigenous People). Not only are these images misrepresentations, they also mask the inequities and tensions that exist between them and the dominant group. Teachers might want to show clips to children to have them critique them for different biases.

All of us who care for children need to put hard economic pressure on the communications industry to shift their programming from violent, racist, sexist, product-driven shows for children to substantive ones. These issues may galvanize teachers and parents to become activists and advocates for their children. They can work together to support and critique public television and local community access channels. They can also pressure local stations to air grassroots programs, to investigate and report local problems and success stories, and to resist the dictates of advertisers and networks to air violent and biased shows. It is a daunting challenge, but lots of people are frustrated, and children, teachers, and parents can collectively become a force for change.

Toys and Materials. Although teachers do not experience the same pressure to purchase advertised products as parents do, they may feel compelled to stock their classrooms with materials that are counterproductive to multicultural education because they are supposed to accelerate children's learning. Teachers in some schools, especially elementary schools, are required to use specific materials such as test preparation packets and state-adopted reading series. In these cases, teachers can try to negotiate with their colleagues and principals to find ways to include other sources and to prevent the mandated materials from defining the whole curriculum.

As much as possible, toys and materials should support children in expanding their views, developing social and cognitive skills, questioning their assumptions, and exploring and solving interesting problems. The following questions may help identify resources and needs in the classroom and guide decisions about new toys and materials:

- What groups are most/least visible? Is the diversity of children in the class, community, and country represented?
- How are different people and places portrayed? Are the figures in the puzzles, the doll area, or blocks stereotyped? or do they represent realistic images that show a range of individual differences?
- What values about the natural environment are conveyed in the images and materials in the classroom?

- How can children use various materials or equipment? Do they accommodate more than one child or only one child at a time? Do they promote cooperative or competitive play? Are they open-ended activities (such as blocks) or do they have defined endpoints (such as a puzzle)?
- Are materials made out of natural or synthetic materials? made by hand or machine? How durable are they? Will they last for a long time, or will they soon be taking up space in the local landfill?
- Before purchasing new equipment, investigate the manufacturers. What are their environmental and employment practices?
- Is a new piece of equipment or toy really necessary? Can the children and adults fix or adapt the old one so it can continue to be used?

In addition to manufactured materials, teachers can provide natural ones (e.g., grasses for paint brushes, small logs for construction) that will challenge children's expectations that tools and materials are all made to exact specifications (e.g., uniform paint brushes and unit blocks). How might these materials enhance children's appreciation for natural forms and their understanding of physical properties (e.g., the challenge of building with uneven logs)?

Books. Children's literature is a valuable resource in efforts to support children's ethnic identity, introduce them to unfamiliar people in a personalized and appealing fashion, challenge stereotypes, raise social and environmental issues, and inspire activism.

However, writing children's stories that fulfill these goals is not easy. Some books that attempt to portray a broad range of human experiences have been criticized for their stereotypical or romanticized portraits. In other cases, authors try so hard to make a political or social statement that the stories have a dogmatic tone and are not appealing to young children. Teachers, together with children and parents, can review and critique a number of books for stereotypes and misinformation and select ones that together authentically represent diverse experiences and perspectives and raise issues in ways that are appropriate for their particular children. Boutte et al. (2011) advocate including a combination of fiction and nonfiction books so that children have authentic and concrete information and do not see issues and groups of people as unreal. The authors also suggest having sources that show multiple perspectives on the same topic and encourage children to identify and analyze the different points of view.

A number of publications (e.g., *Rethinking Schools, Teaching for Change, Teaching Tolerance*) list new resources and review current children's books. I find that reading this material not only gives me information about what is available but also sharpens my own critical analysis of images and issues in other books.

In general, stories written by members of the groups portrayed are preferable. However, due to marketing pressures, publishers often reject books by "unknown" authors or ones that they think will appeal to only a limited segment of the population. Now there is a solution to this problem: With computer publishing software and online connections, children, families, teachers, and community people can create and disseminate their own books and circumvent the publishing industry altogether. For example, the Nunavik Educators' Bookmaking Workshop produced 19 Inuttitut-language children's books based on Indigenous stories and history (Rowan, 2010).

Books authored by people other than those who are represented should be scrutinized carefully for subtle ways in which they may patronize the group or misrepresent their experiences and perspective. The acknowledgments and biographical information also provide information about whether or not the author(s) have worked with, or at the very least consulted with, members of the group that they are portraying. A good example of this type of disclosure is Anne Sibley O'Brien's notes at the conclusion of her book *A Path of Stars*, a story about a Cambodian family living in Maine (2012).

All books, regardless of their content, reflect particular values, even though at first glance they may appear to be "culture-free." For example, although most of its protagonists are animals, *The Story of Babar* (De Brunhoff, 1984) extols the virtues of French colonialism and contains many disparaging images of African people and animals before they were "civilized." The plot of Silverstein's *The Giving Tree* (1964), ostensibly a story about a boy and a tree, reflects our culture's exploitative view of nature, as well as the gender stereotypes of men as takers and women as givers. *The Pirate Princess* (Bardhan-Quallen, 2012) depicts a princess who challenges gender stereotypes by becoming a pirate. However, this message is undermined because her only pirate-worthy talent is the ability to find gold, thereby reinforcing stereotypes of girls failing at physical tasks but excelling at finding and getting material goods (i.e., shopping), especially when it comes to luxury items.

Many books portray a secure and comfortable life as the norm (e.g., classics such as Margaret Wise Brown's beloved *Goodnight, Moon*, 1947; Robert Munsch's *Love You Forever*, 1995; and Jane Yolen's *How Do Dinosaurs Say Goodnight?*, 2000). These three books are ones that I especially enjoy reading to children, and I am not suggesting that they be excluded from classroom and home libraries but rather that these images be balanced with stories that show different and more difficult contexts (e.g., Spinelli's *Night Shift Daddy*, 2000; Tran's *Going Home, Coming Home*, 2003; Woodson's *Visiting Day*, 2002).

Another consideration is the balance between realism and optimism. Books for young children usually have happy endings, and some have been criticized for trivializing complexities and minimizing the pain that people experience. At the same time, children need to learn to hope and work for change. *Wangari's Tree of Peace* (Winter, 2008) is an inspiring example of how one woman and her community faced resistance and innumerable political and economic challenges to reforest large areas of Kenya. *The Story of Ruby Bridges* (Coles, 2010) shows how one young girl had the courage to face hostility and disruption to be a pioneer in school desegregation. *Out of the Dump* (Franklin & McGirr, 1995), a book of poems and photographs by children who live in the dump in Guatemala City, is an unflinching portrayal of the hardships these children face, yet conveys a sense of courage, resilience, and even joy. The children create toys out of scavenged materials and use them for games. Their resourcefulness is a pointed challenge to children who assume that they "need" every new toy and game that is advertised on the media. As the authors and photographers of the book, these children also provide an inspiring example of how children can learn skills and use them to become activists and reveal to the world the plight of a group of poor families in Guatemala.

Nonfiction books are good resources for background information and images of people who are underrepresented in the media. Children's stories can also be used to explore social justice issues and dilemmas. However, many books that allude to injustices and hardships often fail to critique the systemic causes of these inequities. Books that have more critical analyses can challenge these overly benign interpretations of events. (For descriptions of several nonfiction books/series written in the 1990s and how they might be used, see Supplemental Resource 2.7 for Chapter 2, at www.tcpress.com)

Biographies of people engaged in struggles against injustice are also valuable resources. I am not advocating that we return to the "heroes and holidays" approach to multicultural education that has rightly been criticized from many quarters. Rather, I am suggesting that learning about people who have taken risks and have made a difference may inspire children to hope and to persist. Many children are especially interested in how people were able to overcome their fears and limitations in order to act courageously, whether it was refusing to change a seat, leading slaves to freedom, overcoming multiple disabilities, risking serious consequences for acting or speaking out in support of a controversial person or cause, or joining a school or team where no one wanted them. Hearing or reading these accounts can stimulate conversations about being strong and brave in ways that children can understand and can relate to their own lives.

Biographical accounts also provide a compelling antidote to the violent mechanized images of power and strength that dominate the television and toy market. Teachers can point out to children that superheroes have to use their magical powers and weapons to win, but Martin Luther King never used a gun or magic and changed this whole country by using his brain and his words and his faith in people. Questions such as "What do you think is harder? to jump into the Batmobile and to push buttons that provide lots of gadgets or to learn to read and speak when you cannot see or hear as Helen Keller did?" might start some interesting conversations.

Collections of biographies should include not only well-known people but also people who have led relatively ordinary lives. The books in the *Kids Explore* series have biographies of people who are not famous but have overcome discrimination and poverty to become successful contributors to society and agents of social change. With the help of older children or adults, young children can interview family and community members and create their own biographies, which can provide many close-to-home examples of people facing hardships and resisting injustices.

An annotated list of "Suggested Books for Children" can be found at www.tcpress.com, Free Downloads. It is not an exhaustive bibliography but does offer an overview of books that might be used to support a number of different curricula.

This chapter has focused primarily on the cognitive goals of multicultural education—on identifying and challenging assumptions and broadening perspectives. The next chapter will explore the social and emotional aspects of teaching because authentic multicultural education can only occur in the context of caring communities.

CHAPTER 3

Creating Caring and Critical Communities

At the core of all multicultural endeavors is the creation of "communities of critically thinking, morally courageous, and politically engaged individuals, who work together and share power to reform society and who genuinely value diverse realities, voices, individuals, and cultures" (Gay, 1995, p. 181). This chapter will focus on fostering caring and collaborative connections among adults and children that lead to critical involvement with broader concerns.

Adults often assume that caring occurs in private, intimate relationships that protect the innocence of children and provide a refuge from the world. Noddings (1992), however, argues that caring is a way to engage with the complexities and difficulties of the world. She articulates the following eight centers of care: "care for self, for intimate others, for associates and acquaintances, for distant others, for nonhuman animals, for plants and the physical environment, for the human-made world of objects and instruments, and for ideas" (p. xiii). Noddings criticizes most educational programs for being concerned only about ideas and argues that authentic education must address all the centers of care.

Valerie Pang (2001, 2005) echoes these views and states that all aspects of multicultural education flow from caring relationships—among children, teachers, families, schools, and communities. Both Noddings and Pang make explicit connections between caring and social justice work. Noddings (1992, 2002) demonstrates how caring leads to a greater understanding of ourselves and others, a willingness to connect across racial and cultural boundaries, and a critical awareness of how our actions affect others. Pang (2001) asserts that, "Caring and social justice in a democracy are intimately connected. When we care, we act . . . social justice flow[s] directly from what we care about" (p. 63).

Audrey Thompson (1998), speaking from a Black feminist perspective, points out that, for poor people and people of color, caring can never be confined to the personal realm. Because there is no escape from racism and poverty, loving and caring *must* be about confronting and transforming inequities. She asserts that caring in Black communities has always been a shared endeavor and has focused on giving children strategies to survive and challenge racism.

Duhn (2012) makes a similar point in reference to caring for the environment, in particular the urgency of forestalling yet preparing for climate change. This work "inevitably introduces 'reality' into the protected space of childhood . . . children (as future citizens) will have to be able to live in economic, natural, cultural, social, and political environments that are increasingly unpredictable and unstable" (p. 21).

In short, caring is a powerful emotion that energizes concern for ourselves and others and our willingness to confront and change inequities. Thus it is an essential component of multicultural education.

The willingness to collaborate with others is also vital for creating multicultural communities. One of the challenges in this effort is the individualistic orientation of many people and most institutions in the United States. The reverence for individual liberties and achievement has stimulated great creativity, productivity, and innovation. However, it also leads to maximizing self-interest with little attention to others' needs and experiences. Competition, which is a natural outgrowth of individualism, fuels a desire to dominate rather than enjoy experiences; and to ensure victory by sabotaging and undermining others (Johnson & Johnson, 2000). These values permeate educational and economic enterprises. Individuals push themselves to get the best grade or get the highest raise. At an institutional level, schools are judged by their test scores or athletic championships; and businesses expend huge amounts of money and energy to outperform their rivals.

In contrast, cooperative communities, in their ideal form, are energized by members' commitments to contribute to the success of the whole group; to take responsibility for doing one's fair share and for supporting others; to respect and learn from the diverse strengths of community members; to respond with compassion to others' needs; and to strive as individuals— not to win, but to have the intrinsic satisfaction of learning and growing (Johnson & Johnson, 2000). However, in many cases these ideals are elusive, and some tight-knit cooperative communities become hierarchical and repressive and at worst dictatorial and totalitarian. The challenge is to form communities that are sufficiently flexible to support individual growth, yet cohesive enough to work toward common goals.

One way to think about this balance is to consider where the power lies in any institution and community and to distinguish among types of power and how they are allocated. Starhawk (1988) makes the following distinctions. First, there is "power-over," in which an individual or group dominates and directs other people. Second is "power-with" when people collaborate and become a powerful force through sharing their ideas and resources and engaging in collective actions. Finally, "power-from-within" refers to our internal sense of competence and confidence. Ideally classrooms foster children's development of the last two types of power and diffuse the first type. Obviously in all classrooms there is a hierarchy. No matter what we, as adults, say or do, by virtue of our size, experience, and access to resources, we have more power than young children. Often we try to deny our power and may go to great lengths to pretend that we are on an equal playing field with children and families. However, it is better to be honest with ourselves and others about the power we do hold (e.g., setting and enforcing basic health and safety standards in the classroom) and open up possibilities for children to gain "power-with" (e.g., deciding how to ensure that everyone gets a fair chance to play with a new piece of equipment). This process enhances connections with others and respect for their well-being and rights. As an example, Oliveira-Formosinho and Araújo (2011) found that the more children were involved in daily decisionmaking, the more they interacted with their peers. (For additional guidelines to creating collaborative communities, see Supplemental Resource 3.1 for Chapter 3, at www.tcpress.com)

CREATING CARING AND CRITICAL COMMUNITIES AMONG ADULTS

Positive relationships among adults are crucial to creating caring communities and developing shared commitments to work for social justice. In the following sections I discuss relationships among staff members and between parents and teachers and between schools and communities.

Staff Relationships

To create sustainable communities, all staff members, regardless of their roles, must feel secure and well compensated in their jobs40 supported by peers and the administration. They need working conditions and schedules that allow them to enjoy and savor their work and to participate in professional development activities. If teachers are working two other jobs in order to make ends meet, then they are not going to have the time and energy to meet with colleagues and parents, to participate in community activities, or even to connect emotionally with all of the children. Clearly the poor wages and benefits of many early childhood teachers (particularly those in the private sector) are incompatible with these goals. Although many organizations have called for more funding for early childhood education, such support would involve sweeping shifts in national spending priorities. Realistically, adequate funding for early childhood education may happen, but it will take time. Thus, in the short term, staff members can collaborate in setting priorities, making schedules, and allocating responsibilities to ensure that, as much as possible, they have the energy and time to grow personally and professionally and to enjoy their work with children, families, and colleagues.

All staff members, including teachers, support staff, and administrators need to feel that they are valued participants in the decisionmaking of the school. At the same time, the power differentials among staff members should be transparent and acknowledged openly to avoid the demoralizing "inclusion illusion" that arises when the hierarchy is masked by rhetoric about everyone being an equal member of the team. The system also needs to be flexible enough so that all members can grow and expand their knowledge, skills, and roles. When a staff member feels devalued and frustrated, the whole school suffers. In one preschool a teacher from a working-class background, who was financially struggling to keep her family housed and fed, understandably resented more affluent staff members' accounts of their children's' dance lessons and their expensive family trips. Her anger and frustration derailed staff meetings and caused tensions that reverberated throughout the center. After some difficult but productive conversations, her colleagues realized how their own limited economic perspectives had made them insensitive to others' experiences, resulting in unintentionally excluding their colleague. From that point on, they worked to communicate more clearly and honestly and to ensure that their conversations were inclusive and reciprocal and respectful of everyone's experiences. In many public schools the undesirable task of monitoring the cafeteria falls to low-status workers, often disparagingly called "lunch ladies." Some children, fully aware of the status differentials among the school staff, test the limits and act in ways that they would never dare to do with their classroom teachers. The cafeteria workers, who may have little training and support, then react punitively to children, and conflicts escalate and spill into the playground and classrooms. Sometimes racial, ethnic, and class differences are factors, exacerbating the tensions.

Linda Jimenez (personal communication, June 2013) described a positive counterexample. She had a teaching assistant in her classroom who had grown up fending for herself "on the streets." Her rough confrontational style was jarring to her middle-class colleagues, and conflicts and tension ensued. However, in this case everyone was able to learn from each other. As the young woman grew into her teaching role and learned new negotiating skills, she also encouraged the veteran teachers to challenge the early childhood culture of "niceness" and to be assertive and speak up to authorities. As a result, they became more effective advocates for the children and families in their program.

Creating caring communities requires that all members care for themselves, support each other, and recognize and challenge inequities in all forms. By engaging in conversations such as those described in Chapter 2, staff members can become more responsive to colleagues' values, needs, and interests, and help each other analyze and address classroom dilemmas that arise. One center has a system of "critical friends," in which teachers who are wondering how to respond to challenging classroom or family situations can bring their questions to a group of staff members. In these discussions, colleagues help each other examine and rethink assumptions and develop effective strategies. A group facilitator ensures that the discussion stays focused and that time is equally allotted among members (for other examples of this process, see Earick, 2010).

These suggestions may seem overwhelming; teachers understandably may think, "Who has the time for all these meetings and discussions? We already are juggling way too many activities and commitments." Most staff members are under a great deal of pressure and may resist taking time for retreats, full-day workshops, and even regular meetings. It is vital that staff events are planned collectively and thoughtfully to ensure that they are meaningful and helpful. If participants feel connected and energized during and after these sessions, they will be motivated to dedicate the time to attend future events.

In short, the emotional, social, and physical well-being of all staff members is key to creating a caring community for children and their families. If they feel empowered, supported, and respected, they will participate more fully in community decisions and activities and will have the emotional energy to make their classrooms caring communities.

Family-School Partnerships

To engage in meaningful multicultural practice, families and schools need to operate as interdependent, mutually respectful partners. We need to learn from and stand with families and advocate for them and their children (Oliveira-Formosinho & Araújo, 2011; Pelo, 2008b; Schoorman, 2011). However, establishing these relationships is challenging for many reasons.

First, many families are rarely in the schools and have little contact with any of the staff. Their children arrive and depart in a carpool, on a bus, or in the company of a relative or home day care provider. Parents' work schedules and/or lack of transportation often make it impossible for them to get to school when the teachers are available. Except for occasional phone calls or text messages, teachers and parents may rarely communicate with each other. Moreover, if parents feel uncomfortable in the school for any reason, then they will find excuses to avoid contact.

Staff members might experiment with ways to make meetings appealing and accessible to as wide a range of families as possible (e.g., different formats, schedules, locations). Teachers can also use their phone contacts with parents, not simply to exchange information, but to more fully explore the parents' feelings about the school and their child's progress. Many schools and centers are now using social media to stay in touch with parents. Some teachers post descriptions and photographs of classroom activities on secure websites that parents of children in that classroom can access. Others use Facebook and email to tell parents about classroom activities. If scheduling in-person meetings is impossible, parent conferences can be done using Skype or FaceTime. Some parents have started their own email communication or Facebook pages to provide each other with information and support. Social media has great potential for maintaining connections; however, there must be clear guidelines and close monitoring to protect confidentiality of families and to prevent activities such as gossiping about other parents that would undermine rather than support community building. Needless to say, administrators and teachers should be very aware of any parents who do not have access to these media or prefer not to us social media sites and be sure that they are "kept in the loop" in other ways. Finally, social media should support but not replace face-to-face conversations, which are still the best way to truly communicate.

Another impediment to meaningful connections between parents and teachers is the lack of a common language (Gregg, Rugg, & Stoneman, 2012). Every effort should be made to have translators (e.g., bilingual staff, family members, or community members) available at class meetings and conferences. However, using intermediaries makes conversations stilted, and often nuances of meaning are lost. Gregg et al. argue that we need to move beyond simply translating documents or having an interpreter present; they suggest having bilingual staff and parent leaders work with families on an ongoing basis so that they develop authentic and productive relationships with them. Community groups such as local churches and social clubs may be resources for advice and services to aid in creating a comfortable environment for all parents. If teachers find that they are working with many children from a particular language group, they may want to study that language so that they can begin to communicate more directly with parents and their children. In addition, administrators can work with local adult education groups to organize English classes for parents that focus on vocabulary relevant to schools and children.

An additional obstacle to honest parent–teacher communication is the expectation that families and schools have—or should have—common philosophies and practices. Yet many families, particularly those who are new to a community or country, find that the goals and practices of school personnel are incongruent with, if not antithetical to, their childrearing values. These challenges will be discussed in more depth in Chapter 6.

Status and power differentials also interfere with parent-teacher communication. Throughout our educational system, teachers are considered the experts (Silin, 1995). Even open-minded, well-intentioned teachers often slip into the role of the expert, especially with parents who are dealing with poverty, divorce, homelessness, or other hardships. These differences are sometimes reversed in affluent communities, where some parents treat their children's teachers as employees or "institutionalized versions of . . . nannies" (Tobin, Wu, & Davidson, 1989, p. 209). Parents may exert their influence to limit school closures for staff training and handpick their children's teachers; they may expect the teachers to give their children special attention, and ensure that their children excel on future tests. Many teachers understandably resent these high-handed approaches and avoid communicating with the parents. In economically mixed schools, affluent parents (usually White) who are more familiar with the school staffs and accustomed to wielding their power often dominate agendas and conversations and marginalize parents from less advantaged circumstances. (See Irving, 2014, for compelling examples of this dynamic.)

To create communities where roles are flexible and information is exchanged freely throughout the system rather than hierarchically, a whole new approach to family–school relations is needed. As Souto-Manning and Swick (2006) advocate:

> We invite you to reconstruct your own path of curiosity, to learn alongside parents and families, rethinking your theories according to new learnings, and valuing each student and each family for their richness, for all the wonders they bring to the school and classroom community . . . we must learn from the families that make up the intricate fabric of our classroom communities. (p. 192)

The staff of one inner-city elementary school put many aspects of this approach into action by holding a new-parent breakfast, forming an outreach committee to get parents involved, opening a family center, creating a parent leadership team that was involved in the governance of the school, and forming reciprocal relationships between parents and teachers where ideas and feedback were shared and parents' ideas were given equal weight. As a result of this work, parents felt welcomed, honored, and connected with the teachers and administrators of the school (Mapp, 2002).

The funds of knowledge approach (Moll, Amanti, Neff, & González, 1992) demonstrates how reciprocal relationships between teachers and parents can develop to their mutual benefit. By "gathering funds of knowledge from families, teachers can then connect families' cultural knowledge with learning practices and help families recognize these connections. . . . [Families, in turn,] recognize their child and family's strengths and . . . [see] how they [already] help their child learn at home" (Gregg et al., 2012, p. 95). An edited volume by González, Moll, & Amanti (2005) offers many inspiring stories of how teachers, using this approach, create strong collaborative connections between home and school.

For example, through a series of home visits, a kindergarten teacher in a low-income neighborhood in Tucson (Hensley, 2005) learned that a father, in addition to his day job as a groundskeeper, was also a musician. At her encouragement, he wrote a musical for the children to perform. Preparing for this event had a ripple effect as many parents, grandparents, and aunts and uncles, realizing that they too had skills to offer to the classroom, came forward to help with costumes, sets, and choreography. Hensley points out that, when parents bring their knowledge and skills into the classroom, their children see their families and themselves in a more positive light that, in turn, strengthens the bonds between the teacher and the child.

Home visits are a time-honored practice in early childhood education and a key element in the funds of knowledge approach. Although they take a considerable time and planning, they enable teachers to connect with families and to get to know children in their home, cultural, and community environments. Entering the child's world, where family members are the experts, may also equalize the power differentials between teachers and parents. In this more intimate and informal context, teachers and parents can also discuss the child's transition between home and school, especially if there are differences in language and expectations. This shared knowledge may help to prevent or diffuse concerns and tensions in the future.

Hensley (2005) and others who use the funds of knowledge approach urge teachers to make at least two and preferably more home visits in order to develop deeper and more collaborative relationships with families. They also note that sometimes parents prefer not to meet at their homes, and teachers need to respect that wish. Hensley describes meeting instead in places that parents choose, such as a mall, park, or fast-food restaurant.

The possibilities for involving parents are endless, and all teacher–parent contacts can be used to support reciprocal learning and collaborative enterprises (for examples adapted from schools in Reggio Emilia, Italy, see Cadwell, 2003; Gandini, Hill, Cadwell, & Schwall, 2005).

One issue that immediately arises is time. To develop true home-school partnerships, teachers and parents need time to talk, to plan, and to work together. Obviously there are many other logistical problems aside from time, such as transportation, child care, and incompatible work schedules. Here again, social media may help overcome some of these obstacles. The bottom line is: If meetings are supportive and meaningful—leading to more collaborations, insights, and strategies—then teachers and parents will find a way to participate. If not, then logistics and time will always be good excuses. As described in the following sections, parent–teacher conferences and class meetings can be vehicles for initiating and maintaining collaborative and reciprocal partnerships.

Parent-Teacher Conferences. Typically in parent–teacher conferences, teachers, acting in their role as experts, ask parents for background information about their child, then tell the parents how the child is doing in school, raise any concerns and problems, and sometimes offer advice to the parents. Usually teachers reveal little of their own backgrounds and feelings. These conferences, however, could be more reciprocal. What if teachers openly acknowledged their limitations and backgrounds? Parents often perceive teachers' biases and limitations anyway, so trying to mask them is futile. If teachers are not trying to hide their uncertainties, they can more comfortably ask parents for advice on issues that are beyond their personal realm of experience: "One of the children in our class keeps insisting that Sara does not live with her "real mother." How are you explaining Sara's adoption to other kids?" "What words do you and Lenny use to describe what happens when he has a seizure?" "How are you talking to Frank about his father's incarceration? What is your preference and advice about how to discuss it in class?" In cases where children are learning English as a second language, teachers can ask parents (through an interpreter if necessary) how they can complement the parents' efforts to teach English and/or maintain the child's home language.

When a child is not doing well in school, parents and teachers often blame each other. Parents and teachers need to acknowledge their different perspectives on the issue and try to reconcile them—or at least agree to disagree (Gonzalez-Mena, 1992). Optimally they collaborate to find a good solution, but it may take time and requires being honest about their concerns and listening to each other. For example, if an African American parent is worried about her child's discomfort in a predominantly White classroom, the teacher, instead of reacting defensively, can openly admit, "As a White person, I cannot know what it is like to be the only African American child in this classroom. Based on your experience, how can we make the class more comfortable for your child?"

Even if they thoroughly disagree with parents' views, teachers need to listen carefully and respectfully to parents' concerns and suggestions and keep in mind the contexts in which they are raising their children. By hearing how parents handle various situations, teachers can get ideas for coordinating their own efforts with those of the parents, and, when necessary, help children adapt to two different sets of expectations.

In sum, I am not advocating drastic changes in parent–teacher conferences but rather a subtle yet profound shift from teachers as the experts reporting to parents, to teachers and parents openly sharing concerns and collaboratively exploring possible solutions.

Community Building: Class Meetings and Other Gatherings. To encourage broad participation and to create connections among families and school personnel, teachers and parents can plan a number of different events, including class meetings, workdays, potluck suppers, and classroom celebrations (e.g., harvest festivals, exhibits of children's work). This section will focus primarily on suggestions for class meetings, but they can be applied to a number of different formats.

Class meetings for parents are usually held at the beginning of the year and maybe once or twice more during the year. Typically the teacher describes the program and gives a general overview of what the class has been doing and will be doing in the next few months. Often teachers feel pressured to impress parents with the quality of their program and spend hours fixing up their classrooms and setting out materials.

Class meetings can be adapted to support more collaborative relationships among parents and teachers. To make this shift, meetings need to occur more often, especially at the beginning of the year, and be oriented toward reflection and discussion instead of teacher presentations. Ideally, meetings would be planned and cofacilitated by teachers and parents.

In the first one or two class meetings parents and teachers might get to know each other by talking about their own racial, cultural, class, and occupational backgrounds. To get the discussion going in a fun and non-threatening way, parents and teachers can pair up (obviously there are more parent–parent than parent–teacher pairs) with someone they do not know, "interview" each other, and identify one way that the partners are similar and one way that they are different. When the pairs report their "findings" to the whole group, conversations about backgrounds and experiences begin to flow easily, and a sense of camaraderie often arises as all participants discover common interests and life challenges. Starting the first few meetings with this activity helps everyone to get to know more members of the group.

At the first meeting parents can also "introduce" their children, perhaps by describing a recent event that highlights some aspect of their child or sharing how their child is both delightful and challenging. Parents as well as the teachers gain a fuller view of each child, which enables them to support the children's fledgling friendships and respond more knowledgeably to children's questions and comments. For example, if a parent knows that his son's classmate Selina has cerebral palsy, he can challenge his son's misperceptions if he comes home saying that "Selina is just a baby because she can't even walk yet."

At subsequent class meetings parents and teachers might discuss their goals for the children and their ideas about how children learn. One way to start these conversations is to have parents and teachers describe their own experiences with school and their current hopes for their children. These conversations may reveal a range of views about learning, behavioral expectations, and discipline. Although these differences may be unsettling, it is better to have them out in the open and discussed from an attitude of "Let's try to learn from each other and find some common ground or ways to compromise." Examples of children's work; video clips, photographs, and written documentation of classroom activities; and records of children's questions and comments can provide material for parents and teachers to discuss how and what children are learning and how their expectations converge and diverge.

In almost any group some members feel a stronger sense of belonging than others. To create an authentic community, teachers and administrators need to be very aware of parents who feel excluded due to differences in neighborhood, values, religion, race, economics, culture, age (e.g., grand-parents raising their grandchildren) or any other factors. They can ask parents who are involved to reach out to these parents, introduce them to other parents, and ensure that they feel welcome. Teachers also should be aware of which parents are occupying leadership roles and encourage them to avoid dominating and possibly marginalizing other groups of parents. To create a more inclusive environment, one school does not allow fundraising, such as selling items or holding auctions that underscore economic differ-ences among families. For the same reason, teacher gifts are limited to cards and homemade items.

At the same school the staff found supportive and creative ways to make connections among parents. For example, a single mother who is blind and living on disability did not appear to have that much in common with the affluent, married, and sighted parents. Using a funds of knowl-edge approach, the teachers and director worked with the mother to orga-nize a workshop on the "courtesies of blindness." The mother's expertise became visible to other parents who were grateful to learn how to support but not patronize or intrude when interacting with people with disabili-ties. This experience dissolved many barriers, and the mother became an integral member of the community.

To deepen connections and to start thinking about curriculum, a class meeting can be devoted to exploring children's previous experiences and how parents and teachers could build on that knowledge base. As the con-versation develops, the teachers could raise the following questions as they seem relevant:

- How much contact have children had with people from different racial, cultural, and social-class groups? What has been their experience with people with disabilities? Do the families they know represent a range of compositions (e.g., gay or lesbian parents, young single mothers, foster families, grandparents raising children)?
- What have been the families' experiences with community services, such as police, welfare workers, and the schools? with more informal support systems, such as family members, neighbors, and coworkers?
- What workplaces are the children familiar with? Do they know people who do non-gender-stereotyped jobs (e.g., women construction workers)? Have they seen people from diverse cultural and racial groups and with different abilities and disabilities work together and enjoy shared leisure activities?
- What physical environments are the children familiar with? What experiences have they had in wilderness areas? in urban areas? How much do they know about environmental problems?

As they discuss and compare children's experiences and parents' interests and skills, parents and teachers may develop some curriculum ideas and plan field trips and classroom visits that would take advantage of resources and experiences of the families and encourage children to learn about lives of people beyond their immediate world. For example, if children live in the suburbs or rural areas, a parent who grew up in a city might come and talk about and show photographs from her childhood. If the classroom is not culturally diverse, then parents who came from a different country or region of the United States could come and share their experiences. All of these contributions potentially lead to many follow-up activities.

In short, instead of an occasion for teachers to describe a predetermined program, class meetings are opportunities for parents and teachers to become a cohesive teaching team—with everyone sharing their backgrounds and concerns, offering ideas, and becoming involved.

Conversations About Multicultural Education. The preceding suggestions rest on the assumption that all—or at least most—of the staff members and parents are in favor of multicultural education. Of course this breadth of support is rare. Many people resist the idea of multicultural education, and those that support it often disagree on what it means and how to go about it. These conflicts are unavoidable, but approaching them with respect and transparency increases the likelihood of reaching satisfactory resolutions.

First, if a school is committed to a multicultural approach, it should be clear in the descriptions of the program, as well as application materials and intake interviews. Because many people are confused by what multicultural education means, staff members can provide parents with concrete examples of implementation, invite them to observe, and encourage them to ask questions and express concerns. If a program is moving toward becoming multicultural or introducing a particular topic (e.g., economic inequities, same-sex parents, local environmental issues), then parents need to be part of the conversation about why and how teachers and children are exploring this particular issue. If parents have participated in making these plans, then they are more likely to support their implementation. Still, even under the best circumstances, some parents and staff members will be concerned or uncomfortable.

Staff members and parents who are interested in learning more about multicultural education—including those who are resistant to the idea—might organize discussion groups geared toward deepening their understanding and challenging their assumptions about social divisions and the natural world. To get people interested, a parent–teacher committee might sponsor a workshop on an aspect of multicultural practice that would be of particular interest to parents at the school. Parents and teachers who want to pursue these issues can form small ongoing support and discussion groups. To avoid alienating parents and staff members who do not want to participate in a group, no one should feel pressured to join.

Community Involvement and Taking Action. Parents and staff members might also plan discussions about issues that are affecting families, school, and community (e.g., lack of good multicultural materials in the center, concerns about the violent and racist images on children's television shows, budget cuts for local schools, plans to build a hazardous waste dump nearby). As participants share their stories, they may start seeing how social, political, and economic pressures are negatively influencing their lives and their children's futures. They are often eager to "do" something and may get more directly involved. For example, they may write letters to the local broadcasters, use social media to inform and galvanize a wide range of people, go as a group and speak at school board meetings, or attend protests (perhaps with their children) at a proposed hazardous waste site. Lalley (2008) describes how in her early childhood center parents, children, and teachers all join in efforts to pressure the local and state governments on a myriad of issues including immigration reform, dual-language programs, and environmental justice.

Individuals might choose to join local, national, and international movements for causes that are the most meaningful to them (e.g., antiracism, disability rights, hunger projects, environmental justice). Obviously no one individual or group can be involved on all fronts, but by meeting and talking together, parents and staff members can energize each other, stay connected, and explore ways of collaborating. There are a myriad of possibilities for teachers and parents to support each other, to bring multicultural perspectives into the classroom, and to get involved in larger social justice issues.

CREATING CARING AND CRITICAL CLASSROOM COMMUNITIES

To develop connections with each other and with the social and natural worlds, children must learn to be caring and respectful. They need to make "room in [their] mind[s] for others" (Coles, 1996, p. 185)—a space for others' ideas, wishes, and perspectives and a willingness to learn from people with experiences and backgrounds dissimilar to theirs. Connecting and collaborating also require that children be mindful of how their own actions affect others and be willing at times to set aside their own preferences and help others meet their goals and needs.

This emphasis on community building does not mean, however, that children should be compliant and primarily concerned with pleasing others or conforming to expectations. In fact, they should be encouraged to express their views and to challenge others, including adults, when they feel that a rule or procedure is unfair. To engage in social justice work, children need clear values, critical-thinking skills, and confidence that they can be a positive force in the world.

Social development has traditionally been a high priority in early childhood programs. Unfortunately, as discussed in Chapter 1, recent mandates for skill-oriented testing for younger and younger children have forced teachers to spend more time on teacher-directed academic curricula, which reduces opportunities to support children's developing friendships and social skills. However, many teachers have developed creative strategies to teach the required skills in ways that encourage children to interact and collaborate (e.g., using cooperative group activities to teach pre-math concepts).

Teachers and parents play crucial roles in children's social and emotional development by being responsive to children's emotional states and supporting children's efforts to learn social skills (e.g., modeling, coaching, explaining; for specific teaching strategies, see Howes & Ritchie, 2002). Often family and cultural values and expectations about the expression of emotions and the formation of relationships may differ from what children are learning and experiencing in school. For example, if a family believes in strictly differentiated gender roles, then they may be concerned about teachers encouraging both boys and girls to express their feelings openly, to expand beyond gender-typical activities, and to form cross-gender relationships. Becoming aware of such differences through home visits and early meetings with families is critical to identifying and managing these potential conflicts.

Early childhood social goals usually include empathizing with and caring for others, communicating effectively, initiating and maintaining social interactions and relationships with peers, playing cooperatively, and resolving conflicts. These interpersonal skills are relevant to multicultural education because they underlie children's capacities to connect with the larger social world, the natural environment, and social justice issues. They are discussed in more detail in the following sections.

Empathy and Caring

Caring, respect, and interdependence require the ability to empathize with how other individuals feel and to understand how they think. According to Hoffman (2000), children go through several phases in developing these skills during their early childhood years (summarized below), although the sequence and timing vary across individuals and social and cultural contexts.

Humans appear to be born with some innate ability to resonate with others' emotional states as evidenced by the fact that newborns typically cry reactively when they hear other babies cry. As babies get older, they develop a self-referenced empathy, an assumption that others feel the same way that they do. For example, toddlers frequently bring their own favorite dolls or blankets to comfort crying friends. However, they are beginning to see that others have distinct perspectives and needs. Hoffman described how

David, a 2-year-old, first offered his crying friend his own teddy bear. When that did not work, David got his friend's teddy bear from the next room. A teacher told me that the toddlers in her class often help each other if adults encourage them and do not rush in to help too quickly. For example, a child was trying to climb into a box but could not get high enough. A classmate brought him a chair to stand on so he could get into the box.

Preschoolers are learning how to read more subtle emotions and to understand that people have their own information and ideas and may react differently to the same event. When they see a crying child, they may ask questions about what happened rather than assume that they know. They also begin to see how their own actions affect others (e.g., grabbing a toy makes the other child mad) and are able to resolve conflicts, often with some adult help. However, children this age still tend to interpret events in their own terms. For example, when they see a photograph of a father comforting a child, they may begin to talk about a recent incident when they themselves were sad rather than focus on the situation of the father and child in the picture.

Children of elementary-school age begin to realize that they themselves are the objects of others' ideas and feelings. This development enables them to be more considerate of others and better able to collaborate with other individuals and groups. However, this awareness can also make children self-conscious and worried about what their peers think of them. Some children respond by conforming to group norms (e.g., rigid ideas about appropriate dress) or by being antagonistic toward out-group members in order to ensure in-group peer approval.

Asking questions or pointing out how others may feel or think can foster children's developing awareness of and interest in others. For instance, if the class is watching construction workers carry heavy materials, teachers might ask: What do you suppose they are feeling in their arms? What does it mean when they wipe their faces? Teachers might set out some heavy objects so that children can experience those feelings themselves. Many children's stories have plots that encourage children to empathize with others' feelings and to see how individuals and groups often have different perspectives and priorities. Dramatic play, either inspired by one of these stories or spontaneously generated by the children, provides endless opportunities to experiment with taking multiple roles and perspectives.

In one preschool classroom each child gets a "Birthday Surprise," a special gift made by his or her peers that reflects their knowledge of the birthday child's specific interests and preferences. For example, one group of children made a small obstacle course for a classmate who particularly enjoys that activity. This novel approach to birthdays motivates children to observe their classmates and think about what they like and need, as well as work collaboratively to make the "surprise."

As discussed previously, children often develop strong in-group biases and regard unfamiliar people negatively. Young children's capacity to resonate emotionally with others' feelings is a potential "handle" for teachers and parents to use in helping children to feel connected with unfamiliar people and to understand the effects of discrimination. Hoffman (2000) advocates emphasizing emotional similarities among people. Stories that personalize unfamiliar people can help children see beyond differences and to identify and empathize with individuals.

In our highly technological society where machines do most of the manual work, many children, especially those in relatively affluent families, have few responsibilities for the well-being of others (e.g., most do not collect firewood to cook the family dinner). Thus we have to make conscious efforts to teach children how to recognize and respond to others' needs. Teachers can encourage children to help each other get dressed to go outside, put on and take off smocks, move large tables, and hang up large easel paper to dry. Older children might visit preschool and toddler classrooms and read to their younger peers or help them do art projects or make snacks. Caring for classroom plants can become opportunities to observe how plants change day by day and learn how to "read" and attend to their needs. As one preschool girl said to me, "My plant looks really tired, today. I'm gonna sing her to *sleep*."

Communication

Effective communication requires paying close attention to what others are saying, both verbally and nonverbally, and genuinely trying to understand their perspectives, as well as making oneself understood. Children can enhance these skills by using alternative ways to communicate. For example, conveying information nonverbally, pantomiming events or feelings, and "mirroring" each other's gestures or facial expressions make visual information more salient and meaningful. Many activities commonly seen in toddler classrooms, such as using simple sign language and making different facial expressions in a mirror, support this aspect of communication.

In group discussions young children often blurt out comments that have little to do with what else has been said, which often derails any real communication. In individual and small-group conversations, children can learn to slow down and hear others, perhaps repeating the question or statement that they are responding to before they speak. When they have the opportunity to instruct each other on how to do an activity or task, they quickly see how well they have conveyed and heard the information. One activity for kindergarten and primary children is to sit in pairs, back to back; the first child draws a picture or builds a block structure; then the second one replicates it, based only on the first one's oral instruction.

Peer Interactions and Relationships

As children experience the pleasures and challenges of playing with peers, they become more motivated to understand others' points of view, which in turn enables them to develop relationships and get along with a wider range of people. Friendships are critical learning opportunities for children, and we can support them in many ways.

The design of space and the selection of equipment and materials influence the type and frequency of social interactions in classrooms (Kemple, 2004). For instance, one study (Ramsey, 1986) found that single-entrance spaces such as lofts or small houses tended to be the scenes of more exclusionary behavior than were more open spaces. Single swings, which could only accommodate one child at a time, were frequently the scene of disputes and complaints about having to wait one's turn, whereas the horizontal tire swing was more fun with several children who often invited passersby to join, helped each other get on and off, and coordinated their motions in order to make the swing go fast. Although children on the tire swing also had many conflicts, usually about how fast or slow to spin the tire, these disputes required more interpersonal awareness and negotiating strategies than simply vying for turns on the single swings.

The placement of furniture and equipment also influences the kinds of social interactions that occur. If the sand table, water table, and housekeeping furniture are placed against a wall, then children have less eye contact and direct interactions with each other. Moving them away from the wall facilitates more sociable and cooperative play, provided that any freestanding furniture is stable enough to prevent accidents. In primary classrooms, moveable tables and chairs allow children to work with different peers, either at tables or on the floor.

Children have a wide range of social styles and preferences; some may wish to play alone and should not be pressured to interact all the time. Other children, however, may want to join in play but are hesitant for whatever reason and may need adult support. For example, children who have difficulty starting social interactions benefit from having adults serve as a "bridge" between them and their classmates (e.g., "Sally, can you show Mary and me what you are building? Mary, do you see how Sally is making her garage?"). Adults can also "coach" and support children who are having difficulty maintaining contacts (for more specific suggestions, see Supplemental Resource 3.2, for Chapter 3, at www.tcpress.com).

In addition to learning how to interact with their peers, children are also forming relationships. Often they end up playing exclusively with one or two best friends and ignoring or rejecting other classmates. Close, long-term friendships provide rich contexts to learn about oneself and how to manage the ups and downs of peer relationships. However, playing with only one or two children is limiting and puts a lot of pressure on relationships that often fall apart, leaving both parties bereft. Moreover, these tight relationships keep children from broadening their range of friends and connecting across groups. Thus a balance of close friends and a wider range of good friends is optimal. (See Vivian Paley's recommendations in *You Can't Say You Can't Play* [1992] for examples of how to talk with children about exclusionary behavior, why it happens, and how it affects other children.)

Children's friendships often reflect gender, race, social-class, culture and language, and abilities divisions (these patterns will be discussed in more detail in Chapters 4–8). As a result, they are not learning how to play and work with peers who at first may seem different from them. One way to start encouraging cross-group contacts is to identify what factors contribute to the current grouping patterns by considering the following questions:

- How do children respond to overtures from peers who are different from them in some way: race, gender, culture, language, economic class, abilities?
- What reasons do they give for rejecting certain peers?
- What factors appear to influence whether particular children are included or excluded (e.g., play styles, preference for certain activities, language)?
- Are there times and places when groups are more or less segregated? What are they?

When teachers have a clearer sense of reasons for these divisions, then they can try various strategies to support children in crossing borders and expanding their range of relationships. Changes in seating arrangements or the creation of long- and short-term "teams" or classroom buddies for various activities provide children with opportunities to get to know different classmates. Teachers can encourage children to articulate their feelings about exclusivity and introduce photographs and storybooks that portray children playing with friends from different gender, cultural, racial, and ability groups. These legitimize cross-group relationships and serve as a reference point to counteract children's arguments that groups must be exclusive.

Teachers also may want to analyze how the physical environment (location, size, accessibility, and attractiveness of the spaces) may be contributing to divisions. If it is apparent that some groups—be they defined by race, culture, class, gender, or energy level—are always together in certain areas, then rearranging the physical space may support intergroup contact. In one classroom, teachers noticed that some children tended to spend much of the day in their favorite areas with their special friends. After observing this pattern and talking with the children, the teachers realized that the boisterous play that often occurred in the open area in the middle of the classroom intimidated some of the quieter children who stayed in the "safer" areas on the periphery. After several class discussions, the teachers and children agreed to create an area for active play at one end of the classroom and to move some of the other areas into the center of the space. Once these changes were made, the children began to move around more and play with a wider range of peers and activities.

Cooperative Activities

Cooperative activities provide a good counterbalance to our society's obsession with individual achievement and competitiveness. They also promote children's sense of *inter*dependence, their awareness of others, and their flexibility. Moreover, they potentially foster friendships among children of diverse groups (Johnson & Johnson, 2000; Slavin, 1995) and different abilities (Kemple, 2004; Kozleski & Jackson, 1993).

Because most of us have been immersed in competitive activities and individualistic goals all of our lives, we may find ourselves unintentionally undermining children's cooperation. One interesting exercise is to keep an audio recorder running in the classroom and at the end of the day listen to see how many instructions, reprimands, and praises reflect an individualistic orientation (e.g., "That is a really tall tower you made, Sammy") or a more collective orientation (e.g., "You three children are really helping each other on your collage"). Often teachers are surprised at how many times they reinforce individualistic behaviors and attitudes even though they may consciously be trying to encourage children to cooperate.

Many activities and routines can be easily modified to encourage cooperation. For example, when playing cooperative games (Orlick, 1982, 2006), children are learning how to observe their peers' actions and coordinate theirs with each other's. Group art projects, in which all children contribute, also require cooperation and can result in a tangible symbol of the classroom community. The routine of assigning chores to a "special helper" of the day or week can be adapted to having pairs or trios of helpers do the tasks cooperatively.

Children often develop cooperative fantasy play and games on their own. However, they sometimes need support to share responsibilities and to work and play together cooperatively (Kemple, 2004). Adults can monitor and "coach" groups to help them function equitably and to avoid forming hierarchies and exclusionary subgroups.

Conflict Resolution

Children's conflicts are an inevitable part of classroom life. Although adults often regard them as annoying interruptions, they teach children a lot about interdependence, flexibility, and diversity of opinions. Resolving conflicts requires that children know how to distinguish different perspectives; balance their own wishes with those of others; manage anger and aggression;

recognize how their actions affect others; be both assertive and respectful; and know when and how to compromise—all skills germane to multicultural education.

Some teachers try to eliminate conflicts altogether by providing children their "own" materials for each project. Likewise they may try to settle a dispute as expediently as possible by giving both parties equivalent objects so that "each of you can have one." While these strategies may prevent or stop arguments, they also reinforce children's expectations that they can have absolute control over resources and can count on them being distributed fairly, which obviously does not represent the real world. Furthermore, these strategies do not allow children the opportunity to engage in deliberations and to learn how to resolve conflicts.

When a conflict does start, sometimes teachers intervene so quickly that children do not have a chance to manage and resolve it on their own. In his comparison of preschools in different cultures, Corsaro (2003) observed that teachers in U.S. middle-class preschools tended to prevent or quickly mitigate conflicts. He noted that the children in those classrooms perceived themselves as vulnerable and their relationships as fragile, and, when disputes arose, they often turned to adults for help. In contrast, the Italian teachers he observed generally ignored children's *discussioni*, vigorous arguments about many topics, and their playful physical fights. Rather than rely on their teachers, the children themselves usually moderated or resolved conflicts in ways that affirmed their sense of collective identity and connections. This comparison suggests that children benefit when teachers step back from a conflict and give children an opportunity to manage their feelings and negotiate with each other.

If teachers feel it is necessary to intervene, they can help children work out joint solutions that (at least minimally) satisfy all parties. For example, if two children are fighting over a truck, they can be encouraged to talk about why they want it and figure out a way to either take turns or, even better, to play with it together (e.g., loading it up with blocks and making it part of a construction game).

When an injury to a person or a piece of equipment or material has already occurred, children can make some kind of restitution, which is a positive alternative to retribution (Conflict Solutions Center, 2009; Schaffer & Sinicrope, 1983) or empty apologies. By supporting a child to aid the victim (e.g., helping rebuild the block tower that was knocked down or getting a cold compress to put on a bruise), the effects of the aggressive act become a shared problem instead of the focus of vociferous blaming. Furthermore, the aggressor, who may be feeling some remorse, is able to reestablish a positive or at least neutral relationship with the injured child. If the latter is not receptive to help or if direct contact between the two parties is too volatile at the moment, the aggressor might make a more indirect restitution. For example, a child who has torn another's painting could put fresh paper on the easel so that the materials are available if the aggrieved child wants to paint another picture at a later point.

Conflicts can be used to help children reflect on larger social issues and possible solutions; these discussions, in turn, may help children see their conflicts from a broader perspective. For example, if a group of children is excluding others from the block area, a teacher might initiate a broader discussion about how many people are negatively affected when one person (or group) takes over and does not respect the rights of others. Many children's stories have this theme, whether they depict interpersonal or intergroup conflicts (see "Suggested Books for Children" at www.tcpress.com, Free Downloads) and can be used to encourage this discussion.

Critical Thinking and Social Action

Encouraging children to be activists for social change poses some interesting dilemmas. Children need enough guidance to make good decisions and to function responsibly in groups. At the same time, they need to learn how to raise questions and challenge adults when they feel that something is not fair. Also encouraging children to criticize and challenge rules and authority may contradict some families' educational and social values (e.g., unquestioning obedience to authority). Teachers need to be sensitive to these cultural nuances and work with the parents to encourage children to see and respond to inequities in ways that respect their families' values. Another dilemma is the question of how much children do understand about larger social issues. As discussed in Chapter 2, adults often underestimate children's capacities instead of seeing them as capable and proactive citizens (for an example of children participating in municipal decisionmaking, see Supplemental Resource 3.3 for Chapter 3, at www.tcpress.com).

Rules and Procedures. One way to support the development of both critical thinking and activism is to involve children in the process of deciding on classroom rules and procedures. Although the latitude given children varies by age and experience, they should be engaged in as many decisions as possible. For example, children at all ages have ideas about helpful and hurtful interpersonal behavior and are usually eager to contribute ideas about how to make the classroom "safe" for everyone (e.g., no hitting or scaring kids). In the process of deciding on procedures and rules, children experience the interdependence of all members of the class, and the need to be flexible. They learn to articulate their own needs; listen to the opinions of others; and think about the purpose, fairness, and enforcement of the rules. Moreover, children experience the effects of conflicting needs and perspectives. For example, children who are eager to curtail the rights of others realize that, when applied to them, repressive rules have their disadvantages. As children debate the merits of different routines and rules, they experience on a small scale what it takes for a democratic society to function.

Decisionmaking about classroom procedures is often a cumbersome process with young children, who may not have the vocabulary to express their views and may have difficulty weighing various options and making decisions. With time and support, however, they often arrive at fair and wise solutions. Some teachers like to use voting to make decisions. However, with "majority rule," the emphasis often shifts children away from finding a common solution to pressuring each other to vote in a certain way. Also, when one side has "won," the "losers" may resist or undermine the decision. In contrast, when using a consensus process, the group acknowledges different views and encourages all participants to "move" a bit (i.e., show some flexibility in their position). Through this process they collaboratively reach an acceptable decision that is a compromise or, in some cases, a totally new and better plan that everyone can support. Consensus is a slow process but one with a lot of learning potential. If a quick decision is necessary or if the children do not seem to be getting anywhere close to consensus after several sessions, then voting, teacher mandate, or even flipping a coin might be appropriate. Decisions, however they are reached, should not be cast in stone; new (and old) rules should always be viewed as flexible and subject to change.

In one preschool many children loved to chase each other, but other children were scared by the roughness and noise. The teachers and children discussed this problem at some length and made several decisions about how to keep the chasing game safe for everyone (e.g., checking to be sure that a classmate wanted to be chased, letting the chasers know if the game was getting too scary, and rotating the roles of chasing and being chased). Over time, the initial rules were adjusted as their implications became clear and situations changed. (For another example of a teacher who used the consensus process, see Supplemental Resource 3.4 for Chapter 3, at www.tcpress.com)

Participating in critical analyses and social change requires thinking about complex situations and issues. These processes require time and are often in conflict with society's emphasis on speed and efficiency. Teachers can consciously resist these pressures and work with children as together they learn to live with confusion and frustration and to persist in developing new perspectives and solutions.

Routines and Rituals. Classroom routines and rituals can be adapted to be more meaningful and to foster interpersonal connections and critical thinking. For example, instead of just "doing" the calendar every day, it could be discussed less often but in more depth—perhaps when it is a new month or new season. These discussions could be opportunities for all class members to review the year so far and to think about the passage of time in terms of friendships and classroom projects. Children and teachers could talk about what they remember and notice how individuals recall different details of the same experience. To see how they have an impact on their world, children and teachers could also reflect on problems that they were able to resolve together and identify current issues that they want to address.

Likewise, mealtimes can be occasions to talk about families, different traditions related to food, and comparisons of food likes and dislikes. They also offer opportunities to explore children's understanding of where food comes from and to raise issues like hunger and poverty. Teachers can inject relevant information and questions and see how children respond (e.g., "You know when everyone was talking about how starving they were just before lunch, it made me think about the fact that some children have only one meal a day. I wonder how that would feel.").

Conversations. A critical part of multicultural teaching is conversation. As children are trying to understand the many injustices, contradictions, and just plain absurdities of their world, they have many concerns and questions that they need to share and mull over. Adults can also learn and grow from hearing children's views. Thus classrooms should be organized to enable teachers and children to have meaningful, mutually respectful conversations—even if it means letting some other things go.

Family books—that is, photographic books that children and their parents have made about their families—can inspire many conversations about similarities and differences among people and a better understanding of diversity and inclusion (Cleovoulou et al., 2013). In one classroom I observed, each child's family book is read out loud on a separate day during circle time; then it is placed on a special shelf and is available throughout the year. The teachers noted that the family books are among the most popular books in the classroom. Children often look at them in pairs and compare different families and ask each other questions.

Teachers may find it difficult to have long conversations with individual children because other children are often clamoring for their attention. However, one child's questions can often be turned into a group discussion ("Silvio was asking me, why—if the grown-ups want kids to learn to read—are they now closing our town library on Saturdays? It's a good question. Do any of you have ideas about what is happening? . . . What we might do to keep the library open?").

In these conversations teachers do not need to explain all the complexities of an event, but rather to puzzle along with the children and together explore issues and raise questions. When Daniel was 5 years old, he indignantly asked me, "Since Columbus was mean and cruel to the Indians, why do we have Columbus Day? Why don't we have Indian Day instead?" When questions like that come up, adults can invite other children to share their views and questions, affirm their feelings, and look for children's books and other resources to learn more (e.g., about past and current Native American movements to gain justice). Likewise, adults and children can collectively consider possible actions (e.g., "How could we learn more about these problems?" "What group might we talk to or write to about our concerns?").

Many events—big and small—can give rise to conversations, and teachers should be prepared to "seize the moment" to encourage children to ask questions and rethink ideas and assumptions. Strikes or layoffs, reductions in municipal services, a book with stereotyped characters, or exclusionary play are examples of the many occasions when children may be open to challenging the status quo and engaging in efforts for social change.

All of us as adults need to make space for conversations, hear children's concerns, and try to connect with them in a meaningful way. We will make mistakes—I can think of dozens of times when my response missed, and all I got was a blank stare or "I don't want to talk about this anymore." But other times we hit the mark and can have wonderful enlightening discussions with children. In many ways children are natural critical thinkers—they often ask questions that we as adults would rather avoid or have forgotten how to ask. When Daniel was in kindergarten, he and I visited a large city that was a sharp contrast to our small university town in many ways. While there, he saw a lot of homeless people for the first time and asked, "Why don't people like us who have houses invite the homeless people to live with them?" Why not indeed? I did not have a good answer.

CONTEXTS OF LEARNING

This section of the book explores divisions and inequities related to race, economic class, culture (including orientation to the natural environment), gender (including sexual identities and orientations), and abilities and disabilities.

Each chapter begins with questions to encourage readers to reflect about their experiences, identities, and attitudes related to the topic of the chapter. The questions are written in the first person but can be adapted for group discussions.

The second part of each chapter is a discussion of how that particular social dimension affects children's life circumstances. Given the gaps in information and the bias of much research, these reviews cannot be used to predict how specific children will fare growing up in specific circumstances. This information, however, can lead to rethinking assumptions and responding more sensitively to the families and communities connected to our schools.

In the third section I briefly review the research about young children's emerging ideas and feelings related to the topic of the chapter. Each child has a unique way of perceiving the world, but knowing general trends and patterns helps adults hear the nuances of children's concerns and questions and develop meaningful ways to raise these issues.

The final part of each chapter includes specific suggestions for observing and talking with children to find out more clearly what they know, think, and feel about the dimension under discussion. This section also has examples of how teachers might use this information to join children in exploring and challenging their assumptions and the inequities that they experience in their worlds. Because children and families have different histories and circumstances, no curriculum can be applied across the board. I include examples, not to prescribe activities, but rather to encourage readers to develop activities and practices most appropriate for their particular children. You may disagree with some of the strategies and/or feel that they would not work for your group. Use these moments to explore the source of your discomfort and to create strategies that better fit your particular situation.

Dividing these topics into separate chapters has the advantage of allowing readers to focus on each dimension in more depth and not be overwhelmed by too much information at one time. However, the disadvantage is that this organization implies that race, class, culture, gender, and abilities/disabilities are static categories that operate independently. *Nothing could be further from the truth.* Throughout the following chapters I will point out how these dimensions are constantly changing and interacting.

Before turning to the next five chapters, ask yourself "Who am I?" and write down the answers as quickly as possible. This list will give you an idea of which attributes are salient in your identity and which ones you tend to ignore or take for granted. Keep your list in front of you as you record your responses to the questions and reflections at the beginning of each chapter.

I hope that you will find these chapters helpful in developing your own "reflective and clarified" identities (Banks, 1997, p. 138) and gain new insights into how your unique history and worldview influence your identity, your attitudes, and your work with children.

CHAPTER 4

The Context of Race

REFLECTIONS ON RACE

When you were answering the question "Who am I?" posed in the Part II introduction, did you mention race as an attribute? To consider the role that race plays in your life, consider the following questions:

- Why did I include—or not include—race as one of my attributes?
- What is my racial background? Do I have a monoracial, biracial, or multiracial identity? Was I raised by adoptive or foster parents whose race was different from my own?
- What do other people assume about my racial background?
- What are my early memories of my racial identity? How has my identity changed?
- How do I feel about my racial group(s)? Am I proud? ambivalent? Do I sometimes wish (or have I wished) that I belonged to another group?
- What are common attitudes toward my racial group(s)? How are we portrayed in the media? How are we stereotyped? How are we viewed and treated in public spaces? Shopping in stores? Walking or driving through different neighborhoods?
- Where does my racial group(s) fit in the power hierarchy of my community? Country?
- How has my racial background influenced my educational and career opportunities?
- How diverse is my personal social network? Do I have close friends and neighbors in other racial groups, or is my social network racially homogeneous?
- What assumptions and feelings do I hold about particular racial groups? Where and how did I learn these messages? How would I react if I found out that our new principal was Puerto Rican? The new gym teacher was Chinese American? A European American child in my class was on welfare? My new doctor was African American?
- How do I feel when the subject of race comes up in a conversation or conflict? Am I anxious? Do I try to avoid it? If so, why?

GROWING UP IN A RACIALLY DIVIDED SOCIETY

As discussed in Chapter 1,"race" has no biological base but is a socially constructed concept, located in economic, political, and historical power relationships. Moreover, with the increase of biracial and multiracial families and children, racial categorizations have become even more blurred and often contradictory. In fact, using them at all is problematic (Ramirez, 1996), and perhaps someday they will no longer exist. Despite these ambiguities, however, people in this country and many others have been and still are formally and informally classified by "race" and often judged by stereotypes that are associated with their particular group. Regardless of many educational and legal reforms, racial segregation and hierarchies continue to define our lives and "racism is a permanent fixture of American life" (Ladson-Billings, 1998, p. 11).

Racial Advantage and Disadvantage

A system of racial advantage, in which one group has unearned privileges and power over other groups by virtue of their physical characteristics (Tatum, 1992), has prevailed in this country since the arrival of the earliest European settlers to the continent we call North America. The lines of advantage and disadvantage are such that people who look the most different from the Anglo-Saxon settlers have been the most marginalized. Those who have been particular targets for discrimination include Native Americans and Mexicans who were conquered, African Americans who were enslaved, and Asian Americans who faced stringent immigration and segregation rules. Over the past two centuries many immigrants have quickly learned that to be American meant becoming "White" (Barrett & Roediger, 2002), and many have bought into the myth of White supremacy to legitimize their membership in the dominant group and their claims to economic privilege (Roediger, 2005).

Critical Race Theory (CRT) provides a useful framework for recognizing and challenging the persistence of racial inequities in our society and especially in our educational system (Ladson-Billings, 1998). According to Hayes and Juárez (2009, p. 733), the six unifying themes of CRT include:

1. " . . . Racism is endemic to American life."
2. We should be skeptical toward assumptions that legal, economic, political, and educational systems operate with "neutrality, objectivity, colorblindness, and meritocracy."
3. " . . . Racism has contributed to all past and contemporary manifestations of group advantage and disadvantage."
4. The "experiential knowledge of people of color," expressed in a wide range of forms, including personal stories and chronicles,

plays a crucial role in exposing the persistent racism in schools and other institutions.

5. "CRT is interdisciplinary" as all disciplines embody racist assumptions.
6. "CRT works toward eliminating racial oppression as part of the broader goal of ending all forms of oppression."

For people of color, CRT is a space to explore and express their experiences and expose the overt and covert racism that defines their lives and all of the institutions in our society. CRT is a charge to Whites to be vigilant about recognizing White privilege; to question and confront individuals, institutions, and practices that perpetuate it; and to learn from and support the CRT scholarship of people of color (Bergerson, 2003). Ladson-Billings (1998) points out that CRT is not simply an "explanatory narrative for the persistent problems of race, racism, and social injustice" (p. 22), but rather a call to speak and act boldly and to take risks.

Since the civil rights movement and particularly after the election of President Obama, many White people believe that racism is a thing of the past. However, numerous surveys reveal that, in contrast to White respondents, the majority of African Americans still see racism as a serious problem that affects their lives and, in particular, their job prospects. Over half report that they have suffered recent discriminatory incidents (Wise, 2009).

The persistence of racial discrimination and institutionalized racial advantage and disadvantage is clear in economic and other quality-of-life statistics. Consider these 2008 data about young children: Of the children under age 6 living in low-income families, 30% were White, 69% American Indian, 64% African American, and 64% Hispanic (Wight & Chau, 2009). Statistics from current reports reveal the growing gaps between Whites and people of color in both income and wealth (i.e., non-income assets such as houses, cars, investments). According to the Federal Reserve Board's triennial Survey of Consumer Finances (Inequality.org, 2014), the incomes of families of color are only 65% of what White families earn. The difference in assets is even wider; White families have about six times more wealth than families of color. Moreover, this gap is growing; the difference between the wealth of Blacks and Whites nearly tripled during the past 25 years, due largely to inequality in home ownership, income, education, and inheritances (Luhby, 2013). The 2008 economic crash widened these gaps as disproportionately more families of color lost their homes or saw their homes decrease in value.

In addition to the material impact of racism, many families face a constant and debilitating confrontation with racism and prejudice that has been described as "mundane extreme environmental stress" (Carroll, 1998; Grace, 1998; Peters, 1985). For example, when a Puerto Rican American family takes a trip to the mall, they are more likely to be rudely treated, ignored, and/or suspected of shoplifting than a European American family. Needless to say, these conditions profoundly affect all aspects of family life.

In contrast, people who are identified as *White* are racially privileged in every aspect of their lives. Whiteness is the "invisible norm" that sets the standards for everyone else's experience (Derman-Sparks & Ramsey, 2011; Howard, 1999; Kivel, 2002; Levine, 1994; McLaren, 1994; Sleeter, 1994). White people usually are not conscious of the racial advantage that underlies their daily encounters with the world (Irving, 2014; McIntosh, 1995), yet many people who live outside this circle of power and privilege see it clearly.

White people often feel insulted and bewildered when they are seen as racists because they have good intentions and are trying to reach out to other racial groups. However, as Boutte et al. (2011) note, "*good* people can and do contribute to racism and other forms of oppression" (p. 335) because, unless Whites make a conscious and concerted effort, most of them unwittingly contribute to institutional racism, by accepting and participating in social, economic, political, and educational institutions that perpetuate race-based inequities (e.g., media that promote stereotypes, banks with discriminatory practices, political entities with restrictive voting regulations, and schools that embody "savage inequalities," as described by Kozol, 1991).

Because many Whites do not see or vastly underestimate the existence and impact of racism, they can pretend to be "color-blind." Many teachers and parents of young children fall into this trap and insist that all children are the same and that preschoolers are too young to learn about race and racism (Husband, 2012). This stance silences teachers and children alike and leads to misconceptions and poor preparation for dealing with and challenging racism (Boutte et al., 2011).

Obviously those of us who benefit from racial privilege cannot know what it is like to live without it, but we can become more aware of the small, concrete ways in which we experience privilege throughout the day (Irving, 2014). Walking down the street, I wonder if I were not White would that police car make me feel afraid instead of safe? Watching television, I ask myself how would it feel to have my life and my image reflected only in stories about crime and sports? Going into stores, would I be getting this courteous service if I were a Latina instead of a White woman? Would they let me take all seven garments into the dressing room? Would they so readily accept my check or credit card?

Racial Identities and Attitudes

Examining our evolving racial identities and attitudes can help to deepen our understanding of how our lives and views have been influenced by our racial backgrounds. In the following sections, I will discuss three patterns of racial-identity development. The authors of these models label different phases in this process as "stages," which implies a predictable and universal sequence of racial identity development. However, in reality, it is

> [a complex and convoluted] process in which contradiction, opposition, incongruity, gaps, tensions are constantly present. . . . There is no endpoint . . . for the cultural dynamics are always changing, the contexts in which identities are claimed and in which meaning is made, are continually being erased and remade. (Scholl, 2002, p. 6)

As with theories of child development, these models help us recognize, anticipate, and understand nuances and changes, but we cannot assume that the sequence is inevitable or that the process is the same for everyone.

Because of different experiences and contexts, including racial advantage and disadvantage, racial identities and attitudes vary across those who identify as Whites, as members of other racial groups, or as bi- and multiracial individuals. For these reasons, I will discuss them separately. However, identities often shift across time and situation, so these divisions are more permeable and complicated than is implied by this presentation. (For more detailed accounts of how people move through these phases, see Derman-Sparks & Phillips, 1997; Derman-Sparks & Ramsey, 2011; Earick, 2009; Tatum, 1997).

Racial Identities and Attitudes of White People. Janet Helms (1990) formulated the following model of White identity development, based primarily on her work with adults. During the first stage, called *contact*, people understand racism only as overt individual acts, such as cross burnings. They are naïve about their own role in maintaining a more pervasive system of racial privilege. Often these individuals have very limited contact with people of color and believe the stereotypes in the popular press. Many Whites live out their lives at this stage.

At some point a White person may have an experience or a series of experiences, such as working with a person of color, reading a book, or taking a course that challenges present assumptions. This experience sets off the next stage, *disintegration*, during which people become aware of the racism that prevails in society and their own social relationships. They often feel uncomfortable and guilty about their privilege and may try to confront other Whites.

Often the pervasiveness of racism (especially its subtle manifestations) and the resistance of fellow Whites tempt individuals to *reintegrate* and revert to their familiar assumptions. One particularly strong pull is White bonding (Sleeter, 1994), often expressed in snide comments or jokes about people of color that enhance a sense of in-group solidarity and privilege among Whites. Many Whites, even if they disagree, may remain silent to avoid being ridiculed and ostracized.

However, some individuals continue their journey toward a deeper understanding of racism, and they may enter the *pseudo-independent* stage when they begin to question more deeply assumptions about White superiority but possibly still act in ways that perpetuate the system. Some White people at this stage try to deny their racism and prove that they are a "good White person" and distinct from "those other racist, bad Whites" (Hayes & Juárez, 2009, p. 738). To this end they may attempt to affiliate with people of color, who understandably may be suspicious of the Whites' motives and inconsistencies. At this point, learning about other Whites who have struggled with their own racism and have participated in antiracist movements can help White individuals channel their guilt into challenging the social and economic inequities of our society (Derman-Sparks & Ramsey, 2011, includes a list of current antiracist workers and organizations and resources about the history of White antiracist movements). People engaged in this process are at the *immersion/emersion* stage of racial identity development.

The final stage articulated by Helms is that of *autonomy*, when individuals have a clear and positive sense of themselves as White and participate in antiracist movements as a way of expressing their White identity. However, this stage is not an end point but rather a readiness to see and hear new information and be prepared to question and challenge even dearly held ideals and practices. Uncovering and unlearning racism is like peeling layers off of an endless onion: each time individuals think that they have gotten rid of one set of assumptions, they hit another set and have to start working on those.

Racial Identities and Attitudes of People of Color.

People from marginalized groups go through similar stages in their racial identity development, but they start at different vantage points. Whereas most Whites need to unlearn a false sense of universality and superiority, many people from other groups need to overcome false assumptions of inferiority. William Cross (1991) has identified five stages in achieving Nigrescence, the point at which African Americans have a clear and positive identity and a commitment to confronting racism. Although this theory is based on research with Black adults, similar stages have been identified in studies of other groups of color.

The first stage is called *preencounter,* in which individuals accept White dominance. Some may acknowledge that racism exists but feel that they are exceptions and are accepted by Whites. Alternatively, they may deny that they are a member of a marginalized group. Individuals at this stage often internalize the negative stereotypes and the blaming-the-victim ideology of the dominant group that can lead to a sense of hopelessness and victimization.

At the next stage, called *encounter*, individuals may experience racist events or come into contact with peers or teachers who cast a harsh light of reality on former illusions of being accepted by Whites. With this disillusionment—often accompanied by anger and bitterness—individuals then enter the *immersion/emersion* stage, in which they surround themselves with members of their own group, often avoiding contact with Whites and sometimes rejecting all symbols of White dominance, including what they perceive as White definitions of success such as doing well in school. College students' desires for racially separate dorms, meeting places, and dining halls reflect this stage of racial identity development. During this time individuals often immerse themselves in the literature, music, art, politics, and history of their group, which contributes to the formation of a positive racial identity.

With this kind of experience and support, pro–African American—or pro–Asian American or pro–Latino American—attitudes may shift from being anti-White to being more expansive and less defensive, and individuals emerge into the stage of *internalization*. At this point, they are poised to develop positive, healthy, and stable yet flexible racial identities that enable them to maintain close connections with their own racial community *and* participate in equal and reciprocal relationships with Whites. They are more likely to confront Whites who enact their racial privilege. Some Whites may feel threatened and dismiss or criticize their outspoken colleagues as "arrogant," "rude," and "hostile" (Hayes & Juárez, 2009, p. 736). These reactions and their possible consequences (e.g., loss of jobs) can be personally devastating and speak to the importance of having strong support groups and allies. They also underscore the necessity for Whites to understand and "unlearn" their own privilege.

The final stage, according to Cross's paradigm, is *internalization/commitment*. Now the strength of a person's racial identity is translated into a commitment to challenge the status quo and to work to address the inequities of society. As with White identity development, the process is more complex than this model suggests. Often people who have achieved a positive racial identity find that some years later they still have vestiges of their pre-encounter selves and may again go through one or more of these stages as they lay these assumptions to rest.

Identities and Attitudes of Biracial and Multiracial People. Many people identify with more than one racial group. With globalization and worldwide migrations, interracial relationships are more common, and the number of people who identify as bi- or multiracial is increasing. Also children raised in adoptive, blended, and foster families often live with parents from different racial backgrounds, raising the question of "who am I?" in new and complex ways (McGinnis, Smith, Ryan, & Howard, 2009).

In some communities, bi- and multiracial children and adults face the challenges of negative attitudes toward interracial marriage and transracial adoption or a mutual antagonism between their identity groups. Children may feel pressured by peers, schools, and community members to choose one aspect of their backgrounds and to deny the other(s) (Wardle, 1996). Some children do not feel accepted by any of their adoptive or heritage groups (Ramsey & Mika, 2011; Trenka, Oparah, & Shin, 2006; see also the essays in Root, 1992).

Kich (1992) identified three phases of identity development of biracial youth and adults. He links these with developmental stages, but many adults go through similar changes. First, biracial and multiracial individuals become aware of *differentness and dissonance* and often confront questions about who they are. In some cases they find that their differentness is devalued and feel caught between groups. The next stage, *struggle for acceptance,* often occurs during adolescence and is characterized by conflicts in loyalties—between parents and friends, between communities, and between different peer groups. During this time individuals may feel compelled to choose one aspect of their identity and reject the other one(s) but, in that process, feel diminished by "passing" as something they are not. Difficult as this stage is, it is also a time when people can learn how to hold multiple points of view and how to successfully negotiate between groups. Often they engage in a lot of self-exploration and learn about the lives of other multiracial people in the United States and other parts of the world—much as in Cross's *immersion* stage.

Self-acceptance and assertion of an interracial identity, the third and final stage, often occurs in late adolescence or early adulthood. At this point people have developed a stable self-acceptance of themselves as bi- or multiracial and no longer feel threatened by questions about their background. They may feel most comfortable in multiracial and multicultural groups. For example, McGinnis et al. (2009) found that the majority of the Korean transracial adoptees in their study had moved away from the predominately White rural and suburban communities where they had grown up and now lived in diverse urban areas. At this stage, bi- and multiracial people may become involved in activities that address discrimination against multiracial people (e.g., forms and policies that force individuals and families to identify with only one race).

All of these theories of racial identity development are parallel in several ways. People confront their illusions; deal with the tensions, anger, disillusionment, and disequilibrium that result; and then use information about their own group(s) and the larger society to develop more secure and realistic identities and a commitment to change the conditions that made this development so hard in the first place. At some points in the process, individuals from different groups may need to work separately. This temporary division often gives rise to fears of resegregation but can provide safe spaces for people to explore their experiences and to grow.

Racial identity formation sounds very neat and well defined in theory, but in reality it is complex and convoluted. Not everyone passes through all these phases in the prescribed order; many recycle through the same phase(s) several times. Furthermore, even during a given time period a person's racial identity and attitudes may shift across situations.

These models also offer hope—hope that everyone has the potential to transcend the damage that they have suffered from racism and challenge their racist environments. While we can never eliminate all the wounds of racism from our hearts and minds and lives, we can struggle to overcome its most deleterious effects and use our insights and skills to challenge racial injustice.

CHILDREN'S RESPONSES TO RACE

In the last half of the 20th century, largely in response to the civil rights movement and attempts to integrate schools, a number of researchers studied how children view race. However, the first two decades of the 21st century have seen a decline in the number of such studies in the United States. Much of the current research comes from other countries and has enriched our understanding of this complex dynamic.

Most early research in this country compared European American and African American children's responses to same- and cross-race people, often depicted by dolls, drawings, or photographs. Only later did researchers include a broader range of participants and stimulus materials. Thus our knowledge about children's reactions to racial differences is still incomplete and fragmented. However, the trends that have emerged may help parents and teachers to observe, ask questions, and respond to children's concerns more insightfully.

Children's responses to racial differences involve a complicated set of cognitive, affective, and behavioral dimensions (Cristol & Gimbert, 2008; Katz, 1976, 1982), and this review will be organized around these dimensions. However, as will become apparent, they continuously interact and mutually influence each other.

Do Young Children Notice Race?

This is one of the first questions that teachers and parents ask when the issue of race comes up. Often it is asked as a statement of denial: "Do young children *really* notice race? Kids just see other kids; they don't see color!" Husband (2010) describes how parents of his 1st-graders were adamant that their children were "too young" to learn about racism and discrimination. Contrary to this color-blind myth, young children *do* notice race and learn, interpret, rework, and enact the societal discourse about race (Boutte et al., 2011; Davis, 2009; MacNaughton, 2009; Perkins & Mebert, 2005). Infants have been observed to consistently react to racial differences by 6 months of age (Katz & Kofkin, 1997). By the age of 3 or 4, most children have a rudimentary concept of race and can easily identify, match, and label people by racial group (Holmes, 1995; Katz, 1976; Lam, Guerrero, Damree, & Enesco, 2011; Ramsey, 1991b; Ramsey & Meyers, 1990). During their elementary school years children elaborate their concepts of race as they begin to associate social information with the physical attributes that they see (Katz, 1976) and grasp the social connotations of racial distinctions (Alejandro-Wright, 1985).

The fact that race is so salient to young children supports the CRT position that race and racism permeate our social discourse and institutions. As discussed in Chapter 2, children form categories based on attributes that are relevant and visible in their environments, as race clearly is (Bigler & Liben, 2007).

Nevertheless, the timing and clarity of racial awareness appears to be related to children's contacts and experiences with people from different racial groups (Katz, 1976; Lam et al. 2011; Ramsey, 1991b; Ramsey & Myers, 1990). In our interviews, one European American 3-year-old from a predominately White community, when looking at a picture of a smiling African American child, said, "His teeth are different." Then he looked again and said with some hesitation, "No-o-o. [pause] His *skin* is different." However, European American children of the same age who lived in more racially integrated neighborhoods readily categorized the same photographed child as "Black."

Because young children have a hard time coordinating multiple attributes, the children may appear "color-blind" in one situation but intensely aware of race in another, as illustrated in the following conversation I had with one of my White interviewees:

> Four-year-old David was looking at photographs of unfamiliar African American children. "I'm gonna kick all those Black people out of the workplace!" he clenched his fists as he spoke. "They can't be there," he exclaimed. "They're bad! I'll punch and kick them if they go there!" Later in the interview, David was selecting friends from photographs of classmates. Two of his designated playmates were African American. When I casually observed that "some friends are White and some are Black," he emphatically disagreed. "Oh no! Michelle is brown!"

What Do Children Know and Think About Race?

A number of studies have suggested that children may not understand that race is an irrevocable characteristic until after they have acquired gender permanence (usually between ages 4 and 6) (Katz, 1976, 1982; Ramsey, 1987). Young children often confuse skin color difference with color transformations such as sun tanning, painting, and dyeing in which colors usually change from lighter to darker. In my interviews with children (Ramsey, 1982), virtually all of the 4- and 5-year-olds believed that everyone was inherently White and that Black people had been painted, sunburned, or dirtied. Only one child, an African American, had another theory. "If those White kids had left their skin on, they would be nice and black and shiny like me!"

However, as discussed in Chapter 2, we often underestimate children's knowledge. After conducting a series of studies in which preschoolers accurately predicted the race of older children and adults based on their parentage and their characteristics as babies and young children, Hirschfeld (1995) concluded that preschoolers *do* understand that the physical attributes we associate with race are inherited and unchangeable characteristics. Moreover, according to Hirschfeld, children have a relatively sophisticated view of race that includes not only physical characteristics but also the images of race in the popular culture. In a similar vein, Husband (2010) described his 1st-graders' broad and in-depth knowledge about how race and racism function in the United States. These findings clearly diverge from earlier ones and suggest that children may have a more accurate understanding of racial differences than previously thought. Alternatively, their level of understanding may be influenced by their circumstances (e.g., racial composition of the community or classroom; opportunities to discuss race), and by the particular questions that researchers ask.

Do Children Identify Themselves by Race?

Children's racial identity development varies across groups and across historical periods. In many early studies (e.g., Clark & Clark, 1947; Radke & Trager, 1950), European American children never expressed a wish to be Black, but African American children frequently appeared to either wish or to believe that they were White. M. Goodman, who wrote at about the same time (1952), offered a poignant example of an African American child in a predominantly White nursery school who assured her friends, "This morning I scrubbed and scrubbed and it [my skin] came almost white" (p. 56). This attitude was not unique to African American children. In his autobiography, Mexican American author Richard Rodriguez (1981) described his efforts as a child to "shave off" his dark skin with his father's razor. A kindergarten teacher described how one of his Latino students told him, "Maestro, my mom is giving me pills to turn me white" (Segura-Mora, 1999, p. 7). Sadly, this view is not limited to the United States; in many countries, "whitening" creams and lotions have a huge market.

Studies since the 1960s suggest that the positive images of people of color, now more evident in schools and in the media and consciously promoted in families and communities, may be reducing this dissonance. In studies done in the 1980s, African American children usually identified as Black (e.g., Cross, 1985; Farrell & Olson, 1982). In my research (Ramsey, 1983), African American children readily identified themselves as Black or Brown, but the effects of racist images were still clear as some adamantly pointed out that they were not as dark as some of their peers. As one African American child said, "I like Brown people, but not real, real Black people."

Cross (1985, 1987, 1991) suggests that these patterns of White identification and preference may be an attempt to resolve the contradiction between feeling personally valued, yet disparaged because of group membership. As evidence of this, Corenblum and Annis (1993) found that White children's personal self-esteem was positively related to their own group attitudes, whereas the reverse was true for a comparable group of Canadian Indian children. Spencer and Markstrom-Adams (1990) point out that children who have been targets of discrimination have to negotiate the conflict between loyalty to their own group and the negative images that prevail in the larger society.

White children, in contrast, do not have to negotiate between these conflicting messages about their identities and self-worth. Not surprisingly, they consistently identify as White, as shown in numerous studies over several decades (e.g., Clark & Clark, 1947; M. Goodman, 1952; Jordan & Hernandez-Reif, 2009; Ramsey, 1991b; Ramsey & Myers, 1990). Moreover, rather than expressing the ambivalence and misgivings about their identities as some children of color do, White children often go to considerable lengths to affirm their Whiteness and distinguish themselves from their peers of color (Van Ausdale & Feagin, 2001). (For reviews of more recent research about White children's construction of racial identities, see Derman-Sparks & Ramsey, 2011.)

How Do Children Feel About Racial Differences?

Children's emotional reactions to racial differences reflect their cognitive capacities and their interpretation of their social contexts (Cristol & Gimbert, 2008; Enesco, Lago, Rodríguez, & Guerrero, 2011). First, young children have a tendency to exaggerate the intergroup differences and minimize individual ones (Aboud & Amato, 2001; Holmes, 1995; Katz, 1976, 1982; Ramsey, 1987; Tajfel, 1973). This phenomenon is not limited to children; adults often sheepishly admit that they have trouble identifying individuals from cross-racial groups.

Children's constructions of race are influenced by what they hear and see as they grow up. Inevitably they will be exposed to racism in its many forms. They may hear explicit racist stereotypes and comments from the media, family members, or peers. They may also observe implicit manifestations of racism, such as noticing that people of color are doing more menial jobs or that they live in poorer neighborhoods (Quintana & McKown, 2008). By the preschool years, children begin to express or enact stereotypes of different racial groups (Ramsey, 1987, 1991; Ramsey & Williams, 2003; Tatum, 1997; Van Ausdale & Feagin, 2001).

One time a woman whom I introduced as an Algonquin visited our classroom of 3-year-olds. She had long braids and wore some beaded jewelry, but the children did not realize that Algonquians were "Indians." The children happily heard her stories and sang with her, until she told them that she was an "Indian," whereupon several children shrieked with fright and refused to stay in the group. Here a pleasurable experience was overwhelmed by the children's preconceived and stereotyped notions of "Indians."

Children's in-group preferences and racial bias tend to increase while they go through their preschool and early elementary years (Doyle & Aboud, 1993; Raabe & Beelmann, 2011). Lam et al. (2011), observing a multiracial group of British preschoolers, noticed that during their 4th year, all the children (regardless of race) showed an increase in White preference and began noticing and talking about intergroup differences.

The development of stronger in-group preferences does not necessarily mean that children feel negatively about out-groups (Kowalski, 2003). In describing preschoolers' responses to racially different dolls, Kowalski noted that

> Despite their clear in-group bias, children's evaluations of ethnic and racial out-groups . . . were generally positive and appeared to be influenced more by the social dynamics of the local context . . . than by any desire to elevate their own-group status by lowering that of others. (p. 687)

Enesco et al. (2011) found a similar pattern with Spanish preschoolers who generally expressed positive attitudes toward out-group members (in response to photographs). However, the effects of prevailing social attitudes were also evident in the children's derogatory comments about Latin Americans, who are negatively stereotyped by many Spaniards.

In my conversations with children, both African American and European American children frequently made disparaging remarks about the colors black and brown when referring to African Americans. Some researchers (e.g., Williams & Morland, 1976) argue that this aversion stems from an innate fear and dislike of the darkness. It could be argued, however, that these feelings also reflect the negative connotations of darkness (e.g., *blackball, blacklist,* and *black lie*), in contrast to positive connotations of lightness (e.g., *pure white, whitewash,* and *white lie*) that prevail in our society. Most environments and materials designed for children are brightly colored; dark colors are avoided or only used to depict evil or frightening figures. Earick

(2009) described the distress of one of her Black children when he learned from his White friend that the Black Knight is always the bad knight, in contrast to the good White Knight. "The conceptual metaphors 'White is good' and 'Black is bad' exemplify the embedded messages children are exposed to during . . . their racial identity construction/deconstruction" (p. 72). Colors are not benign; the values they are associated with carry strong and persistent racist messages to young children.

How Does Race Affect Children's Friendship Choices?

Across 4 decades of research White children have consistently shown stronger same-race preferences than their African American classmates do (Fox & Jordan, 1973; Hallinan & Teixeira, 1987; M. A. Newman, Liss, & Sherman, 1983; Ramsey & Myers, 1990), and this difference appears to increase with age (Aboud & Amato, 2001). Two recent Italian studies showed that White Italian children (ages 3–6) also showed strong same-race preferences (Castelli, Carraro, Tomelleri, & Amari, 2007; Castelli, Zogmaister, & Tomelleri, 2009). This pattern is not surprising because White children's in-group preferences in the United States and in Europe are generally supported by the prevailing power codes and social attitudes.

Exactly how children learn these views is unclear as results from studies examining the relationship between children's and parents' racial attitudes have yielded inconsistent and contradictory findings (Castelli et al., 2009). However, parents may play a role but in a more subtle and indirect fashion. Katz (2003) found that children whose parents spent more time talking about photographs of same-race individuals than different-race ones expressed more negative bias toward other racial groups than those whose parents divided their time equally among the photographs. A study of White Italian preschoolers and their parents showed that children's attitudes were not related to their parents' explicitly expressed views. However, mothers' implicit attitudes were linked with children's perceptions of positive and negative attributes of White and Black age-mates (Castelli et al., 2009). Lam et al. (2011) found that White British 5-year-olds generally assumed that their mothers would prefer that their children play with White classmates. The children who inferred that their mothers had particularly strong racial views expressed more consistent White preferences in their playmate choices.

Only a few researchers have studied children's actual cross-racial behavior, and the findings about younger children are mixed. Some studies revealed few signs of cross-race avoidance or antagonism in young children's choice of play partners (Holmes, 1995; Porter, 1971; Singleton & Asher, 1977; Urberg & Kaplan, 1989). In other studies, however, cross-race avoidance was more apparent, especially with White children (Finkelstein & Haskins, 1983; Fishbein & Imai, 1993; Ramsey & Myers, 1990). In some cases White children overtly rejected and demeaned their peers of color (Mednick & Ramsey, 2008; Van Ausdale & Feagin, 2001). In one observation, a White child refused to let her African American classmate hold a White doll because "I don't want an African taking care of her. I want an American. You're not an American, anybody can see that" (Van Ausdale & Feagin, 2001, p. 86).

Despite the number of studies that have been done, many questions about children's understanding and feelings about race remain unanswered. However, we can generally assume that children are not color-blind and that, by the age of 3 and probably even younger, they are aware of differences in skin color, hair, and facial features and can label and categorize people by race. Early on children begin to construct views of themselves and others by learning, interpreting, and incorporating racial stereotypes and other explicit and implicit messages about particular groups. Although they are sometimes confused about causes and implications of racial differences, they learn about racial hierarchies and what they should and should not say in front of adults. Children commonly express a dislike of dark colors that may reflect societal attitudes and reinforce negative associations with darker skin tones. Many children prefer same-race people, especially when they are choosing among unfamiliar people. White children in particular are at-risk for developing racial bias and a sense of racial superiority.

LEARNING AND CHALLENGING WHAT CHILDREN KNOW, THINK, AND FEEL ABOUT RACE

The previous sections have shown that young children are constructing views about race and enacting them in their play and in their interactions with others. These overall patterns provide helpful background information for teachers. However, each child has a unique history and perspective, and each group has its own dynamics, so teachers have to observe and talk with children to learn about their assumptions and interests and to engage them in creating meaningful activities to challenge and expand their views.

Researchers have found that teachers are often unaware of children's biases. Van Ausdale and Feagin (2001) observed as child participants (i.e., they avoided taking adult roles) described the teachers' disbelief and horror when they read the observations from their classrooms. The children were adept at hiding their racist views and comments from their teachers, similar to surreptitious bathroom talk and gun play. Likewise, the teachers in the 2nd-grade classroom my student observed seemed unaware of racial power differentials and often supported them (Mednick & Ramsey, 2008). In several cases they punished or reprimanded children of color based solely on a White child's report. Moreover, they frequently put White children into positions of authority by asking them to do special jobs (e.g., hand out papers, stack chairs, and so on). The children, in turn, often used these responsibilities to dominate or intimidate their peers (e.g., threatening not to give some children needed materials).

Thus teachers need to observe as unobtrusively as possible in order to learn what children really feel and do in reference to racial differences. In classrooms with little or no racial diversity, teachers can closely watch children's responses to stories, pictures, dolls, and puppets that portray different racial groups.

A few of the many possible activities designed to elicit children's ideas about race more directly are described below. Children's responses, in turn, may lead to extended activities that challenge misinformation and stereotypes that arise.

1. Show children photographs of people who represent a range of racial groups and ask them to describe all the things that they notice about each person or to tell stories about the people. Children's responses may reveal how much they notice race and what racially related assumptions they are making. If children reveal particular assumptions (e.g., "Indians live in teepees," "All Chinese people eat at restaurants"), find or make materials, images, and stories to encourage children to question and rethink their ideas.

2. To get a sense of children's assumptions about intergroup relationships, ask them to put photographs, dolls, or puppets representing different racial backgrounds into groups of those "who might be friends with each other." You can also show them different groupings of photographs, dolls, or puppets—some that are racially homogeneous and others that are racially mixed—and ask them questions like, "Do you think that these kids play together a lot or not so much?" Again, depending on what children say, you can set up dolls in the role-play area or doll house and read books and show images to provoke conversations and questions to challenge children's assumptions and expand their perspectives.

3. Use the color black and different shades of brown as often as possible when making Play-Doh, filling the water table, and putting out paints, markers, and paper. Observe the children's reactions. Do they avoid the black water in the water table? make assumptions about how brown play dough might smell? complain about being limited to five shades of brown at the easels? Encourage children to rethink their reactions by pointing out the richness of the colors, the effects of mixing them, the possibilities of creating images with black and brown, and the many shades of brown in the natural world.

Aside from setting up activities designed to elicit children's ideas about race, teachers can also build on "teachable moments" that arise, as described in the example that follows:

Janet, a White preschool teacher, overheard Sara and Alison, two White girls, say that Amanda, a Black classmate, could not play in the water table because she would get the water dirty. Janet was concerned, so she and her colleagues, Andrea, who was Black, and Lauren, who was White, developed multiple responses that reflect several of the goals mentioned in Chapter 1. First, Janet worked with the three girls to resolve their conflict. She encouraged Amanda to express her frustration and anger at being rejected and seen as "dirty"; Sara and Alison acknowledged that they had been wrong and apologized (albeit a bit reluctantly).

For the next few days the teachers listened closely to conversations of all the children to see if other children were making negative racial comments. Although they did not see a general pattern, the teachers knew that all of the children were growing up in a world of positive images of Whites and racist images and assumptions about people of color; they realized that this incident may only have been the tip of the iceberg. They introduced some class activities to elicit and challenge children's assumptions. For example, they organized water play with soap bubbles and had children wash dolls with different skin tones to give children a chance to explore and express their questions about skin color and what does and does not come off in water.

This incident also prompted the teachers to take a hard look at the books, photographs, and dolls in the classroom. They invited parents to be part of the process, and a small group of parents joined in the project, as did several children. As they all scrutinized their collections, they realized that, despite efforts to portray a wide range of people, the majority of the images, books, and dolls portrayed White middle-class families. They also noticed that many of the images of people of color were "touristy" and one-dimensional. In many cases they were portrayed in foreign countries, wearing traditional clothing, and celebrating festivals. The children, parents, and teachers went to the school library and the town libraries to look for better books. The local librarians listened to their concerns and spent some time looking at their collections and talked about what they could do to make them more representative of all people. In the process, the librarians also spoke about municipal budget cuts that were making it harder to expand their collections. This information prompted the class and some of the families to write letters to the city council about the need to keep the libraries well funded in order to ensure that their collections were current and accurately represented the diversity of the community and country.

The teachers and children read and looked at the books that they had found in the libraries. The ensuing conversations revealed questions and assumptions about race that led to further explorations. Several children seemed confused about why skin color varied and what these different shades meant. The teachers and children read books about the physiological basis for skin color differences, which led to self-portraits using skin-toned paints. As children mixed paints and came up with a range of colors, they saw skin-color gradations in a more realistic and less polemic way (e.g., no one was "white" and no one was "black"). The teachers and children invited families to join them for a late afternoon event where everyone used the paints to make self-portraits and enjoyed comparing how skin color differed within as well as across families. The whole group brainstormed names for the myriad of colors they had created.

After a few weeks the teachers noticed that the children learned to discern and describe nuances of colors and to see these distinctions in the world around them as they looked at food and the natural environment. To encourage children to think more broadly and not feel locked into creating the "correct color," to represent their skin tones, teachers also encouraged them to create portraits with other colors. In one project, children painted half of their face with their "real" color and half with their fantasy color

After several weeks of focusing on skin color, the teachers wanted to push the children to see other attributes as well. So they took facial photos of all the children and, using various computer programs, created posters that showed just the eyes or mouths of children. Then they challenged the children to see if they could identify their classmates based on these limited images. The children had difficulty at first, but began to look more carefully at their classmates and see subtle differences in their facial features.

The teachers had anticipated that some parents might be resistant to discussions and activities focused on race. For this reason, before they began their activities, they wrote a letter to the parents discussing their plans and rationale and invited parental input and participation at every step.

Despite their efforts, some parents were uncomfortable. A number were sure that their children did not "see race" and were too young to be discussing this topic. The teachers provided some brief summaries of research on children's racial awareness and shared observations of children's comments in response to books and images. As parents learned more, they rethought their assumptions about children being "innocent" of any racial beliefs and saw that talking about race was an antidote to, rather than an indicator of, racism.

A couple of White parents felt defensive and assumed that the teachers were accusing them of being racists. They also indicated, using code words, that they were uncomfortable about the increasing racial diversity in their community (e.g., "Before all of these new families moved in, we had such a nice friendly community"). Janet had several ongoing conversations with these parents, openly talking about her struggles recognizing and unlearning her own racist attitudes. She also created situations to bring those parents into nonthreatening collaborative interactions with parents of color (e.g., a committee to plan the end-of-the-year party). Obviously the parents' views did not immediately or drastically change, but they became more comfortable with the curriculum and more at ease with other groups of people.

The teachers had no illusions that they had completely stopped children and parents from thinking and expressing racist beliefs. However, they felt that the conversation was "on the table" and that they, in collaboration with the children and parents, had created a context for meaningful conversations about race and a safe space for asking questions and challenging racist attitudes and actions.

CHAPTER 5

The Context of Economic Class and Consumerism

REFLECTIONS ON ECONOMIC CLASS

Imbedded in much of the discussion about racial power and privilege is the question of social class, or the more transparent term "economic class" (Derman-Sparks & Edwards, 2010). In your responses to the question asked in the Part II introduction, "Who am I?" did you include your economic background? The salience of economic class in our lives varies but often is stronger the further one is from the "norm"—in this case, middle- or upper-class lifestyles that are erroneously viewed as the way most Americans live.

To clarify your own background and your assumptions about different economic-class groups and possible causes and remedies of unequal income distribution, ask yourself the following questions:

- What are my worries about money? Am I afraid that I won't be able to pay the rent or feed my children? Or am I concerned that I might have to forgo a vacation trip or the purchase of a new car?
- How do I imagine my future financial situation? Do I have a savings account? money for retirement? Or do I have to spend all of my available funds on day-to-day necessities?
- What do I assume about the race, gender, education, and character of people in different income groups and jobs? What images come to my mind when I hear that someone is a homeless person? a lawyer? an assembly-line worker? an executive? a chambermaid? a manager?
- When I think about people in different jobs or life circumstances, which ones do I assume are more like me? What are the economic backgrounds of members of my social network?
- What are my assumptions about why some people are affluent and others are poor? Do I think it is fair? inevitable? the natural course of events?
- Who or what is responsible for disparities in wealth, education, and job opportunities? Individual effort? luck? racial discrimination? the economic system? political system?

- What do I think needs to be changed about our economic system? What reforms do I or would I actively support?
- What would I be willing to give up to ensure that everyone in the world had adequate shelter, food, and education?

People who enjoy at least some financial security are often unaware of the role it plays in their lives. A number of years ago I worked for a federally funded child-care center in a low-income neighborhood. At first I was impatient with families and fellow teachers who seemed to have "a crisis a minute." After a while, however, I realized how much my crisis-free life depended on my relative affluence. For one thing, I owned a car and did not have to rely on public transportation or hitch rides to get to work. Furthermore, if my car broke down, I could get it repaired right away and did not spend weeks relying on friends and family members for rides. Having a car and sufficient money meant that I could take care of numerous errands quickly and easily. When I needed to go to a doctor, I made an appointment, went, and was back in an hour or so. I did not have to spend a day waiting in an emergency room or clinic to get the same service.

A 1st-grade teacher came to a similar realization (Earick, 2010). Initially she was frustrated by a child from a low-income family who engaged in a lot of challenging behavior (e.g., stealing, disrupting, and not doing her homework). She was especially critical of the child's mother for not helping the child with her work. As the teacher worked with an inquiry group of colleagues, she became more aware that her assumptions about good behavior and parenting were based on her own middle-class upbringing. She worked hard to monitor and change her responses and approached the child and mother more openly and supportively. With much effort on everyone's parts, the child became more engaged in the classroom and in the end was a successful student.

The myths of equal opportunity, meritocracy, and guaranteed upward mobility have made it difficult for people in the United States to face the fact that we are economically divided into distinct classes and that those divisions affect every aspect of family life, childrearing, and children's future prospects. Recently many politicians and journalists have been talking about these inequities and urging that we change our ways and live up to our egalitarian principles. However, research has shown that, although many people express discontent with economic inequalities, very few actually *support* egalitarian reforms (Furnham & Stacey, 1991). Most people resist change because they do not want to give up their own resources and fear that major economic changes might mean the loss of their familiar way of life. Even individuals who are economically disadvantaged are committed to the current system because they buy into the American dream and expect to be upwardly mobile in the future. As an example, in the 1st decade of the 21st century low-income and working-class people were part of the political force that resisted raising taxes on the most affluent members of our society, even though it was against their self-interest. Likewise, many politicians extol the virtues of universal high-quality preschools, especially for low-income children. Yet they balk at any suggestion of raising taxes on the wealthy to pay for these initiatives.

One reason that we as a society do not face the reality and consequences of economic inequities is that most of us are entangled in consumerism that keeps us focused on chasing the latest fashions and gadgets and searching for the best deal. Consumerism both reflects and exacerbates economic gaps. Moreover, it affects many aspects of children's lives, including their views of themselves and others, as will be discussed later in this chapter.

SOCIOECONOMIC DIVISIONS IN THE UNITED STATES

Despite our egalitarian principles, the United States has been moving *away from*, not toward, more equitable distribution of wealth, especially since the 1980s (Huston, 1991; McLoyd, 1998). The 2010 U.S. Census revealed that, since 1979, the share of the aggregate income for 80% of the population has declined (56.40% to 44.76%), whereas the wealthiest 20% have seen a significant increase in their share of the aggregate income (43.60% to 50.24%) (Boho, October 11, 2011). Most analysts attribute this trend to the reduced numbers of well-paid semiskilled and low-skilled jobs available to Americans because of outsourcing to developing countries, cutbacks in federal programs that supported poor families before the 1980s, welfare "reform" that further eliminated these supports in the 1990s, deregulation and tax cuts that favor the wealthy and penalize poor and working-class families, and the changes in family configuration that have resulted in higher numbers of female-headed households.

The Great Recession in 2008, in which millions of people lost their jobs and homes, further widened these gaps. According to R. Newman (2014), personal wealth, which includes assets such as real estate, savings, investments, and cars, but not income, dropped by 43% for the median American family. However, households in the top 10% lost only 18% of their wealth, whereas those in the lowest 25% lost 75% of their wealth. These differences are reflected in current consumption patterns. Schwartz (2014) notes that the "recovery" from the 2008 recession has been driven by the spending of the most affluent 5%. As a result middle-class restaurants, hotels, stores, and clothing and appliance lines are losing money, whereas those that attract the affluent are thriving. One particularly painful comparison for early childhood educators is that in 2013, "25 hedge fund managers made more than twice as much as all of the kindergarten teachers in America combined" (Krugman, 2014, p. A25). As discussed in Chapter 4 these inequities intersect with race, gender, and age, with disproportionately more families of color, female-headed households, children, and elderly people falling below the poverty line.

The increasing economic disparities have had a profound effect on children. Since the 1980s the numbers of children growing up in very poor (deprived) households and in very affluent (luxurious) households increased, whereas the number of children growing up in "frugal" (i.e., working-class) or "comfortable" (i.e., middle-class) households declined. The number of children raised in poverty continues to rise. From 2006 to 2011 the percentage of children living below the official poverty line increased from 18% to 22%, and when we include the "near poor," the percentage has changed from 40% to 45%—almost half—of all children in the United States under 18 (Addy, Engelhardt, & Skinner, 2013). The statistics are even worse for younger children: 49% of children under 3 years of age and 48% of those between 3 and 5 years of age are currently living in poor or near poor households.

By being aware of the economic circumstances of the families in schools and centers, teachers can work with parents and children to recognize, challenge, and, as much as possible, overcome the effects of economic inequities. The next sections provide descriptions of family life in different economic groups based on Annette Lareau's (2011) well-known ethnographic study. As you read these descriptions, be aware that all families have unique histories and circumstances, so these accounts are suggestive rather than definitive. Moreover, as Li (2008) points out, many families straddle more than one class as their education and aspirations may differ from their current economic conditions (e.g., highly educated immigrants who were professionals in their home country but are now doing menial work; formerly comfortable middle-class families who have suffered recent financial losses).

Lareau and her colleagues observed and interviewed poor, working-class, and middle-class families. Each income group included 2 White and 2 Black families, making a total of 12 families (4 in each income group and 6 White and 6 Black). The children were in elementary school during the first part of the study, and follow-up interviews were conducted 10 years later, when the participants were young adults (ages 19–21). It should be noted that Lareau and her colleagues conducted this study before middle and working classes had been battered by the 2008 recession. Moreover, while some of the poor families were threatened with eviction, none of them were homeless, so I will add some information from other studies about raising children under those circumstances. I definitely recommend reading Lareau's entire book, *Unequal Childhoods: Class, Race, and Family Life* (2011), as it vividly and comprehensively portrays how economic circumstances affect every aspect of childrearing and family life. Furthermore, it illustrates how teachers and other professionals are often blind to those effects and unintentionally exacerbate them.

Growing Up Poor

Lareau's (2011) observations and interviews with the four poor families vividly illustrated how they lived on the edge, with the constant strain of stretching every last penny to support family members. Food was often short, and children learned never to ask for second helpings or to take any food items without permission. Empty refrigerators were the norm. The families lived in decrepit and sometimes dangerous housing, and they faced the threat of eviction when they could not come up with the rent. Because they had no cars or convenient public transportation, they shopped at small local overpriced stores, and buying a treat for their children was a rarity. Their lives were filled with inconveniences. Lareau described how for one family, doing the laundry was an ordeal of first finding a store where they could get change and then carrying bags of laundry to and from the laundromat on public transportation. Likewise, getting to a doctor's appointment required complex logistics of timing and transportation.

However, their lives were not necessarily bleak. Relatives often lived in the same apartment building or nearby; children played with cousins and visited with aunts and uncles and grandparents on a daily basis. Kinship was important, and children developed strong bonds with their extended families. The children also enjoyed a lot of autonomy from adult oversight (in contrast to the middle-class children in the study) and were responsible for taking care of themselves, doing household chores, and running errands. To the best of their ability adults ensured that the children were fed and clothed, but they did not monitor their play, nor did they praise and encourage their creative endeavors. Lareau termed this approach to childrearing as "accomplishment of natural growth" (p. 67), letting childhood and events unfold without worrying about children's achievements and future prospects. Children did not participate in organized after-school activities that cost money, but instead spent a lot of relaxed time hanging out with friends and relatives; they invented games and entertained themselves, and watched a lot of television.

One salient difference among the income groups was the distribution of power and use of language. In contrast to the middle-class parents, the low-income adults treated the children in an authoritarian manner, issuing directives and often administering or threatening physical punishment in the face of disobedience. They did not negotiate or explain their decisions; when parents were frustrated, they asserted their power through curses and threats. In contrast, when the parents were talking to professionals such as teachers or doctors, they often were passive and confused and intimidated by professional aloofness and jargon. Parents wanted their children to succeed in school but did not have the time to help children with homework or the confidence to advocate for their children. As a result of these dynamics within families and between families and institutions, children did not learn how to use the more indirect language and negotiating strategies that are common in schools and other middle-class organizations.

In the follow-up interviews 10 years later, three of the four children Lareau had observed had dropped out of high school; all worked minimum wage jobs and lived with relatives (usually their mothers); no one had a driver's license. Neither they nor their older siblings had married. Some of their older siblings had children, and a few of them had been arrested. Most of their younger siblings were still in school, but some were struggling with behavior and academic issues.

Although Lareau did not include homeless families in her study, an increasing number of children live in temporary shelters and face particularly difficult challenges. Without a home, parents face huge obstacles supporting their children's development and education (Stronge, 1992). Homelessness is associated with severe physical problems (e.g., poor nutrition, lack of immunizations, high lead levels in the blood); socioemotional stressors (e.g., depressed parents, abuse and neglect); and poor educational experiences and outcomes (e.g., inconsistent attendance, grade retention, poor performance on tests) (Molnar, Rath, & Klein, 1990). Children often face bureaucratic and logistic barriers to attending school (e.g., lack of permanent addresses and transportation to school) and frequent disruptions in their schooling due to moves. Once they get to school, they are often stigmatized by peers and teachers. When they get "home" to the shelter or the cramped quarters of a temporary placement, they do not have a space free of distractions to complete homework assignments or to get adequate rest. Tim, a child living in a shelter, illustrates how homelessness can affect a child's experience in school: "She [my teacher] hates everything I do—she made red checks on all my worksheets and anyhow I can't do homework and stuff in the shelter—there's always noise and stuff going on" (Polakow, 1993, p. 145). The observer in Tim's classroom also noted that when children ate lunch or worked in pairs, Tim was always alone, and the teacher did not attempt to help him find a partner or become part of a group. Tim fell asleep several times in the afternoon and each time was "jerked back to attention by Mrs. Devon's voice calling his name" (p. 145).

Growing Up in the Working Class

The four working-class families in Lareau's (2011) study shared many similarities with the poor families in terms of language and discipline styles and children's activities. They too had to be careful about how they spent their money but did not have the extreme constraints and constant anxiety that the poor families faced in terms of keeping children housed, fed, and clothed. They lived in modest dwellings but not in the decrepit housing of the poor families. Like the poor families, the working-class families had many relatives nearby, and family events and connections were extremely important. Occasionally children requested and were allowed to participate in organized activities (e.g., one child played on a football team for a year), but they were not a high priority for the parents. Some parents wanted to enroll their children in extracurricular activities but did not have the money. By and large, parents were content to have their children spend a lot of relaxed time with cousins and friends. When they heard about the hectic schedules of the middle-class children, some of them felt those parents were wrong to pressure their children to do so many activities.

The children were relatively free of adult supervision and invented informal games and activities. Often the boys would gather in fairly large groups (5–10 neighborhood friends) playing sports, going to the store, and telling stories. Lareau points out that these long-term friendships provided a good context for children to learn how to relate to people of all ages and how be creative and independent. However, she notes that they were not "getting training in the enactment of *organizational* rules" (p. 81) as they would if they participated in organized extracurricular activities.

As with the low-income families, the working-class parents were authoritarian and directive with their children. Also some were assertive with people like landlords and utilities personnel. However, they were quite passive and intimidated in school conferences and other interactions with teachers and counselors. Educational professionals often spoke quickly and used a lot of technical terms but never checked to see if parents understood the information. Even when children were experiencing difficulties, and teachers and administrators were offering confusing and contradictory advice, the parents (usually the mother) waited to see what the experts decided and accepted their plans. Teachers and counselors on their part acknowledged that the parents were caring and supportive of their children, but they were frustrated that the parents were not more proactive in helping their children with their schoolwork or demanding services for them.

Like the low-income parents, the working-class parents worried about their children and wanted them to succeed in school. They did their best to provide clothing and food so that their children would be prepared for school. However, they believed that school was the domain of the experts and their role was to attend parent conferences but not to intervene or advocate for services.

In the follow-up interviews when the children were in their late teens or early 20s, three of the four child participants had graduated from high school and the fourth had earned his GED. One was in college; two were working full-time in a trade (construction and painting) and living with their parents; one was a homemaker, living with her husband and child. One had a driver's license, and one had had his license suspended; two did not have a license. In terms of their siblings, two younger ones were still in school; two older ones had tried postsecondary education but had dropped out and, in the process, had accrued significant debt in student loans. One sibling was in the navy, and others were working at fairly stable jobs.

Growing Up in the Middle and Upper-Middle Class

The four middle-class and upper-middle-class families in the study provided a stark contrast to the working-class and low-income families in terms of values, relationships with children, educational goals, and interactions with the outside world. Instead of the "accomplishment of natural growth" (Lareau, 2011, p. 67), the parents actively engaged in "concerted cultivation" of their children's cultural capital (p. 165). Middle-class parents saw raising children as a project and worked hard to groom them for future success (i.e., to be accepted into competitive colleges and launched into professional careers).

The parents were very attentive to the details of their children's academic work, often spending long hours helping with homework and school projects. High grades were a clear priority, and parents constantly encouraged their children to do well. When their children were struggling, they obtained extra supports either through the school or private tutors or therapists. Parents kept in close contact with teachers and administrators and did not hesitate to intervene on behalf of their children or to advocate for change in particular school policies or practices with which they disagreed. They populated the parent organizations such as the PTO and exerted considerable influence through them.

To further cultivate their children's cultural and social capital, parents encouraged their children to join multiple extracurricular activities to develop and hone skills in sports and the arts. Whereas the working-class and low-income children had many hours of relaxed leisure time when they could hang out with friends and relatives, the middle-class children often rushed from activity to activity. They spent little time away from adult supervision and expected—even demanded—that adults pay attention to them. Parents devoted much of their own leisure time to taking children to classes, practices, and sporting and musical events, offering advice and cheering them on.

Family relationships were quite different from the other two groups. Because of busy schedules and the priority to cultivate children's skills children spent most of their time with same-age peers in organized activities and little time with siblings, cousins, and neighborhood friends. The sense of kinship with family was not as strong. Sibling rivalry was often fierce, and children frequently announced that they hated each other. Unlike their autonomous counterparts in the other groups, children often turned to their parents to settle conflicts. Moreover, expectations related to the extended family were different. One middle-class child decided, with his parents' consent, not to attend his cousin's graduation. In the other two groups, this decision would have been an unthinkable breach of kinship expectations.

The middle-class families were more apt to live far away from extended family members, which may account in part for this difference. However, even when relatives lived close by, busy schedules precluded more than occasional visits, usually for special occasions, not the frequent casual contact that the other families had.

The power dynamics within families and between them and the world varied considerably from the other two groups. In terms of discipline, middle-class parents generally avoided directives or threats. They reasoned with their children and explained their expectations and requests. Whereas the working-class and poor children usually complied with parental demands with no comment, the middle-class children often argued back and negotiated for changes and exceptions to rules.

Children also witnessed their parents' assertiveness with professionals and organizations. Unlike the parents in the other two groups, these parents understood technical terms and jargon and often argued with teachers and school administrators when they did not like what was happening with their child. They also had the resources to influence the outcomes of school decisions. In one case, the parents were unhappy that their daughter did not test into the gifted and talented class, and so they had her tested by a private psychologist and used those results and their clout to get her into the class. Parents often "coached" their children on negotiating skills, having them role-play what they might say to their coach or teacher. Thus, while these children did not have the opportunities to learn how to manage their own lives and to function autonomously, they did learn how to talk with professionals and how to negotiate with institutions and organizations.

Efforts to ensure the best experiences and outcomes for their children were not always successful. One girl with severe learning disabilities continued to struggle academically despite help from tutors and considerable advocacy and support from her parents. To her parents' anguish, ultimately she did not to college. Another mother expressed disappointment that her son did not get into a top-tier college. On the whole, however, these families moved through the world expecting and getting the services, supports, and success that they expected.

The follow-up interviews showed that all of the middle-class children had graduated from high school; three were in college, one of whom had been accepted into medical school; the fourth was attending cosmetology school. All four had their driver's license. Of their siblings, two were still in high school, and two were in college, and one had dropped out of college.

Comparing Families Across Economic Classes

Despite their vastly different circumstances and values, the families in all three economic groups also shared many similarities. All families had moments of connection, affection, and fun. They also had rituals such as favorite meals, television shows, games, and outings that strengthened the sense of membership in the family. Regardless of financial circumstances, family members spent a lot of time in daily routines and chores such as getting up, dressed, and out the door to school or work; preparing and eating meals; cleaning clothes and living spaces; and doing homework. Contrary to popular stereotypes, the degree of organization did not vary across income groups. In fact, the lower income homes were often described as very tidy, and some of the middle-class ones as chaotic. None of the families were immune from tragedies, disappointments, and anxieties, showing that wealth cannot buffer people from all adversity. Finally, across all groups family members had a range of temperaments and skills and interests.

Even with these similarities among the families, the gap between economic classes is wide and troubling yet all too often ignored. As one of the research assistants said after a day when he visited both a middle-class and a poor family, "I . . . was distraught for days. . . . Every day there are poor people and comfortable people living in the same world, ignoring (or not seeing) each other and having wildly divergent experiences. But we generally don't see this" (Lareau, 2011, p. 354). The follow-up interviews also demonstrate how much economic class determines adult outcomes. In their early 20s, the children were living lives very similar to those of their parents. Furthermore, they show how the American dream of "rags to riches" and equal opportunity is beyond the reach of most poor people. Despite the hard work and hopes of their parents, children growing up poor and to some extent those in the working class did not have the skills and credentials to move into a more affluent life.

Many of the institutions that serve families from different income groups also reflect and reinforce these gaps. In a study comparing a day care center that served low-income and working-class families with one that served primarily children of professional parents, Nelson and Schutz (2007) found differences that echoed those in Lareau's families. In the first center, the "accomplishment of natural growth" was reflected in fewer interactions between adults and children, authoritarian discipline strategies, and offhand praise and attention directed at children's work. In contrast, the teachers at the center serving more affluent families sounded very much like the parents in Lareau's middle-class families. The "concerted cultivation" approach was evident in the teachers' frequent interactions with the children, their intense interest in children's efforts, and their reasoning orientation to discipline.

Stephanie Smith (2012) notes that the directive style of teaching in low-income schools may put poor children at a further disadvantage in terms of their future schooling. She compared the authoritarian and explicit methods and the democratic and implicit ones in two Head Start programs. Both groups of children were from low-income families, but those in the democratic classrooms were more likely to internalize and follow school behavioral expectations than those in the authoritarian ones.

For all of these reasons, children who are poor are less likely to be successful in school than their more affluent peers. The high rates of school failure among children from poor families is especially ironic and frustrating because Stipek and Ryan (1997) found that, across all racial groups, economically disadvantaged preschool and kindergarten children entered school equally optimistic of school success and as motivated to do well in school as their middle-class peers were. However, they were already behind the middle-class children in academic skills. This disadvantage, along with the other pressures described in this section, eventually eroded their optimism and motivation. Unfortunately, teachers often do not recognize and build on the skills that children do have, and the current emphasis on testing is making it even harder to look beyond academic "deficits." The strategies discussed in Chapter 3 to build strong family and school partnerships and to use family "funds of knowledge" (González et al., 2005) may enable teachers to recognize the skills that children are learning at home and to develop teaching strategies that build on these capabilities. In describing her work with Mexican-origin families, Tenery (2005) noted that "the harder their lives, the more coping and survival skills [family members] develop. Strategizing households are rich resources for learning . . . [skills and practices that] may be utilized in the classroom" (p. 129).

How can we create schools where children from all economic backgrounds learn and thrive? A vital first step is to push for equal funding for schools, to reduce the "savage inequalities" (Kozol, 1991) that relentlessly exacerbate the achievement and opportunity gaps between economic groups. This effort includes full funding for federally sponsored early childhood programs such as Head Start. Then parents and teachers can work together to develop challenging and rigorous educational experiences that provide tools for children to critically understand their circumstances and create ways to overcome and change them (e.g., learning math skills by analyzing the extent and causes of the unequal distribution of wealth; studying history from the perspective of economic inequities and how people have challenged them). All of us—children, parents, educators, and community members—have to learn about the causes and costs of increasing economic polarization and collaborate to reverse this trend.

CHILDREN'S AWARENESS AND FEELINGS ABOUT ECONOMIC CLASS

Young children rarely notice indices of economic class such as educational level and occupational prestige, but they do take note of concrete clues such as differences in clothing, homes, and possessions. Moreover, they daily experience the effects of economic privilege or disadvantage by watching how their parents interact with teachers, retail personnel, agencies, and institutions. They interpret this information and construct their ideas and expectations about the role that economics plays in the world. In the last 3 decades of the 20th century, a number of researchers studied children's awareness and understanding of economic differences; however, the past 2 decades have seen little work in this area.

As children experience economic disparity, they are exposed to many images and stories that reflect the prevailing attitudes that being rich is better than being poor (Leahy, 1983). Even preschoolers assume that rich people are happier and more likeable than poor people (Naimark, 1983; Ramsey, 1991c). Children also develop expectations about their own futures. Echoing Lareau's observations, one low-income child interviewee said, "Rich folks like you are lawyers and poor folks like me go into the army" (Cottle, 1974, p. 136).

Leahy (1983), who conducted a major research project (720 subjects, aged 6 through adolescence) on children's views of social class, found that children's understanding goes through three phases. Early elementary school children are likely to both describe and explain poverty and wealth in observable concrete terms, such as types of possessions and residences. At about 10 years of age, children begin to refer to psychological traits, such as motivation, in their explanations of why people are in different economic circumstances. Finally, adolescents are capable of seeing the role of social and economic structures in the unequal distribution of wealth. During childhood and adolescence, children increasingly make the connection between having a job and getting money and learn more about the status and financial benefits associated with specific occupations (Furnham & Stacey, 1991).

Young children are developing a sense of fairness that reflects increasing capacities to notice inequities and see others' perspectives (Damon, 1980). They often hold strong views on what is and is not fair. When I asked preschoolers if it was fair that some people had more money than others, only a few of them tried to answer, but those who did said that it was not fair and some suggested that the rich should share with poor people (Ramsey, 1991c).

At the same time, young children are also learning stereotypes, especially about poor people. On the walk back from dropping off food at a soup kitchen, the director of a middle-class preschool heard the following conversation among the children who had accompanied her. They were talking about the people they had seen waiting for lunch (Williams & Norton, 2008, p. 108):

Jack: Those kids were dirty.
Robbie: Yeah . . . dirty.
Jack: I bet they were hungry.
Robbie: That's because their daddies don't work for them to get them food. Their daddies are lazy. My daddy isn't lazy. He works to get us food.

Jack: It's a good thing for them that we got them food.
Robbie: Yeah . . . They should get to work . . . and take a bath!

Needless to say, this observation triggered many conversations among the school staff about the source of these stereotypes and the pitfalls of doing activities related to homelessness without a great deal of reflection and preparation. This conversation also suggests that middle-class children (like adults) may claim to want more equitable distribution of resources when responding to interview questions, but when they actually see and interact with poor people, they are repulsed and, at best, have an attitude of "noblesse oblige" to help, but not to respect or befriend, the poor (Williams & Norton, 2008, p. 109). Sadly, these latter attitudes become more prominent as children get older (Leahy, 1983, 1990).

Taken together, these findings illustrate how children in our society, even as they are developing their ideas about fairness, are caught in one of the underlying contradictions of our society: the ideal of equality versus the economic competitiveness and individualism that inevitably result in inequality (Chafel, 1997).

Many schools are economically segregated, but even when children from different class backgrounds are together, they often divide themselves along economic lines. As Lareau describes, they are learning different social goals and skills in their homes and neighborhoods and may gravitate toward those with similar values and play styles. Moreover, many already know each other from neighborhoods and previous school experiences. Low-income children, if they have attended school at all, have probably gone to Head Start or other publically funded programs, whereas more affluent children usually attend tuition-based preschool programs. A series of observations of peer interactions in a racially and economically diverse 3rd grade (Kang & Ramsey, 1993) showed that children divided themselves more by gender and economic class than by race. In their conversations children talked about possessions, interests, and activities that often reflected varying levels of affluence and different neighborhoods that potentially inhibited cross-class contacts. Mednick and Ramsey (2008) found a similar pattern in a 2nd-grade classroom, in which the White middle-class children frequently talked about after-school activities (e.g., gymnastics, piano lessons, organized sports) and expensive family vacations. These topics excluded their low-income peers of color.

These economic divisions often extend to parents, who, like their children, usually feel more comfortable with others from similar backgrounds. This segregation exacerbates the children's economic divides because parents usually make plans with parents they know well. Teachers and administrators need to find creative ways to bridge these gaps. In one school teachers were concerned about a low-income child who was isolated from his more affluent peers. His grandparents were raising him because his parents were incarcerated, and they too did not fit in with the younger wealthier parents. In the course of a conversation with the grandparents, the teachers learned that the family had an old dump truck that was ideal for transporting the soil for the school garden. The arrival of the dump truck and the soil was a great occasion for everyone. All the children were thrilled to see how a dump truck works, and the child and his grandparents became instant celebrities. As a result of this event, the family felt appreciated and more comfortable at the school, and the child developed more peer connections.

In summary, young children have a limited understanding of social-class differences. However, in preschool and early elementary school, they are developing ideas and attitudes about rich and poor people and their own economic futures. Moreover, they are learning the values and social skills that prevail in their own economic groups, and these differences may lead to segregated friendships and peer groups. Through close collaboration and mutual respect, teachers, children, and families can work to reduce these barriers and to recognize and challenge the economic inequities that define the lives of all people.

One impediment to engaging children in critiquing the economic system is the fact that they (and all of us) are so imbedded in it—in particular the hyperconsumption that has become a way of life for many people in our society. Thus we need to consider how this pressure affects children, families, and schools.

REFLECTIONS ON CONSUMERISM

All of us engage in the market economy, but the relative importance of consuming varies across cultures, families, and individuals. Raising these issues with children requires an understanding of how we as adults feel about acquiring and owning goods and how these views affect our relationships with others. Some questions to ask yourself are:

- How often do I engage in nonmonetary activities, such as watching a sunset or enjoying the company of friends versus activities that involve spending money, such as shopping, going to the movies, or taking expensive trips? Which type of activity do I tend to value more?
- How much time do I spend shopping at stores? online? looking at printed and online catalogues? home shopping networks? How do I feel when I see these tantalizing products?
- How do I feel when I see friends buying new products (e.g., clothes, sports equipment, latest media device) or taking expensive vacations? Do I feel envious? pressured to "catch up"?

- How do other people's material wealth and ability to keep up with the latest fads affect my opinion of them?
- What proportion of my income do I spend on food, shelter, and transportation? on charities and social justice work? on nonessentials?
- What factors do I consider when I am contemplating a purchase? How essential is the item? How will this purchase affect my life? Do I consider if the new item is worth the raw materials and energy to produce it? How do I feel about buying the item secondhand?
- What are my motives for shopping? Do I only shop when I need a specific item? Do I shop for fun or to be with others? Do I shop to feel better about myself?

An interesting historical perspective on our consuming habits is that in earlier times (and now in some remote areas), towns and villages had "market days," one day a week or month for everyone to do their shopping and bartering (Bowers, 2001). As we think about the role of consuming in our lives, we can ask ourselves how we would feel if we were suddenly transported to that time rather than living in a society where we have "24/7" shopping.

LIVING IN A CONSUMERIST SOCIETY

Over the years I have watched in dismay as more and more open land near where I live is covered by malls. At the same time, the population in the area is not growing, which means that I and my neighbors are buying more, and that does not include our online purchases. This hyperconsumption is not unique to my town—it is a national trend. The fact that many of us have far more "stuff" than we need is evident in the self-storage units that have also sprouted up all over the country.

What does this material abundance mean? Are we happier? According to a number of studies, the answer is "no." Once people have sufficient food, shelter, and clothing, increased material wealth tends to bring, not happiness, but rather a "hankering for more; envy of people with the most perceived successes; and intense emotional isolation spawned by resolute pursuit of personal ambitions" (Luthar & Becker, 2002, p. 1593). Moreover, pursuit of material wealth often squeezes out alternative sources of satisfaction such as developing physical skills, creating works of art, or spending time with family and friends (Csikszentmihalyi, 1999).

Consumerism in different forms has been part of society for millennia, but over the last few decades it has changed. "What is novel about [contemporary consumerism] is the amount and number of consumer goods that are [now offered] . . . and the rate at which they are changed, exchanged and thrown away and how fast new consumer items are developed" (Benn, 2004, p. 108).

Another change is that "consumerism has become a global, universal, and unifying movement" (Benn, 2004, p. 108). Many products that were once only available in particular countries or regions now show up everywhere (e.g., jeans, T-shirts, electronic devices). As a result, there is a worldwide common culture, especially among young people who enjoy the same clothes, music, movies, and videogames regardless of where they live.

Despite this unifying effect, competitive consumerism aggravates economic divisions. Even if people have sufficient food and shelter, their inability to keep up with competitive consumerism makes them "feel poor," which affects their psychological functioning (Csikszentmihalyi, 1999; McLoyd & Ceballo, 1998) and can lead to shame and, in some cases, violence (Vorrasi & Gabarino, 2000).

Consumerism, class, race, and gender interact in some particularly damaging ways. As mentioned before, a disproportionably high percentage of people of color, female-headed households, and children are in the low-income groups and excluded from many of the opportunities that come with affluence. For people denied other avenues of success and satisfaction, "with a limited capacity to ward off self-contempt and self hatred" (West, 1993, p. 17), purchasing power may become an exaggerated source of self-esteem and sense of well-being. Also people who are targets of discrimination are judged more harshly on the basis of their appearance and possessions and often feel pressured to purchase the latest of everything—clothing, nail and hair treatments, cars and equipment. Merchandisers, fully aware of these dynamics, mount intensive advertising campaigns in poor communities (Nightingale, 1993), especially for alcohol and tobacco products (Stephen Smith, 2010). Thus people who can least afford it often end up going into debt to purchase expensive highly advertised items. The resulting financial pressures, in turn, can cause interpersonal tensions and undermine the sense of community and care for others and potential for political action (Haymes, 1995; West, 1993).

CHILDREN'S UNDERSTANDING AND EXPERIENCE OF CONSUMERISM

Children's worlds today are saturated with consumerist messages claiming that purchasing power brings happiness and therefore everyone should buy, buy, buy. As a result of media deregulation in the 1980s, television programs and websites for children are filled with overt and covert commercials. Child development research and sophisticated neurological technology are used by marketers to "hook" children onto particular shows, brands, and products (Barbero, 2008; Schor, 2004). In 2009, corporations spent $15–17 billion on advertising to children (Shah, 2010). According to some accounts,

American children under 12 spend $18 billion a year, and teens around $160 billion. By some estimates children and teens are a $670 billion dollar market when their influence on parental spending is factored in (Shah, 2010). This means that the U.S. child-related market is bigger than the total economies of the 115 poorest countries in the world (Barbero, 2008). Aside from viewing thousands of commercials on television, children frequently accompany parents on shopping trips and see aisle after aisle filled with enticing objects packaged and placed to elicit children's desire to have them. A subtext of all of these messages is that satisfying a never-ending desire to own new items takes priority over other considerations, such as the needs of family members and friends, environmental sustainability, or equitable distribution of resources. (For a comprehensive review of the pervasiveness of consumerism and its effects on children and families and ideas for neutralizing these pressures see *Kids Unbranded: Tips for Parenting in a Commercial Culture,* created and distributed by newdream.org (The Center for a New American Dream, n.d.)

What are the psychological effects of growing up in a consumerist society where children are bombarded by messages that they need more and more? Schor (2004), reporting on her research study of children as consumers, observed that a high level of consuming is associated with lower self-esteem in peer and family relationships, suggesting that "consumer involvement may push out strong social connections" (p. 173). She also observed that the more children are "enmeshed in the culture of getting and spending . . . the worse they feel about themselves, the more depressed they are, [and] the more they are beset by anxiety, headaches, stomach aches, and boredom" (p. 173). She further notes that the psychological costs of consumerism fall hardest on poor children who often feel deeply inadequate because they lack the means to buy all the current fads.

Teachers and parents often share their concerns about children's obsessions for particular products and the control that comes with ownership. Recently one teacher was shocked to hear a child in her toddler group tell a classmate, "You can come over to my house if you bring [name of a popular toy]." Another teacher reported that one of her preschoolers tried to make classmates "pay money" to move their trucks along "his" block structures. Moreover, children often use their "consumer identities" to jostle for social power and control (e.g., one-upping each other about their possessions) (Saltmarsh, 2009, p. 55).

As they grow up in a consumerist society, participating in the marketplace becomes central to many children's sense of self and the basis for friendships (Shah, 2010). Moreover, children are learning to relate to physical objects, especially toys, in terms of *getting* and *having* instead of *using* and *enjoying* (Kline, 1993). Many begin to identify themselves solely as consumers, and consumerism comes to dominate children's peer culture (Shah, 2010).

Many of the toys promoted on television and computer games are specific to that program; when the fad fades, the toys lose their appeal. Furthermore, children's play with these toys often revolves around the media-created identities—not around the children's own ideas and feelings. Many scripts are saturated with sexualized and stereotyped messages (e.g., Bratz dolls) and violence (e.g., action figures). In contrast, children create elaborate and ever-changing play with non-scripted toys such as blocks and stuffed animals. Once, many years ago, I kept track of the different roles our sons assigned their two favorite teddy bears over the period of an hour. In this short time, the bears were spectators, misbehaving and crying babies, karate kickers, bicycle riders, water skiers, naughty dogs, and pirates' parrots. Meanwhile, the much-begged-for action figures remained untouched.

In this context, children's sense of efficacy rests not in contributing to the family or community welfare or creating games but in getting the resources to purchase new toys and clothes. Children are also learning to judge each other—and themselves—by the desirability and quantity of toys that they own. "It's mine!" and "I had it first!" have echoed in schoolyards in the United States for generations. Nowadays, however, the competition and exclusion based on the latest toys or clothing are fierce, often triggering demands to parents to buy yet another product.

Teachers sometimes unintentionally encourage children's consumerism. Discussions around Christmas holidays often revolve around anticipated toys—a time when children from low-income families (not to mention those who do not celebrate Christmas) may feel left out. In some classes, children bring in toys for "sharing," which can aggravate possession-oriented competition. One parent told me about how her kindergartner worried for days about what to bring in for sharing; if his toy was not the glitzy attention-grabber of the day, he came home bitterly disappointed.

We need to be asking ourselves: What are the long-term effects of this passion for consuming on children's self-images and their social relationships? Of particular relevance to multicultural education is the question, what does hyperconsumerism mean in a world of limited resources and unequal distribution of wealth? How can children think about racial and social justice, equality, and community when their sense of well-being is tied to getting more toys or clothes than another child? "In fact, [when] . . . most of one's psychic energy becomes invested in material goals, . . . sensitivity in other [nonmaterial] rewards . . . atrophy" (Csikszentmihalyi, 1999, p. 823).

As a start to generating possible approaches to address these concerns, consider the distinction between ecocentric and egocentric consumerism (Benn, 2004). Ecocentric individuals make purchasing decisions with the well-being of themselves, their families and communities, and the environment in mind. Egocentric consumers, in contrast, focus only on fulfilling their own needs, with no thought of the consequences. Most people engage in both kinds of consumption, with their behavior varying across contexts.

Our children will inevitably grow up to be consumers, and some may always have to prop themselves up with the latest gadget, outfit, car, or piece of sports equipment. Moreover, their children will also learn to be consumers. As one critic observed, "Childhood makes capitalism hum over the long haul" (Cook, quoted in Shah, 2010). However, if children grow up learning an ecocentric orientation to life, they may be able to see beyond the momentary pleasure of new possessions to develop other dimensions of their lives and relationships, and to challenge the pressures of consumerism.

LEARNING AND CHALLENGING WHAT CHILDREN KNOW, THINK, AND FEEL ABOUT ECONOMIC CLASS AND CONSUMERISM

Children are not likely to talk explicitly about economic class since they probably have only a vague awareness of what it means. However, as teachers, you can observe to see how economic backgrounds are affecting children's social contacts and play themes and ask more direct questions to learn what economic concepts and attitudes children are developing. In contrast to their ideas about economic class, the role consumerism plays in children's lives may be obvious in children's conversations about possessions they have and wish they could have. As explained in Chapter 4, all of these observations and conversations with children can lead to activities that broaden understanding and challenge assumptions and misinformation, as seen in the following examples:

1. To get an idea of how economic class might be affecting children's relationships, you might observe grouping patterns and playmate choices to see if there are economically based divisions. If so, what factors seem to be contributing to it (e.g., after-school activities, play styles, possessions, friendships among parents)? If there is evidence of class-based divisions, you might organize children in cross-class groups for projects or snack and in those contexts encourage them to talk about shared experiences such as an upcoming event or ongoing project in the classroom. Although I generally discourage promoting movies and television programs, they do have a wide appeal and talking about them may foster initial connections. Children's family books (see Chapter 3 for a description) provide opportunities to learn about each other's lives and see how every family has an interesting story and does fun activities regardless of economic circumstances. Discussions about what children did on vacation or over the weekend can generate competitive stories about exciting trips and activities. To deflect this dynamic, you can ask them to talk about who was with them or describe one particular activity, and be sure that an afternoon

at a grandmother's apartment gets as much acclaim and interest as playing on a beach at a resort. If children start competing about their glamorous trips (e.g., "I've been to Disneyworld three times and have ridden the . . . "), shift their focus back to describing why a particular activity was fun rather than rattling off lists of places and experiences. Using the funds of knowledge approach (González et al., 2005), talk to parents and invite them to visit and share their skills and hobbies with the children. Be sure that numbers of parent visitors are balanced across income groups.

2. To learn what knowledge and beliefs children are developing about economic class, show children photographs of people who have different kinds of jobs and represent different levels of affluence (with a good distribution of different racial, gender, and ability representation across occupational and income groups to avoid reinforcing stereotypes). Ask children to describe what they notice and/or to tell a story about a person in the photograph to see what (if any) characteristics, especially stereotypes, they associate with particular jobs and income levels. In response to children's questions and assumptions about jobs, read stories about people who do different types of work and illustrate how each person makes a contribution. (See "Suggested Books for Children" at www.tcpress.com, Free Downloads.) In order to broaden children's awareness of how everyone plays an important role at the school, invite some less visible staff members (e.g., cooks, custodians, administrative assistants) to come to the class and talk about what they do. These visits also may challenge the implicit staff hierarchies and power differentials that children often notice. If children express negative views of poor people, then introduce stories using books, persona dolls, or puppet shows that demonstrate how many people suffer hardship through no fault of their own and how they can be strong, creative, and caring despite many challenges. You and the children can critically read stories about beautiful (and rich) princesses and their handsome princes and consider questions that challenge these romantic images (e.g., "What do you think these people are really like? Are they ever sad? Mean? Make a mess? How do they treat other people? Do you think it is fair that they have so much money and others have only a little?"

3. To get a sense of the role consumerism plays in children's lives, observe children's dramatic play and listen to conversations to see how often they describe and compare new clothes or toys or enact shopping. How concerned are particular individuals with getting a particular product? What roles do possessions play in their sense of self? in their social interactions? Do children include or exclude

others or compete with them on the basis of owning or not owning popular items? If children are focusing on the thrill of "getting" a highly prized item, teachers can acknowledge those feelings but also encourage children to see the utility and purpose of the item rather than just its logo or connection to a movie (e.g., "I know you are excited about your princess sneakers: are they comfortable? Do you like running in them?" "That was very nice of your nana to buy you the Spider-Man sweatshirt; it looks cozy and warm." When children get clothes and toys from donations or thrift stores, be sure that they are honored as much as new items. Children who always try to "prop themselves up" with their possessions (e.g., using them to gain friends or outshine others) are probably masking their lack of confidence and feelings of inadequacy. Encourage them to develop more "power-from-within" and "power-with," as discussed in Chapter 3. Draw attention to their pleasure in making a block tower, molding play dough, playing with peers—activities that do not require a fancy new toy. Finally, if children are convinced that certain foods, toys, and clothing are more desirable because they are advertised and or attached to a movie or show, collaborate with them to develop some counternarratives. One humorous approach is to put on puppet shows where the characters are making outlandish promises about a particular product; then of course, when it is revealed, the item is nothing like the advertised version. Children can also look at advertisement clips and see what words and images are used to make an item look bigger, better, or tastier than it really is. Children might create their own overblown "commercials" with skits or drawings or small video cameras.

4. Observe how different children speak and act in regard to distribution of classroom materials. Do they readily share or try to gain control over certain items? Do they encourage others to join in their play, or do they try to "sell" or "charge" classmates for use of items or structures they have made? As with all of these inquiries, individual children will vary a great deal in their expectations and behavior. You can challenge assumptions about private ownership and the need to control materials by encouraging collaborative projects (see Chapter 3). If a child is being overly protective of something she has made, she can be encouraged to experience the satisfaction of seeing others enjoy her work (e.g., drive their cars on the ramp she made, eat the "food" that she has prepared and set out in role-play). If a particular object is the source of a lot of conflict, then you and the children can talk about creating ways for everyone to have access to it (e.g., the highly coveted "knight" in the Lego collection could be housed in a collaboratively built castle).

Often children's activities and interests open up the opportunity to explore their ideas about economic class and consumerism and challenge their assumptions, as the following vignette illustrates. (For other examples, including a research study in which teachers used story books to stimulate discussions, see Supplemental Resource 5.1 for Chapter 5, at www.tcpress.com)

Anita (Filipina) and Silvia (Argentinian) taught in a child-care center in a diverse, low- and lower-middle-income neighborhood in the city. They noticed that their preschoolers spent much of their time "going to the store" and often referred to highly advertised products in a competitive way while they were "shopping." The teachers decided to use this interest to expand and challenge some of the ideas that children expressed during their play. The teachers set up a store in the pretend area, where each item cost one bill of play money. Then they gave each child a bag with different numbers of bills. As the children came and "shopped," some were delighted, and others dismayed at how many or how few items they could "buy." At the end of the activity, the teachers had the children stand in a circle, next to their "purchases." As the children saw the discrepancies and expressed their outrage at the lack of fairness, the teachers talked about how these discrepancies affected everyone in the country. Several children chimed in with how their parents worried about money and often did not have enough. The teachers followed up by reading several stories about families from different economic backgrounds. Then the teachers worked with the children in small groups to think about ways to make the game and—in some conversations—the larger world more fair. Each group had a chance to "run" the store for a day to try out some of their ideas.

A week or so later, the teachers put new empty containers into the "store," some of which had labels of highly advertised products and others no brand labels at all. They also included plastic replicas of vegetables and fruits. They then gave children equal amounts of money but assigned different values to the products—the advertised ones cost two bills, whereas the brand-free items and the fruits and vegetables each cost one. They watched as children were first drawn to enticing brand names and then struggled with deciding how to spend their money. Afterwards the teachers and the children discussed why certain products were more appealing than others. This conversation led children to look at advertisements in magazines and describe ones they had seen on television. They pointed out specific ways that advertisements make children want particular products (e.g., showing close-ups of gooey cheese or chocolate) even if they were expensive and not good for them.

The annual classroom Harvest Festival was celebrated right before Thanksgiving and "Black Friday," the epitome of competitive hyperconsumption in the United States. After everyone had eaten, the children enacted several "advertisements" that highlighted the disparity between the tantalizing images and the disappointing reality of many products. These hilarious skits made everyone laugh and opened up a lively discussion about the financial pressures of the holiday season. Parents particularly bemoaned the unrelenting advertisements for expensive toys, clothes, and vacations that made their children yearn for gifts that the parents could not afford. The teachers suggested that everyone brainstorm ideas for money-free gifts (e.g., family outings, game nights, a favorite home-made meal, back rubs, assistance with chores) and stress-free holidays (e.g., inviting friends for dinner or going for a walk to see holiday lights instead of heading to the mall or watching TV). As children, parents, and teachers called out ideas, two parents wrote them down on paper placed on a couple of easels. Pretty soon four large sheets of paper were filled, and one of the parents offered to type them up and send them out to all the parents by email and to print up copies as well. The gathering ended with people still laughing about the skits and making plans for "stress-free" and "money-free" holidays. Some were promising to stay in touch and help each other not get "sucked back" into the mall or online shopping. On his way out, one father told the teachers that he had hardly seen his family for months because he had been working overtime in order to "give my kids a good Christmas." "I have a lot to think about . . . " he said as he walked out of the door.

CHAPTER 6

The Context of Culture and the Natural Environment

Culture is a multifaceted, fluid, and amorphous concept, yet it profoundly affects how we perceive the world and relate to people, objects, and nature. The first part of this chapter describes how cultural values influence social relationships, particularly those between families and schools, and how teachers and children can explore cultural differences and mitigate tensions. In the second section I discuss how interactions with the natural world also reflect cultural values and how children can expand their perspectives, deepen their connections with nature, and learn about sustainability.

REFLECTIONS ON CULTURE

To help readers identify the complexities and influences of their cultural backgrounds, this section consists of several discussions including two sets of questions, each addressing a different aspect of culture.

Because culture is typically associated with specific countries and bygone traditions, many people, especially those whose families have lived in the United States for several generations, assume that they have no distinctive culture—that they are "just plain American," as one of my students told me. Yet everything individuals do reflects their cultures—from singing a good night lullaby to a child, to ordering in a restaurant, to stopping at a red light (Bowers, 2001). These conventions are not biologically encoded on human brains; they are rituals and rules that have evolved within cultural contexts. However, because they are taken for granted, they are often seen as a universal norm and not expressions of a "culture."

Culture is also usually associated with specific customs or artifacts. However, it is a "multitude of values inherited from past human activity" that guide rituals, beliefs, and rules of behavior (Boyer, 2013, pp. 153). Garcia (1990) notes that cultures function on two levels: the *explicit* culture includes overt symbols and expressions, such as clothes, food, tools, holidays, music, and crafts; the *implicit* culture embodies the values, meanings, and philosophies that underlie the overt symbols. For example, shopping malls that have evolved from open markets, small shops, and downtown shopping areas are expressions of our culture's competitive consumption. Graduation ceremonies mesh traditional and contemporary rituals and reflect our national interest in formal schooling.

Take a few minutes to think about the cultural influences in your life, at both the explicit and implicit levels.

- On my list of identifying attributes, did I include language? religion? ancestral country of origin?
- When I think of my family and childhood, what foods, rituals, holidays, and artifacts come to mind? What culture(s) do they represent? What underlying values do they reflect?
- How do people in my family and communities relate to each other? How do they define family and community? How do they prioritize or balance the needs and desires of individuals, families, and community?
- How do I define success? What are my aspirations? fears? How do these reflect in my family's values and childrearing practices?

Many people see cultures as clearly defined and frozen in time, with static rituals and artifacts being passed down through generations. In fact, cultures are not pure or fixed entities with clear boundaries. They continuously change, merge, and diverge in "restless uneasy processes in which the fusion of elements is often . . . dislocating, jarring, and discomforting" (Scholl, 2002, p. 6).

With new experiences, insights, and knowledge, people adapt traditions to meet new realities. For example, think of how the tradition of schooling has evolved during the last 3 millennia. In a recent study Tudge (2008) observed that all over the world some children are now attending day care centers, an option that was rarely available or desired 30 to 50 years ago. Embracing both tradition and change is challenging but can also lead to innovative and empowering programs. As one example, an elementary school teacher in Tucson (Amanti, 2005) knew that working with horses was a traditional occupation and passion for her students and their families who lived in Arizona and Mexico. She developed a comprehensive and vibrant curriculum based on horses that blended students' cultural roots, current activities with families, and state-mandated requirements for literature and writing, science, and math.

Many individuals, especially in the United States and other highly mobile societies, belong to a number of cultures (e.g., family of origin, school, workplace, recreational activities). They shift among groups many times during their lifetimes and even in the course of a day, sometimes with ease and at other times with discomfort and conflict.

To consider your own cultural affiliations and how your values and behaviors are evolving, ask yourself the following questions:

- What cultural groups do I belong to? How do they interact? Do I move easily from group to group? Do I sometimes feel tension among different dimensions of my life? How? Why? Where do I feel most/least comfortable?
- How do my values and practices as a parent and/or teacher differ from those of my own parents and teachers? What traditions and priorities have I discarded, maintained, changed, or reclaimed?
- How is my current life influenced by intergenerational knowledge passed down in my family or community?
- What new values and traditions have I incorporated into my life? Where did they come from?
- How do new and old values influence my goals and decisionmaking? How do they interact? Are they complementary or contradictory? How do I navigate between them?

Cultures also intersect with racial, gender, and economic backgrounds, and we need to be mindful of the heterogeneity of all groups (Tudge et al., 2006). In some cases, race and culture overlap, but not always, and one cannot assume that people who may look alike to outsiders (e.g., African Americans and Haitian Americans; Anglo Americans and recent Russian immigrants) share the same culture. Gender groups and disability groups also develop distinctive cultures, as do occupational groups, which, in turn, may reflect economic-class differences. Tudge et al. point out that many cross-cultural studies conflate culture and race with economics and type of community. As examples, middle-class suburban European Americans are often compared to poor urban African Americans; children in rural Kenya have been compared with urban street children in Brazil. Thus, when learning about "cultural differences," it is necessary to view information and comparisons with a critical eye and avoid making sweeping assumptions.

Finally, it is to critical bear in mind that a culture can never be "learned" through a few activities and information (Moule, 2012). An individual can learn *about* cultures and respect and appreciate their values, traditions, rituals, and changes but must live within a culture to truly know and understand it.

CHILDREN AND CULTURE

Cultural values guide virtually all practices including how parents raise and teach their children. Because people in this country come from diverse backgrounds, many children and families experience cultural discontinuity when they encounter schools and other institutions.

Cultural Influences on Childrearing

How a society wants children to grow up is defined by cultural values and mores that influence every detail of sleeping, feeding, playing, and schooling routines. The following questions highlight a few of the many daily decisions that parents and teachers make that reflect culturally defined childrearing goals.

- Should toddlers feed themselves, or should they be fed? Should they be carried or encouraged to walk alone?
- At what age should children be toilet-trained? How should they be toilet-trained?
- When should children start doing chores? At what age is a child old enough to care for his or her younger siblings? Is it more important that children do household chores or get their homework done?
- How should children act around adults? Should they be respectfully quiet or seek attention and praise?
- How do children learn? by observing and imitating adults in the community or by being "taught" by professional teachers?

As indicated by the questions above, cultural contexts influence a wide range of childrearing goals, strategies, and outcomes, such as the following:

- Level of independence (Gonzalez-Ramos, Zayas, Cohen, 1998)
- Discipline practices (Kobayashi-Winata & Power, 1989)
- Play patterns (Farver, Kim, & Lee, 1995; Farver & Shin, 1997; Roopnarine, Lasker, Sacks, & Stores, 1998; Whiting & Edwards, 1988; Whiting & Whiting, 1975), play themes (Riojas-Cortez, 2001), and peer conflicts (Martínez-Lozano, Sánchez-Medina, & Goudena, 2011).
- Types of daily activities (Tudge et al., 2006)
- Sleeping patterns (Lebra, 1994)
- Family responsibilities (Whiting & Edwards, 1988)
- Emotional development and regulation (Boyer, 2013; Farver, Welles-Nystrom, Frosch, Wimbarti, Hoppe-Graff, 1997)

Learning about the cultural roots of the children is critical to understanding the interface between families and schools (DeGaetano, Williams, & Volk, 1998). Yet, as pointed out above, cultures are always changing, and individuals within groups vary a great deal, so this information can guide questions and observations but should not lead to assumptions about particular children and families.

Cultural Discontinuities Between Home and School

Many children and their families feel culturally alienated from schools at some point in their lives. They may have recently immigrated to this country or perhaps have moved to a new region, or from the country to the city or vice versa. They may have lived in the community all of their lives but find that their cultural values do not mesh with those of the schools. Whatever its cause, cultural discontinuity can be the source of considerable stress for children and families *and* for teachers who realize that their classrooms are not "working" for at least some children and their parents. The following discussion focuses primarily on the experiences of recent immigrants, but many of the dilemmas described are relevant to families who feel culturally alienated from schools for other reasons.

Children of recent immigrants suffer from the dislocation and confusion that inevitably accompanies leaving a familiar place and coping with a whole new language and school structure (Guo & Dalli, 2012). Kennedy, Cameron, and Greene (2012), who studied young immigrant children in England, argue that, rather than focusing solely on children's readiness for school, the emphasis should be on the *school's readiness* to receive children from different cultural groups. Similar to the funds of knowledge approach (González et al., 2005), the authors urge staff members to learn about the children's cultural backgrounds, spend time with the families, and understand the "emotional journey" (Kennedy et al., 2012, p. 27) that children undertake when they transition away from familiar friends and places and enter a new school.

Language. Immigrants to any country usually have to learn a new language. This is an enormous challenge for children and adults alike and can delay children's academic progress and integration into the social world. Social isolation can be particularly acute if only one or two children speak a particular language (Guo & Dalli, 2012). (For more details about this study, see Supplemental Resource 6.1 for Chapter 6, at www.tcpress.com).

Bilingual education programs have been successful in easing transitions for children and families by providing comfortable language environments and support to maintain their home language. Unfortunately, because of political opposition beginning in the 1990s (see Crawford, 1999; Minami & Ovando, 1995; Moran & Hakuta, 1995), many bilingual programs have been curtailed or eliminated in the United States. This change is unfortunate because being bilingual is a tremendous advantage in our increasingly globalized world. In many countries children routinely grow up fluent in two, three, and sometimes more languages. In the United States we all must challenge the assumption that children can learn only one language and push for programs that support children and families to maintain their home languages while they also learn English. (For an account of one family's efforts to raise their children to be bilingual, see Supplemental Resource 6.2 for Chapter 6, at www.tcpress.com).

In the current "English-only" climate, many children not only lose the asset of speaking two languages, they may also become more distant from their families. Moreover, because language and culture are inextricably bound (Boyer, 2013; Nieto & Bode, 2012), the loss of language also diminishes children's cultural knowledge and connections. Children usually learn the new language and customs more rapidly than their parents do because they are in school all day. As a result, they frequently serve as translators, negotiators, and teachers for their parents. This role reversal enables children to take more responsibility and to hone their English language skills, but it can also undermine respect for parental authority. In some cases children refuse to speak their home language, with the result that parents and grandparents cannot pass on their values, beliefs, and wisdom; and families become less intimate (Wong-Filmore, 1991).

Immigrant parents often wonder how they can assist their children to learn a new language and also maintain their home language. One center started a support group for parents of dual-language learners so that they could talk about these issues, understand the tensions and conflicts, and help each other devise strategies to support their children to learn both languages. The parents felt that this group was a wonderful resource for both practical and emotional support. In this case all of the parents spoke enough English so that they could communicate with each other. When parents do not have a shared language, then staff and parents can arrange for translators.

Different Approaches to Education. In addition to cultural and language differences, many immigrants arrive with their own educational experiences, philosophies, and expectations that often clash with the views of early childhood teachers. (For several examples of conflicts related to educational philosophy and parent involvement, see Supplemental Resource 6.3 for Chapter 6, at www.tcpress.com) For example, Latino parents of children in a Head Start program studied by Tobin and Kurban (2010) expressed concern that their children were not learning their numbers and letters and would not be prepared for kindergarten. The teachers, also Latinas, were adamant that the children were learning those skills but doing it through play not the didactic instruction that the parents would recognize. The teachers saw the "parents' wishes . . . as misunderstandings needing correcting rather than as ideological differences needing negotiating" (p. 84). Tobin and Kurban point out a perplexing dilemma that many progressive educators, such as myself, face: We want to be responsive to parents' concerns, but often parents have internalized the well-publicized emphasis on learning specific academic skills and preparing for high-stakes testing. Thus they want us to teach in a didactic, skill-oriented manner that contradicts our educational values and practices that ironically include being culturally responsive. To make matters more complicated, often the parents who express these views are marginalized by our society—recent immigrants, people of color, and working-class and poor people from all racial groups—the very families that we want to empower.

In response to these dilemmas, Adair and Tobin (2008) suggest that, rather than defend their educational philosophies and practices, early childhood teachers should enter into dialogues with parents "in which the starting assumption is one of respect for all points of view" (p. 147). Sharing video clips of a typical day at the center can trigger discussions, in which "both teachers and parents . . . talk through their uncertainty and ambivalence about what is best for children, rather than stake out and defend positions" (p. 148). Finally, teachers need to be aware of the stresses that immigrant families face (e.g., discrimination, poverty, legal issues) and try to help families find resources and develop connections with each other. Even if teachers cannot meet these needs, they can at least listen and provide emotional support.

Alienation and Distrust. Cultural gaps between families and school are often aggravated by mutual distrust, poverty, and politics. Many current immigrants face resentment and hostility in their new communities. Relationships between White school personnel and families of color, even if they have lived here for generations, are often tainted with racism, poverty, and decades of exclusion. Tensions can arise even in in the absence of obvious cross-group differences. For example, in some ethnically homogeneous rural communities, loggers and hunters are incensed by environmental curricula that advocate preserving trees and wildlife.

Ironically, Native American children, whose families have lived in North America the longest of any group, have particularly difficult transitions to school (Hare & Anderson, 2010). Rather than the immigrant experience of leaving familiar people and places, Native People suffered brutal conquest, genocide, expulsion, and colonization in places where they had always lived. Moreover, thousands of children were forcibly removed from their families and communities and sent to residential schools that were designed to erase children's cultures and language. While less draconian than the forced removal of children in previous decades, current educational philosophies and practices are in many respects antithetical to indigenous ways of living and learning (Niles, Byers, & Krueger, 2007; Nxumalo, Pacini-Ketchabaw, & Rowan, 2011). For all of these reasons, many parents understandably distrust the schools. (For more examples and in-depth discussions of tensions between indigenous people and schools and possible strategies for ameliorating them, see Supplemental Resource 6.4 for Chapter 6, at www.tcpress.com)

Classroom Interactions. Aside from the more obvious variations in experiences, languages, and philosophies, subtle differences in how teachers and children interact often cause misunderstandings. Tharp (1989) describes four dimensions of cultural differences that account for some children's discomfort and underachievement in classrooms:

1. Social organization (e.g., emphasis on individual accomplishments versus peer cooperation)
2. Conventions and courtesies of speech (e.g., the length of time one waits for a response, rhythms of speech and responses)
3. Patterns of cognitive functioning, in particular the difference between verbal/analytic and visual/holistic thinking
4. Motivation (e.g., responses to rewards versus affection)

As a result of these differences, children's behaviors at school are often misinterpreted, and their skills are underestimated by teachers and peers who do not understand a child's culture. Children who are taught to quietly respect adults may be seen as withdrawn when compared with their outspoken, attention-seeking peers. In contrast, children accustomed to more spontaneous conversations may feel frustrated waiting for teachers to call on them.

Cultural variations in language use and construction also potentially disrupt communication. Souto-Manning (2007) describes how her 1st-grade student George was seen as a "behavior problem" largely because he used African American Vernacular English (AAVE) and had a more direct, assertive way of speaking than is "acceptable" in American classrooms. Souto-Manning describes how she had to acknowledge her own limitations to recognize and reconsider her initial negative responses to George's speaking style. As she and the other students became more familiar with George's language patterns, they were able to hear what he was saying and to appreciate rather than "correct" the grammatical structure of AAVE. As George felt more accepted, he became an eager participant in the classroom, and everyone, teacher and students alike, gained a broader understanding of the richness and variety of language.

Working With and Through Cultural Discontinuities. Beyond simply adjusting to and surviving in an unfamiliar culture, children are also developing their identities and orientations to two (or more) cultures. Darder (1991) describes four possible outcomes for children growing up biculturally, including those in groups who have been historically marginalized (e.g., Latin Americans, African Americans, Native Americans) as well as new immigrants:

1. *Alienation*: Children identify only with the dominant culture and do not acknowledge any ties to their home culture.
2. *Dualism*: Children separate their lives, behaving and thinking one way at home and another way at school.
3. *Separatism*: Children live totally in their home culture and avoid or reject the dominant culture.
4. *Negotiation*: In this most positive outcome, children live in both worlds and affirm both identities but maintain a critical stance and use experiences in one culture to understand and critique the other one.

These outcomes provide a framework for understanding children's evolving identities and attest to the complexity of growing up in two or more cultural contexts. The challenges children and families face when transitioning to a new school environment are often underestimated; all too often difficulties are blamed on poor parenting (Hare & Anderson, 2010). Both parents and teachers need to be aware of how cultural and language discontinuities affect children and make every effort to collaboratively support children as they learn to negotiate between home and school cultures (Darder's positive outcome). Through conversations with parents and home visits, teachers can reflect on their practices and develop new approaches to make their classrooms more accommodating and empowering to a wider range of children and families (Delgado-Gaitan & Trueba, 1991; González et al., 2005; Phelan & Davidson, 1993; Preston, Cottrell, Pelletier, & Pearce, 2011).

This process entails reaching out to families long before a child enters school (Hare & Anderson, 2010) and assessing whether and how the curriculum and teaching practices are compatible with community and family values. For example, learning isolated academic skills as required by mandated tests is inconsistent with many indigenous children's experiential learning in meaningful activities (Preston et al., 2011).

As part of this process, teachers need to recognize and work with the strengths of families and ethnic communities (Grace & Trudgett, 2012; Valdés, 1996). Much of the literature presents a "pathologized" view of immigrant families, Native American communities, and other marginalized groups as disorganized and overwhelmed. In fact, many families have extended kinship and friendship networks that provide social and financial support. Social and religious organizations give communities identities and provide families with a sense of security and continuity. These formal and informal networks are valuable resources that can help teachers learn about the children's histories and needs and find ways to help children and families negotiate between two (or more) cultures. The good news is that when children, parents, community people, and teachers *do* work together, they *can* create effective programs for children who otherwise may feel alienated and unsuccessful in school. (For examples of this work in a number of different communities and regions, see Grace & Trudgett, 2012; Hare & Anderson, 2010; Nagel & Wells, 2009; Preston et al., 2011; Tharp & Gallimore, 1988; Wubie, 2005. Some of these are described in the Supplemental Resource 6.5 for Chapter 6, at www. tcpress.com)

Children's Understanding of Culture

Despite the profound influence of culture on all aspects of learning and development, the concept itself is abstract, and most children are not consciously aware of their own or others' cultures. Based on an ethnographic study of children's "ethnifying practices" in Germany, Seele (2012) notes that "children themselves, just as most adults, have no elaborated or consciously reflected opinion or theory about ethnicity that could easily be articulated. Rather it gains importance in concrete interactions . . . in everyday practice" (p. 312). During our first year in Mexico, I tried several times to get Alejandro (then 4 years old) to talk about the differences between our lives in the United States and in Mexico. He invariably answered, "I miss my red tricycle." Although his life had greatly changed—food, language, and social context—he had not constructed a concept that encompassed these differences. Even Daniel, at age 7, described concrete differences, often more related to climate than to culture (e.g., "it's warmer," "there are more flowers and prettier houses," "people wear hats more"). At the beginning, he frequently talked about people speaking Spanish, but as the year wore on and he became more fluent, he rarely mentioned it. As illustrated by the account in Chapter 2 of the kindergarten children arguing about whether or not English was spoken in a particular town, most children have only a vague idea of how geography relates to national, cultural, and language differences (Lambert & Klineberg, 1967; Piaget & Weil, 1951). Perhaps for this reason, there are virtually no research studies on young children's understanding of culture.

At the same time, culture shapes children's expectations of the world at an early age (Boyer, 2013; Grace & Trudgett, 2012; Hare & Anderson, 2010; Longstreet, 1978; Preston et al., 2011; Tudge et al., 2006; Wubie, 2005). A teacher of 2-year-olds heard a great outburst in the housekeeping corner one day. When she arrived at the scene, she discovered an Israeli girl (whose parents kept a kosher home) pushing a play milk bottle from the table that was set for "dinner." Her playmate who was not Jewish kept putting the milk bottle back on the table. Although neither child had a concept of kosher laws, each one had internalized particular expectations about serving milk with dinner.

Furthermore, when confronted with the practical demands of cultural differences, children adapt. From a young age, children hold "distinct assumptions about who shares . . . [similar] socially available knowledge"

(Diesendruck & Markson, 2011, p. 189). For example, bilingual preschoolers anticipate what languages particular classmates use and switch depending on their current playmates and also on the particular fantasy roles they are enacting (Orellana, 1994). Unfortunately, they also sometimes divide themselves along these lines. In a study of Canadian classrooms containing both French- and English-speaking children, Doyle (1982) found a striking amount of segregation between the two ethnolinguistic groups. Because many children were competent in both languages, Doyle concluded that the segregation was not simply a matter of linguistic fluency. She attributed these patterns to the following cycle: children play more actively with same-culture partners and develop common repertoires, which means that their play is more engaging; children then seek out same-culture playmates more often, precluding opportunities to create the same shared experiences with children from the other group. Guo and Dalli (2012) found a similar pattern with immigrant Chinese children in New Zealand early childhood programs. While those who had several other Chinese classmates fared better than those who were alone, in neither case did they interact much with their Anglo New Zealand classmates.

Preschoolers also notice and remember concrete cultural differences, especially when they emerge in a familiar realm such as food and clothing. In my interviews, 3- and 4-year-old African American and European American children often labeled pictures of Asian American children as "Chinese" and then talked about Chinese food and "those stick things" [chopsticks] (Ramsey, 1987). One 4-year-old rural White child insisted that "all Chinese people eat in restaurants," which probably reflected the fact that her contact with Chinese American people (and any Asian Americans, for that matter) had been limited to eating in a few local Chinese restaurants.

At the same time children are not passively absorbing cultural meanings and expectations. Seele (2012) observed how children in a multinational group created and enacted their identities through peer-directed discussions about language, physical appearance, national origins, and flags. Through conversations, role-playing, and fantasies, children explored and reworked their own and others' identities. Although some of the comments reflected the larger societal hierarchy (e.g., negative comments about darker skin), the children did not passively absorb these values, but constantly negotiated the meaning of ethnicity. For example, in one conversation children claimed their own national origins (e.g., "Iiiitaly . . . Italy, it's mine!") and assigned them to others (e.g., "you *are* Turkey") (p. 320).

As children approach middle childhood, they begin to acquire a sense of cultural relativity—the ability to see familiar conventions as unique to one's particular culture rather than as universal. However, they are also acquiring a positive in-group bias that may make them dismiss or demean unfamiliar cultures, as discussed in Chapter 2. Thus early childhood teachers can take advantage of young children's flexibility and convey the notion that "there are many ways of doing things" in order to provide them with knowledge and tools to resist peer and media pressures that assume that "our way is the best—or only—way."

One kindergarten teacher noticed that several children in the class were calling a boy from India "garbage head" because they noticed the smell of the coconut oil on his hair. In response, the teacher planned a series of activities in which she and the children compared the scent of coconut oil with a variety of shampoos, cream rinses, hair sprays, gels, and mousses. The children were interested, especially since some of these products had the cachet of being heavily advertised by glamorous media stars. As they noticed the different textures and scents, they made up new words to describe and differentiate them and, with the teacher's help, set up a hair salon for boys and girls (using pretend products—not the real ones!). After many activities and discussions about the different products that people put on their hair, the children had reworked their original narrow assumptions and developed broader conceptions about hair and the way people take care of it.

Culture influences the language, behavior, interactional styles, and expectations of young children, even though they usually do not understand it at a conceptual level. Moreover, they do notice and increasingly reject people who do speak or act in unfamiliar ways. To counteract this tendency, teachers can encourage children to construct and maintain open and flexible views of how people function in the world.

LEARNING ABOUT AND CHALLENGING WHAT CHILDREN KNOW, THINK, AND FEEL ABOUT CULTURE

Finding out what children know, think, and feel about culture is difficult because, as noted above, they, and often their families, may not recognize or talk about their culture. As part of many early childhood programs, parents make family books or posters that show their daily life, favorite activities, and meaningful objects (see Chapter 3). Teachers often report that, when they ask families to include descriptions of their culture(s), the adults, unless they are recent immigrants, usually demur and say that they do not have "any particular culture." However, when they talk about family activities and rituals (e.g., Friday night pizza, favorite bedtime stories and songs) and the values that underlie them (e.g., spending time together), they often begin to recognize their unique family culture that embodies their histories and interests. So whether families have built their lives around gardening, tinkering with old cars, cheering on particular sports teams, practicing a religion, spending time with family or friends, or combinations of all of these, they are engaged in activities that represent their cultural values and define their family.

The following activities and questions are potential strategies for generating conversations about culture, learning what children know and feel
about this dimension of diversity, and challenging them to rethink misinformation and assumptions.

1. When children are looking at the family books and see pictures of
   peers' families doing unfamiliar activities, how do they respond? Do
   they ask questions and want to learn more, or do they laugh and
   assume that the activities are "yucky" or weird?

   Family books are an excellent resource to address these types of
   reactions. They provide concrete examples of the fact that people
   children know do some things differently. Moreover, the children
   of the family being discussed are available to explain how and
   why their family does a particular activity or how an unfamiliar
   food tastes. You can support these discussions by introducing the
   books one at a time and encouraging children to ask and answer
   questions. When the books are available for children to look at
   independently, it is a good idea to monitor comments and use any
   negative reactions to unfamiliar ways of doing things to develop
   activities to challenge those views. Using a funds of knowledge
   approach (González et al., 2005), you can work with parents
   to plan some activities to introduce children to a wider range of
   activities, games, foods, clothing, or whatever is appropriate and
   feasible.

2. When children hear their classmates speak different languages,
   how do they respond? Do they laugh at the unfamiliar sounds and/
   or assume that their peers "cannot talk" (a common conclusion
   for young children), or are they interested in learning new words
   and sounds? Do children divide themselves along linguistic lines?
   How do children with a first language other than English feel about
   speaking their home language in the classroom? Do they deny that
   they speak it, or are they comfortable using words and perhaps
   even teaching some to their classmates?

   If many children seem to be confused or wary of unfamiliar
   languages, then incorporating a range of languages in songs,
   stories, and poems may help children get accustomed to the idea
   that there are lots of ways of speaking. One teacher who was
   fluent in Italian challenged her English-speaking preschoolers'
   assumptions that their Chinese classmate was unable to talk
   by speaking only in Italian to the class. As children expressed
   confusion and even outrage, she initiated a discussion about how
   it feels to not understand a new language. Teachers and children
   can perform skits that carry a similar message. Several children's
   books are written in two languages (usually English and one

other). By hearing the story in both languages, children experience the concrete reality that the same story can be told with different words. If teachers cannot speak one of the languages, parents or community people could make recordings to be used in this activity.

3. If all the children in the class are English speakers, then you can play recordings with songs and stories in different languages to raise children's awareness and stimulate discussion about the fact that people speak in many ways. Activities similar to those described above can be used to challenge the limits of children's knowledge and their wariness about unfamiliar languages.

4. Once children have had a chance to explore the cultural diversity in their own classroom, slowly and carefully introduce photographs and stories about people engaging in familiar activities (e.g., cooking, eating, going to school) in ways that are unfamiliar to the children and see what feelings and questions they have. Likewise, carefully selected clothing, tools, and food items in the dramatic play area can elicit children's views about cultural differences. Are they curious and eager to use them? Or are they dismissive or derisive? Introducing photographs, tools, or clothing from different cultures must be done with utmost caution and forethought to prevent children from associating them with stereotyped images or from missing the point altogether. For example, I have often observed the croissants that are usually included in sets of "multicultural breads" being used as guns (usually surreptitiously, of course). While on one hand the children are being creative, this adaptation underscores the need to introduce "multicultural" materials thoughtfully.

REFLECTIONS ON CULTURE AND THE NATURAL ENVIRONMENT

Besides defining our social relationships, cultural values also influence how people relate to the natural world and experience the rhythms of the day, the year, and their own life spans. Because this relationship is key to the goal of creating equitable and sustainable societies, I will explore it in some depth.

To examine how you and your communities/cultures relate to nature, you can ask yourself:

- How attuned am I to the natural rhythms of the day and year?
- How connected do I feel to the place where I live—the climate, landforms, vegetation, and animal life?
- What do I know about the history of human habitation where I live—especially traditional and contemporary wisdom about how to live sustainably in this area?

- How conscious am I about my daily and yearly consumption of natural resources such as oil, gas, water, and food? Do I know where these resources come from and how much they really cost in terms of environmental impact? How do I balance convenience (e.g., using my car instead of public transportation) with sustainability (e.g., using renewable energy sources, riding my bike to work)?
- How often do I think about how much I contribute to sewage systems, landfills, or air pollution in a day? a year?

I am not asking these questions to make you feel guilty. Many of us are caught between trying to live sustainably and struggling to keep up with the time and financial pressures of our daily lives. Not only are we all too busy with multiple responsibilities, but the infrastructure of many communities does not support sustainable lifestyles (e.g., lack of public transportation or bike lanes). I have to admit that, despite my deep concerns about climate change, I invariably choose to drive 20 minutes to work rather than take the 90-minute bus ride.

Reflecting more deeply about connections with the natural world often reveals cultural beliefs that may not have been obvious before. I have always loved the outdoors and have enthusiastically supported environmental causes. However, after reading works by American Indian writers, I saw how my "appreciation" for nature embodied the European tradition that nature exists to be used and enjoyed by people like myself. Paula Gunn Allen (1992) helped me to recognize the profound difference between my *homocentric* perspective that places people in the center and the *biocentric* view that we are all part of the same ecosystem—plants, animals, water, landforms, and humans:

> The notion that nature is somewhere over there while humanity is over here or that a great hierarchical ladder of being exists on which ground and trees occupy a very low rung, animals a slightly higher one, and man (never woman)—especially "civilized" man—a very high one indeed is antithetical to tribal thought. The American Indian sees all creatures as relatives . . . as offspring of the Great Mystery, as co-creators, as children of our mother, as necessary parts of an ordered, balanced, and living whole. (p. 59)

This view profoundly challenges the Western scientific assumption that "progress" means increasing our control of natural forces and developing ever more complicated technologies to fulfill our basic needs (e.g., the highly mechanized cultivation and preparation of food) and to create new ones (e.g., our increasing dependence on electronic media) (Bowers, 2001). We all rely on modern technology to varying degrees (e.g., I am using a computer to write this book). Thus I am not suggesting that we condemn and/

or rid ourselves of all scientific discoveries and inventions, but we do need to take a hard look at the downsides of the constant push to mechanize and control the natural world. As Ritchie (2012) points out, "We can choose to promote either the metaphors of dominance [over nature] of the Western canon or those of respectful interdependence with nature, as reflected in the narratives of Indigenous peoples" (p. 63).

Cultural and economic contexts also affect our views of spatial and temporal relationships. In the United States and most other industrialized market-based economies, spaces and natural resources (including plants and animals) are precisely defined and measured by standard units (e.g., meters) and evaluated for their potential economic productivity, a contrast to Allen's (1992) concept of all beings as co-creators. Similarly, in some cultures time is linear, and in others it is more cyclical. Most of us in the United States see time as linear and continually race against it, using our planners and app-laden cellphones to make the most of every second with tight schedules and multitasking. The passage of time has a different meaning, however, when we stop racing against it, live in the present moment, and let our lives be determined by the rhythmic and cyclical nature of days and years and our lifetimes. (For examples of how some children's books reflect these different views of time and the natural environment, see Supplemental Resource 6.6 for Chapter 6, at www.tcpress.com)

As we become more conscious about the values and priorities that guide our decisions, we can understand and respect other cultural values and expressions. This broader perspective, in turn, opens up our minds to new possibilities beyond exploiting natural resources and rushing to pursue individual material success.

CHILDREN'S KNOWLEDGE, ATTITUDES, AND FEELINGS ABOUT THE NATURAL ENVIRONMENT AND SUSTAINABILITY

In the United States and many other countries, people, and especially children, are becoming increasingly distant from their natural contexts. To support themselves and their families, many adults are working longer hours, and their children are spending more time in school, after-school care, or in organized activities. Moreover, the lure of the electronic media keeps many adults and children indoors and close to the electric outlets when they do come home.

Many teachers and psychologists have expressed concern that the precipitous decline in the number of hours that children spend in nature may negatively affect children's cognitive, social, and emotional development. Davis (2009) talks about "bubble wrapped children" (p. 228) who are protected from every risk and denied opportunities to challenge themselves in unpredictable natural settings. In *Last Child in the Woods*, Louv (2008) eloquently points out the losses that children suffer as a result of their detachment from nature. In contrast to the organized activities and commercialized materials, where everything is scripted and predictable, nature provides children with complexity and unexpected challenges that, in turn, promote cognitive and emotional development.

Children's physical and mental health are also compromised by this shift. The indoor and sedentary life contributes to obesity and other manifestations of poor physical fitness. Louv (2008) hypothesizes that the epidemic of children diagnosed with attention deficit disorders (ADD and ADHD) in the United States is related to what he calls a "nature-deficit disorder" (p. 10). Without natural outlets for their energy and curiosity, many children have great difficulty sitting still and concentrating in school. Louv cites several studies that demonstrate a number of other advantages of outdoor play. Children who spend more time in relatively wild places have longer and more in-depth social interactions than children who are mostly indoors. They also tend to have more positive views of themselves and others, greater confidence in their skills, and higher levels of creativity. Moreover, they have access to nature as a source of solace as they go through the emotional vagaries of growing up. In short, as children withdraw from the natural world, they lose many physical, cognitive, and emotional benefits.

In addition to the negative impact on children's development, this disconnection also has implications for preparing children to live in a world of climate change and to work toward sustainability. Many studies have shown that most adult environmental activists grew up having strong experiential and emotional connections to the natural world, often wild areas near their homes (e.g., Chawla & Cushing, 2007; Hinds & Sparks, 2008). Ann Pelo (2008a) notes that having a sense of place means that you love it and you want to be in it, to learn and enjoy everything about it, to be transformed by it, and to fear its loss and protect it fiercely. Thus a first priority in early childhood sustainable education is for children to develop a strong attachment to the natural environment that is closest and most meaningful to them.

Many educators—interestingly, mostly from countries other than the United States—point out that children, as future world citizens, must learn about sustainability (Elliott, 2010; Kahriman-Öztürk, Olgan, & Güler, 2012). They note that, in the face of devastating climate change and diminished resources that threaten future generations, sustainability is an essential, not optional, human concern. Moreover, it is a critical part of every movement for social and economic justice (Duhn, 2012; Kahriman-Öztürk et al., 2012. To develop relevant curriculum, teachers need to consider what children know and feel about the natural world and about environmental problems.

What Children Know and Feel About the Environment

Little is known about how young children develop concepts about nature and sustainability and how this development varies across cultures (Davis, 2009; Kahriman-Öztürk et al., 2012). The following discussions are based on the few available studies (from several countries including Australia, Greece, Mexico, Poland, and Turkey) and informal observations and anecdotes. Although there are cultural differences among these nations, all of them are fairly industrialized, so children's knowledge and feelings described here may be different from those of children being raised in more traditional and rural cultures.

According to Palmer and Suggate (1996), who studied children in the United States, 4-year-olds know quite a lot about different environments such as the Arctic and rain forests. Their knowledge is a mix of accurate and inaccurate information and often is limited to unfamiliar and striking animals (e.g., monkeys, polar bears). However, they are "active thinkers in the realm of environmental issues and distant places, thinkers who constantly try to make sense of the challenges presented to them in terms of their own experience and understanding" (p. 317). Palmer and Suggate also note that between the ages of 4 and 7, children gain more accurate information and begin to understand the link between causes and effects related to environmental problems.

In terms of their emotional responses, preschoolers often approach the natural world with a sense of wonder and excitement. They eagerly watch and ask questions about natural phenomena (e.g., sprouts popping out of seeds, water freezing, brown grass turning green in the rainy season). At this age, children usually relate to the environment in a personalized way such as taking care of plants and pets or observing seasonal changes in a particular tree. In a similar vein, Kahriman-Öztürk et al. (2012) found that, when young children considered environmental problems, they were most concerned about potential damage to plants and animals because they could empathize and connect with them. Hyun (2005) noted that young children often experience the natural environment in a "deep and direct manner" in which "perception conducts thought" (p. 204). Hyun also observed that boys tended to express their excitement physically (e.g., by pretending to be a particular animal), whereas girls were more likely to express their interest by describing and drawing many details about plants or animals.

In contrast to children's close and direct connection with nature, adults tend to see nature through preset assumptions, and their "perceptions obey thought" (Hyun, 2005, p. 207). In her classroom observations, Hyun noted many incidents when young children's excitement and curiosity were dampened by adult responses that reflected "biophobic" views (i.e., seeing nature as frightening and in need of control). Instead of joining young children's enthusiasm, adults would often tell them to kill the insect, avoid the snake, or close the windows. A study of preservice early childhood educators affirmed this pattern. The aspiring teachers clearly preferred manicured park-like environments for outdoor education over more natural and wild settings because of safety concerns (Ernst & Tornabene, 2012). These attitudes are pervasive in our society, and it is not surprising that Simmons (1994) found that urban elementary school children (in the United States) valued school playgrounds or small green areas in the city over more remote wilderness areas. When asked about visiting wilderness areas, the children said that they were afraid of natural hazards (e.g., drowning, falling, getting lost); threats from people in isolated areas; and physical discomforts (e.g., lack of shelter from sun or rain).

Children's perceptions and feelings about natural settings may be related to the location of their homes and their outdoor experiences. Wals (1994) found that suburban children saw nature as a threatened place that was rapidly disappearing because of new construction, and they wanted to protect the wilderness. However, in the same study, urban children, whose sole contact with the natural environment had been visiting city parks, saw nature as a threatening place where "murderers and rapists use the trees to block what they're doing" (p. 190). A Polish study showed a parallel pattern with children from rural areas expressing stronger feelings about preserving the environment than their urban and suburban counterparts (Grodzińska-Jurczak, Stępska, & Nieszporek, 2006).

Children's Awareness of Environmental Problems

Although some educators believe that children should not learn about environmental problems that might frighten them (e.g., Rosenow, 2008), others, especially those in countries other than the United States, believe that children are capable of learning about these issues and, as future citizens, need to have this information. A study of Greek preschoolers showed that young children are able to predict the short-term and long-term consequences of destructive human activities on habitats, animals, and food chains (e.g., setting forest fires, hunting all the rabbits, or catching all the fish) (Ergazaki & Andriotou, 2010). When responding to a story about a forest fire, they also expressed concern for the plant life, suggesting that they may hold biocentric views that all living beings have rights. In similar studies, Polish (Grodzińska-Jurczak et al., 2006) and Turkish preschoolers (Kahriman-Öztürk et al., 2012) tended to hold pro-environment views. However, when asked why they wanted to conserve resources and protect animals and plants, most children provided homocentric reasons (e.g., "I would not disturb the animals around me . . . they are dirty"), rather than biocentric ones (e.g., "wild animals . . . should not be killed . . . they have a right to live and everyone should protect them") (Kahriman-Öztürk et al., 2012, p. 640). The Polish researchers also asked parents about their views.

Like their children, they expressed pro-environmental sentiments but were not willing to inconvenience themselves—especially when it came to driving private cars—to conserve energy. Thus young children are capable of understanding concrete environmental problems, but many of them, like adults, see the problems and solutions in homocentric terms. Moreover, they may be learning from their parents and other adults that personal convenience overrides environmental concerns.

Children's Understanding of Sustainability

In terms of children's understanding of potential solutions to environmental issues, Kahriman-Öztürk et al. (2012) noted that preschoolers in Turkey have some knowledge of sustainable practices, including the seven "Rs," core principles of the Education for Sustainable Development (OMEP). In particular, the children understood those that involve concrete actions, namely, *reduce, reuse,* and *recycle,* but they did not grasp the more abstract principles of *reflect, rethink,* and *redistribute.* Although *respect* is somewhat abstract, the children expressed it through their empathy with other living beings (e.g., "I never disturb [animals] . . . because they can get sad . . . " [p. 2992]).

As children get older and able to think about larger ecological systems, they can grasp more fully environmental problems and solutions (see Barraza & Robottom, 2008; Barraza & Walford, 2002). However, most children in the United States (and many other industrialized countries) are learning that nature is something to tame and exploit. Children from families and groups that believe in the sacredness of the Earth may feel alienated by the "conquering Earth" assumptions that prevail in the mainstream culture. Likewise, it may be difficult for children who admire backhoes and construction sites to understand those misgivings. (For more information about older children's views and how their views vary across countries, see Supplemental Resource 6.7 for Chapter 6, at www.tcpress.com)

LEARNING AND CHALLENGING WHAT CHILDREN KNOW, THINK, AND FEEL ABOUT THE NATURAL ENVIRONMENT

Teachers can learn how children know and feel about the environment by observing what fantasies they enact in their play and what they say and do when they are in natural settings or see pictures of animals and plants. Here are a few of the many possible questions and activities that you can tailor to the available resources and local environmental issues:

1. Take children to different natural sites (e.g., city parks, wooded areas near the school, quiet corners in the schoolyard). Listen to

their questions and comments to see what ideas they are developing about the natural world. Observe their reactions to plants and animals. Do they whack at plants with sticks? stomp on ant hills? Or do they seem respectful and curious about the natural world? If they see litter, what do they say? do?

2. Take a walk to a construction site or show children pictures of one and see how they react. Are they mostly interested in the machines and progress of the building, or do they also notice the number of trees that were cut down and think about the animals who have lost their habitats?

3. Observe what themes arise when children play in the sandbox or with blocks. Are they intent on building roads and making towers? Or do they sometimes talk about protecting the land? What do they do when small replicas of animals and plants are placed in these areas?

4. How do children react to evidence of changing seasons? Do they notice changes in plants and shadows and quality of light? What do they notice in pictures of different natural settings? the same setting at different seasons and at different times of the day? What are their questions and comments? How attuned are they to the rhythms of days and seasons?

5. How do children respond to photographs of litter and air and water pollution? clear-cut forests? stories about animals and people whose habitats have been destroyed?

Having learned about children's attitudes toward the natural environment, how can we encourage them to become sustainability activists? Early environmental education requires a transformative approach that "values, encourages, and supports children as problem-seekers, problem solvers, and action-takers around sustainability issues," in the words of Australian educator Julie Davis (2009, p. 230). She describes the holistic approach used by programs in Norway, New Zealand, Australia, South Korea, and Hong Kong and points out that early education for sustainability forces us to think in new ways and to take advantage of "new synergies created by intersections with health . . . sociology, psychology, urban planning, architecture . . . organizational change, and economics" (p. 238).

As discussed earlier, environmental activists often attribute their passion to having had close and meaningful connections with the natural world as children. To nurture this attachment and grow the next generation of environmental activists, children of all ages should spend a lot of time exploring and enjoying their natural surroundings. Although wild places offer the most variety and challenges, the sense of place can be fostered anywhere (e.g., roof gardens, small pocket parks, abandoned lots where plants and animals are finding new homes). It is never too young to start, as seen in

Pelo's (2013) description of how she and a toddler spent a year exploring their "place" from soaring views to small patches of dirt and how a sense of place became ingrained into the fibers of their beings.

Developing a sense of place and forming intimate connections with nature are powerful. The outcomes of environmental education programs show that children learn the most when they actually spend time outdoors seeing and experiencing firsthand natural ecologies, solving practical problems, and enjoying nature, as well as learning information (Dressner & Gill, 1994; Milton, Cleveland, & Bennett-Gates, 1995; Simmons, 1994). McHenry and Buerk (2008) describe how their infants and toddlers learn about the natural world through hands-on play and exploration with leaves and pinecones and by close observation of small-scale ecologies such as the residents of a fish tank. Among others, Wilson (1993, 1995) urges teachers to avoid relying on organized nature walks and/or factual lectures, and instead encourage children to enjoy and feel competent in natural environments (e.g., scrambling up rocks, climbing trees). Unfortunately, these findings and suggestions often clash with the risk-aversive rules that dominate early childhood education in the United States. These regulations are driven by fears of parent disapproval and law suits and the view of young children as fragile beings in need of constant protection. These constraints not only make it difficult to raise challenging topics (as previously discussed) but undermine efforts to encourage children to be confident adventurers.

Despite these dilemmas, educators are working on a number of fronts to foster connections between children and the natural world. Wells and Zeece (2007) advocate using story books about familiar natural settings to enhance children's sense of place. Some programs stress the connections between nature and diversity and caring for others. Nimmo and Hallett (2008) report how working in the school garden helped children learn about different cultural practices and environmental issues and connect with individuals of different ages and abilities. Likewise, Satterlee and Cormons (2008) describe how a family-based nature program in a low-income rural community enhanced children's learning and family participation in the school. Rosenow (2008) writes about how Nature Explore Classrooms enhance stronger social connections and interest in creating and maintaining natural spaces. Many early childhood programs in countries other than the United States offer inspiring examples of teaching sustainability and environmental and social justice. One of the best examples is the TitiroWhakamuri, Hoki Whakamua in New Zealand that is based on Maori (the indigenous people in that country) principles of caring for self, other, and the environment (Duhn, 2012; Ritchie, 2012). (For more information about this program and several excellent programs in other countries, see Supplemental Resource 6.8 for Chapter 6, at www.tcpress.com)

Sustainability may seem to be a vague concept to many children and their families, so programs that emphasize local and pressing environmental problems may stimulate more involvement than abstract information about rain forests and melting glaciers (Sutherland & Ham, 1992). Also exposure to environmental problems needs to be balanced with optimism that they can be solved or at least mitigated. By actively addressing local environmental problems children may gain the confidence that they can make a difference. One preschool curriculum was developed around studying and sustaining the wood duck population in southern Louisiana, an issue closely tied to the children's experiences of boating, hunting, and fishing with their families (Blanchard & Buchanan, 2011). The children investigated the duck population and learned why it was declining. Then they made nesting boxes for the ducks and, with the help of local environmentalists, placed them in the waterways.

The following story describes how one group of children, parents, and teachers worked together to create a garden that generated many activities and conversations about culture and the natural environment as well as providing healthy food for everyone in the class.

Marisa (Puerto Rican American) and Maya (African American) were lead teachers of a kindergarten class in a child-care center in a diverse, working-class, urban neighborhood. They realized that their preschool children knew very little about where food came from and had almost no contact with the natural environment. They frequently walked to small nearby parks, but the high cost of transportation precluded trips to farms or wilderness areas.

At the beginning of the school year, the parents and teachers discussed potential curriculum priorities (as described in Chapter 3) and came up with the idea of having a classroom garden in an available vacant lot next to the schoolyard. This goal reflected several parents' desire to share their own rural farming backgrounds and a common concern about children clamoring for junk food. After getting permission from the school director, the teachers, parents, and children spent the rest of the fall and the winter preparing for the garden.

First, everyone came to a work day on a late fall Saturday and cleaned the area, which had been buried under a lot of debris and litter. (Before offering the lot to the school, the owners had already cleared out all hazardous materials.) This shared effort, which included a pot luck lunch, brought families and school staff together in an informal, convivial way and generated a lot of excitement and ideas for the garden.

As the families and teachers cleaned up the area, the children made frequent comments about the "yucky garbage" and were angry at how much litter there was. Maya and Marisa realized that this interest was a good segue into talking about larger environmental issues. They kept some of the "found materials" and used them in the class the next week to stimulate discussions. These conversations led to several neighborhood "litter walks" where the children and teachers photographed and counted the amount of and type of litter that they saw in different areas. They noticed that streets with fancy houses had less litter than those with run-down ones. With this information, the children wrote letters to the city public works department about the most littered areas and asked them to do a better job of cleaning up the neighborhood. They also visited and talked to the managers of a couple of local fast-food restaurants that had been the source of the most frequent litter. After these discussions, the children made colorful signs pleading with patrons not to litter their neighborhood and posted them near the restaurant exits.

As the garden planning got underway, Maya and Marisa invited families and community people to come in and share their knowledge about particular plants and gardening. Several visitors (ranging in age from 20 to 80) brought in seeds and plants and told the children about the gardens that they remembered from their childhoods. On occasion, they also brought in food that had been made from particular plants and told stories about how these dishes had been part of their families' traditional fare. These moments provided opportunities for the teachers to observe children's reactions to unfamiliar foods and to encourage them to overcome their reluctance to try new things.

A local gardener helped the children make a composting box so that they could start making compost to fertilize the garden. Throughout the year, the children in the class faithfully collected scraps from their meals and cooking projects to put in the compost pile. A couple of other classes became interested and added their materials as well. This project generated many discussions and investigations about decay and life cycles and what plants need to grow.

As spring approached, the families and community people again gathered to prepare the garden, turning the soil and adding the compost and a few weeks later planting the garden. The children created a planting celebration that was an amalgam of several rituals and songs that they had learned about during the course of the year. And of course there were pot luck lunches on both workdays, which provided more opportunity for informal sharing of family traditions.

Once the garden was planted, the children took turns watering, weeding, and reporting on the progress of particular plants. As questions arose about how much water, sun, shade, and space different plants needed, the children and teachers devised classroom experiments that involved growing plants under different conditions. Throughout the summer the growing plants enthralled the children and were the topic of many discussions, drawings, paintings, sculptures, and role-plays. When a few plants died, the whole class mourned their passing.

As vegetables and fruits were ready for harvesting, they were incorporated into meals and snacks. In some cases, family members came in and showed children how to prepare dishes using the produce. Again, these occasions gave rise to memories and stories about different cultural traditions.

Finally, in the fall as the weather cooled, the children and teachers observed the changes in the garden and realized that it was time to do the final harvesting. With the help of family and community members, the children prepared a harvest feast that featured a number of dishes and songs from families and several new songs and poems that the children had written about the garden.

The teachers also encouraged the children to use this time of harvest to think about people who are hungry, which led to a number of related activities such as donating some of the produce to a local soup kitchen and learning more about the causes of hunger.

I would like to end this chapter with an inspiring example of how early childhood education, sustainability, and community activism can be woven together (Lalley, 2008). In Seattle, Washington, El Centro de la Raza has a program in which young children and families participate in many projects, from protesting unfair practices at the local university to pushing for equal funding and dual language programs in the public schools. Their first principle is environmental justice, and parents, teachers, and children all promote sustainable practices in the city and take the following beautiful Ecological Oath:

I promise	*Prometo*
To use my eyes	*Usar mis ojos*
To see	*Para ver*
The beauty of nature	*La belleza de la naturaleza*
To use my hands	*Usar mis manos*
To help	*Para ayudar*
Protect	*A protger*
Earth	*Suelo*
Water	*Agua*
Forests and animals	*Bosques y animales*
And with my good example	*Y con mi buen ejemplo*
Teach others	*Enseñar a otros*
To take care of	*A cuidar*
And use correctly	*Y usar adecuadamente*
Our natural resources	*Nuestros recursos naturales*

CHAPTER 7

The Context of Gender and Heteronormativity

Children live in a world filled with messages about gender roles and sexual identities and orientation. The prevailing heteronormative view is that all individuals should identify as male or female, enact gender-typical roles, and form heterosexual relationships. Clearly, this assumption excludes many individuals, in particular those who are gay, bisexual, lesbian, or transgendered (GBLT). The first part of this chapter will focus on recognizing and challenging gender roles. The second section will explore particular challenges faced by GBLT parents, and the resistance to representing and talking about sexual orientation and identities in early childhood classrooms.

REFLECTIONS ON GENDER IDENTIFICATION AND ROLES

In your answer to the question in the Part II introduction "Who am I?" you probably included gender. In the United States (as in many countries) gender is often the first way we classify people, including ourselves. To consider how gender has influenced your identity and relationships with others, ask yourself:

- How has my gender influenced my life? How has it limited me? sustained me? opened up possibilities?
- If I had been identified as a man instead of as a woman or vice versa, how would my life have been different? How would that have changed my personal relationships? What jobs might I have had? Would I have occupied more or less powerful roles in my family? at work? in the world?
- On a day-to-day level as I go to work, do errands, spend time with my family and friends, would I be reacting to situations the same way if I were identified as a woman instead of a man or vice versa? Would others be responding to me in the same way?
- What assumptions do I make about other people's actions and roles based on their gender? Would I be surprised if a woman made a

daring rescue? the new teacher at the child-care center was a man? the newly appointed CEO of a company was a woman? and her administrative assistant was a man?

- For those in heterosexual partnerships and/or in mixed-gender workplaces: How does my gender define my responsibilities at home? at work? How would the dynamics change if I did all the jobs usually done by my opposite-sex partner or coworkers?
- When I am talking to someone, how does that person's gender influence my tone of voice and facial expressions? my level of assertiveness? my body language?

Interpretation and reactions to children's behavior also reflect gender-related assumptions. For example, loud, rambunctious boys are often tolerated more than girls with similar behavior. Likewise, parents and teachers are often worried and even horrified when boys want to dress up in frilly clothes and wear nail polish, whereas the media extols these behaviors for young girls. To examine your assumptions and awareness of dynamics in the classroom, ask yourself the following questions:

- When I think of two classroom events, one that involved a girl and one a boy, how would my responses have differed if the first one had involved a boy instead of a girl and the second one a girl instead of a boy?
- When I put out art materials, which children do I expect will use them? What about blocks and trucks?
- When I select materials such as photographs, books, and puppets, how conscious am I of the images of males and females that are conveyed? What is the balance of stereotyped and counter-stereotyped images in terms of activities and occupations?
- What attributes of children do I praise? Are there gender differences (e.g., do I compliment girls on their appearance more often than boys, or boys more on their physical prowess than girls)?
- How often do I notice whether children are playing in same-gender or mixed-gender groups? How aware am I of gender-related domination patterns (e.g., boys intimidating the girls)?

As you think about these questions, note that I am using the binary terms of *man/boy* and *woman/girl* as though the two groups were distinct and mutually exclusive, which is commonly assumed. However, with a deepening understanding of sexual orientation and greater awareness of transgendered and intersex (see note at end of chapter) people and those with multiple or evolving sexual identities, gender, like race, economic class, and culture, has become a complex and fluid set of categories. As Dykstra (2005) posits, "gender is a social construction . . . [and] not synonymous with biological sex" (p. 8).

In most cultures gender is assigned based on an infant's genitals; then individuals learn the gender roles that prevail in their communities and are congruent with those assignments. Yet there is growing evidence that "gender runs along a spectrum and is a fluid choreography over a lifetime between the human organism and the environment" (Ehrensaft, 2009, p. 14). It is usually assumed that individuals considering gender reassignment are adults or maybe adolescents. However, some children as young as three do not feel at home with their assigned gender (Ehrensaft, 2009). In earlier times gender nonconforming children would have undergone treatment to learn how to accept and conform to expectations of their natal sex (Lev, 2010). Now, however, more affirmative therapies are "centered in accepting the children's emerging identity as authentic" (p. 284). Lev describes one 5-year-old boy who desperately wanted to be a girl, even to the point of trying to cut off his penis. After months of therapy and agonizing decision-making, his parents agreed to let him start elementary school as a girl.

Although this level of gender nonconforming may be rare at that age, many young children experiment with gender roles and talk about switching genders. These explorations do not necessarily have any bearing on future sexual identities or orientation; rather they allow all children to explore and embrace many possibilities and develop a wider range of behaviors. If ultimately a child begins to question her or his sexual identity and orientation, having grown up in an environment that encouraged these explorations will ease difficult decisions and transitions.

GROWING UP IN A GENDERED AND HETERONORMATIVE WORLD

The assumption of heteronormativity that prevails in our society is embedded in our views of children and families and permeates early childhood studies and curriculum (Janmohamed, 2010). Heteronormativity embodies the expectation that all individuals identify as male or female and form heterosexual relationships as the basis for the ideal family. Heterosexuality and gender stereotypes are both part of these expectations and mutually reinforce each other. (For a fuller explanation of the term heteronormativity and its implications, see Blaise & Taylor, 2012). For example, Barbie dolls, little girls' makeup kits, and domestic play reflect the assumption that girls want to attract boys and grow up to be homemakers in the ideal heterosexual family. Likewise, action figures, toy weaponry, and trucks encourage young boys to imagine becoming highly masculine, dominating mates for docile and highly ornamented young women. Blaise (2005, 2010) observed that when children are playing out these gender-typed roles, many peers enthusiastically join in. However, when children resist these roles and assumptions (e.g., a girl announcing "I don't want to get married"), other children rarely respond and often turn away.

Gender roles and related inequities emerge in almost all societies (Liben & Bigler, 2002; Whiting & Edwards, 1988). In the United States, despite a great deal of legal and attitudinal change, girls and boys are still not treated equally in schools (see Sadker & Sadker, 1995; Sadker et al., 2007). Girls are often overlooked by teachers and not encouraged to excel, particularly in math and science and in physically challenging activities. They do, however, learn to be nurturing and emotionally expressive and often are more skilled at maintaining personal relationships than boys are. Boys, on the other hand, are encouraged to be aggressive, to excel, to take physical risks, and to hide their emotions (Sadker & Sadker, 1995). Boys potentially grow up to be leaders and to earn more money than their female counterparts, but, at the same time, they are more likely than girls to fail in school or to engage in violent and dangerous activities. Although the Sadkers' original research was done more than 2 decades ago, a more recent review (Sadker et al., 2007) documents how these patterns still exist in many schools and how gender equity is still a low priority in teacher education programs and professional organizations (see also Fulmer, 2010).

Gender roles and related stereotypes are often unconscious yet are resistant to change and are re-created with each generation. Freeman (2007) provides a compelling example of how hard it is to change unconscious views and behavior. In her study young children predicted how their parents would react if they chose to play with gender typical or atypical toys (e.g., daughters versus sons choosing to play with dolls). These predictions were compared with the parents' self-described, gender-related beliefs. Despite the parents' explicit rejection of gender stereotypes, their children, probably responding to their parents' unconscious actions, expected that their parents would approve of their gender-typical choices and disapprove of their atypical choices.

Another study further attests to how parents often unintentionally impart gender stereotypes (Sutfin, Fulcher, Bowles, & Patterson, 2008). Despite many parents' explicit rejection of typical gender roles, most of the children's bedrooms were decorated in gender stereotypical colors and decorations. Thus children "woke up each morning and went to sleep each night in bedrooms that served to remind them of their gender and the roles customarily associated with their gender" (p. 510).

One reason for this intransigence is the prevalent use of gender in our society to divide and differentiate people (Bem, 1981, 1983; Liben & Bigler, 2002; Martin & Ruble, 2004). This pattern is exacerbated by the consumerist pressures that were discussed in Chapter 5. Many writers (e.g., Aina & Cameron, 2011; Cunningham & Macrae, 2011; Freeman, 2007) note that, despite many legal sanctions against gender discrimination and a growing understanding of sexual identities as flexible and evolving, gendered marketing is more pervasive than ever. Go to the toy or clothing aisles of any store, and there will always be what I call the "pink aisles" (loaded with pink and purple outfits, sneakers, and toys) and the "grayish-brown" aisles (filled with darker colored clothes and action figures, vehicles, war toys, and guns). While colors themselves may seem innocuous, research has shown that, by the age of 2 and a half girls have a definite preference for pink, whereas boys dislike it (LoBue & DeLoache, 2011). Moreover, in a series of experiments, Cunningham and Macrae (2011) found that the colors pink and blue triggered gendered associations and stereotypes in young children and adults, indicating that these color associations are entrenched at an early age and shape responses and assumptions throughout the life span.

Many films, television shows, computer games, and other electronic media target either boys or girls and model gender-specific fantasies and sell gendered products (Aina & Cameron, 2011). Often films developed around fairy tales (e.g., *Little Mermaid, Cinderella*) reinforce heteronormativity by promoting highly sexualized images of men and women and glorify heterosexual romantic relationships (Lester, 2007). Even movies that depict strong active girls or women usually end in heterosexual romantic bliss (e.g., *Beauty and the Beast, Frozen*).

Gender differentiation and related inequities intersect with race, culture, and class. Stereotypes of males and females vary across race (e.g., Asian "China dolls," African American "gangsters," "macho" Latino men); and the flexibility of gender roles varies considerably across cultural groups (Liben & Bigler, 2002; Whiting & Edwards, 1988). Race and economic status also intersect with gender inequities. For example, White, middle-class, college-educated women managers may enjoy a more equal relationship with male colleagues (at least officially) than Latina chambermaids or factory workers who are supervised by men. However, as with any generalization, it is important to keep in mind that, within groups, individual responses vary widely; some people conform willingly to prevailing gender roles, and others resist them (Liben & Bigler, 2002). Furthermore, individuals may also change over time.

CHILDREN'S RESPONSES TO GENDER

In contrast to discussions about race, one question that parents and teachers *never* ask is: "Do young children notice gender differences?" They don't need to. Everyone who interacts with children knows that from an early age they identify and divide themselves by gender. Children start to use gender labels as early as 19 months and begin to show sex differences in play around 17 months (Zosuls et al., 2009). As discussed previously, gender differences are not as biologically defined or as permanent as commonly believed. However, in the lives and minds of most children, gender differences are alive and well and *very* important. As Alejandro announced one morning shortly after his 4th birthday, "I am a boy because I am 4 years old and I *hate* girls!"

Gender Stereotypes

As children grow up, they construct their gender identities and concepts from overt and covert messages in their environment (Cunningham & Macrae, 2011; LoBue & DeLoache, 2011). During preschool, children learn stereotypic beliefs and attitudes about gender roles that affect a wide range of behaviors, psychological constructs, and aspirations, including peer interactions, self-identity, self-esteem, and social, educational, and vocational goals (Bigler, 1997; Martin & Ruble, 2004). These beliefs tend to become increasingly rigid until around the age of 7, when children begin to see gender roles as more flexible (Trautner et al., 2005).

A number of researchers have proposed that children construct their views about gender using schema—theories about the characteristics of males and females that influence how children interpret information (Bem, 1981, 1983; Martin & Halverson, 1981). These schema are complex and often contradictory. Liben and Bigler (2002) found that many children had different gender expectations for themselves than they did for others (e.g., a girl might think that both boys and girls could do carpentry, but she would not endorse that for herself). However, once they are established, gender stereotypes are self-perpetuating, and children often deny information that challenges them. One 4-year-old girl told me that her mother was a doctor (which was true), but later in the interview when I asked her what mommies did, she emphatically told me, "Mommies stay home and take care of their babies and kids."

Gender Exclusion

Most children clearly prefer same-sex peers; all of their hypothetical and actual playmate choices demonstrate this over and over. Gender segregation begins before preschool and becomes increasingly entrenched during the early childhood years. In a year-long study of the social dynamics of preschool classrooms (Ramsey, 1995), children in the younger groups (average age of 3) stated that they preferred same-sex playmates, but in the classroom they played in many mixed-sex groups throughout the year. However, in the 4-year-old groups, children's time in same-sex groups increased dramatically during the year, suggesting that the 4th year may mark the beginning of separate peer cultures and more rigid geender roles. While teachers often watch these divisions solidify with some dismay, Boldt (2011) reminds us how much children enjoy "performing gender" and affirming the same-sex connections, often with high spirits, shared humor, and affirmations of similar likes and dislikes.

Gender segregation continues to rise during the early elementary years and is reaffirmed by children's engagement in "borderwork" between the two groups (Thorne, 1986). These interactions include contests (e.g., boys' and girls' spelling bee teams), cross-sex chasing games that sometimes include pollution rituals (e.g., giving cooties to each other), and invasions in which one group disrupts the play of the other. Yet this borderwork is complicated because, despite its ostensible purpose of separating the sexes, it invites contact, often with sexual allusions (e.g., the kiss-kiss chase game described by Bhana [2007]). (For more details on gender-defining rituals, see Bhana, 2007; Blaise & Taylor, 2012; Robinson, 2005; and Supplemental Resource 7.1 for Chapter 7, at www.tcpress.com).

As children work to "get their 'real girl' or 'real boy' play right" (Blaise & Taylor, 2012, p. 91), gender roles and sexual identities become increasingly rigid, causing difficulties for children who do not fit heteronormative expectations. Girls who like rough play and, particularly, boys who enjoy dressing up in female clothing and playing with dolls are often rejected and ridiculed by peers bent on enforcing strict gender roles (Aina & Cameron, 2011; MacNaughton, 2000; Robinson, 2005).

Because children readily divide themselves by gender, teachers often unintentionally support and reinforce this segregation by using gender as a way of organizing their classes (e.g., seating, work groups) (Thorne, 1986). In a comparative study, Bigler (1995) found that in elementary classrooms explicitly organized by gender (such as boys' and girls' teams and lines), children developed more gender-stereotyped views of individuals and occupations than did their peers in classrooms where gender differences were not emphasized. Breaking down the gender divide and, in particular, equalizing power between the two groups is difficult and requires teachers to be conscious of their own gender biases and to proactively intervene (Aina & Cameron, 2011; MacNaughton, 2000).

Strategies to reduce gender segregation are not always successful. Some teachers have tried merging the block and housekeeping areas to encourage boys and girls to play together. However, these efforts often result in children simply avoiding the areas or playing in separate gender groups in the combined spaces (MacNaughton, 2000). In our campus kindergarten a teacher assistant placed four dolls in the block area to see if the children would try out new roles. The children were unhappy—to put it mildly. The boys were vehement that the dolls did not belong there (e.g., "Let's get these babies out of here!"). One girl seemed bewildered by the new arrangement—"Then how will I play with them?"

In the same kindergarten several years ago, we went one step further by not only merging the block and role-play areas, but also removing toys, clothes, and props that were associated with gender-specific play. We recreated the areas into an outer-space environment with materials carefully designed to be equally appealing to both boys and girls (Theokas, 1991). The teachers initially assigned girls and boys to the combined area in order to establish the precedence of mixed-gender groups. Over the month-long curriculum, the boys and girls played together and developed gender-inclusive themes. When the teachers stopped assigning groups, the children still chose to play in gender-mixed groups more than they had before the project started. We believed that this intervention was effective because we did not rely on proximity or rewards but proactively encouraged girls and boys to develop common interests. Nonetheless, gender power differentials persisted. A close reading of the observations revealed that in many (not all) mixed-gender groups, the boys still played more dominant roles. The fact that these power differentials were not obvious to the teachers or observers during the intervention illustrates the "invisibility" of these dynamics. Because they align with our unconscious expectations, teachers, and often the children themselves, do not notice them (Blaise & Taylor, 2012).

In short, during early childhood, children are forming their ideas about gender and the related power differentials. They actively look for gender-related cues and find an abundance of them in highly sex-differentiated and stereotyped media images and consumer products. As they get older, many children divide themselves by gender, and play out heteronormative roles and vigorously exclude peers who do not conform to them.

REFLECTIONS ON SEXUAL ORIENTATION AND IDENTITIES

In answer to the question of "Who am I?" did you mention your sexual identity or orientation? If you are gay, lesbian, bisexual, or transgendered, you may have. If you are heterosexual, you probably did not, because your sexual orientation is another invisible norm. Yet all of us have distinct sexual histories and evolving roles, identities, and values that reflect our physiological and psychological traits, our culture, and our family situations. These perspectives in turn influence our responses to children's developing understanding of sexuality (Andrew et al., 2001).

The questions below are designed to assess your knowledge and feelings related to your own and others' sexual orientation. These queries are primarily directed to readers who identify as heterosexual because these concerns are probably all too familiar to most GBLT individuals. However, no matter how individuals identify, they can still harbor misinformation and stereotypes about others, so I hope that all readers will take the time to reflect on their responses to these questions.

- Where do I fit in the spectrum of sexual identities and orientation? Bisexual, gay, lesbian, transgendered, gender nonconforming, gender questioning, heterosexual? How have these identities changed during my life? What has influenced them? As you reflect on the following questions, think about how your current and past identities affect your responses.

- What images come to mind when I think of gay men? lesbian women? bisexual individuals? transgendered people? intersex people? To what extent do they fit prevailing stereotypes of these groups?
- What assumptions do I make about individuals whose sexual orientation is different from mine? Would it change my feelings about my child's teacher if I found out that she was lesbian? Would I still admire a particular athlete if I knew that he was gay? How would I react if I learned that one of the senators from my state was bisexual? if one of my coworkers was undergoing gender reassignment?
- As you walk around your community and watch television, imagine that you are gay, lesbian, bisexual, or transgendered, and ask yourself: where and when would I feel safe? threatened? What images do I see that represent my life in store windows? advertisements? magazine covers? television shows? films?

Teachers often unwittingly support heterosexist assumptions because they are the invisible norm. Think about your assumptions, teaching goals, and practices, and ask yourself the following questions:

- What assumptions about gender and families were woven into my courses in child development and early childhood education? To what extent was heterosexism the assumed norm? Were there exceptions?
- When I learn that a child's parent(s) are gay, lesbian, or bisexual what questions, concerns, and expectations come to mind? What about a child whose mother or father is undergoing gender reassignment treatment?
- How do I react when I see children dressing in cross-gender clothes? engaging in cross-gender behaviors and activities? What has influenced my reactions?
- What images of families are represented in classroom photographs, calendars, and story books? Are families with one male and one female parent the implied "norm," or are other family constellations including ones with one parent or two mothers or two fathers also visible?
- In the doll house and puppet collections are there multiple figures of all ages, genders, and races so that children can enact stories about a range of family constellations?
- How do I respond to children's questions about same-sex parents? Or a sexually ambiguous or gender-nonconforming person? Do I encourage or stifle discussions? What makes me anxious about the prospect of having these discussions in my classroom?

GROWING UP IN A HETEROSEXIST WORLD

Most people in this country are not judged by their sexual practices, but lesbian, gay, bisexual, and transgendered individuals are often judged *exclusively* by their choice of sexual partners and by others' assumptions about their sexual practices. For example, bisexual individuals can go through life working and living alongside others, but as soon as their sexual orientation is known, they are often defined *only* in terms of their sexual partners and activities.

Most politicians and community leaders, regardless of their true feelings, avoid making overt derogatory remarks about race and gender because they know that discrimination on those bases is illegal. In contrast, many vociferously denounce GBLT individuals and seek to exclude them from equal protection under the law. Although they often base their arguments on religious and/or moral beliefs, these condemnations create a climate of hatred in which homophobic insults and violence occur with frequency and impunity.

In the United States the range of sexual orientations and identities are more openly acknowledged than they were 2 or 3 decades ago, and there are more legal protections for GBLT people. The number of GBLT networks and publications has grown. Several popular television series and movies have featured gay and lesbian characters, playing a wide range of roles. Individuals who are transgendered are more openly accepted in many institutions, and the number of support networks for them and their families has grown (see Kids of Transgender Parents at kidsoftrans@colage.org). Several states have either legalized same-sex marriage or are considering doing so. At the same time other states have passed laws prohibiting it. Despite much progress, discrimination based on sexual orientation and identity is far from over.

Dilemmas of GBLT Parents

GBLT parents face many dilemmas about selecting schools and disclosing their family relationships and constellations to their children's teachers and other parents (Brown, Smalling, Groza, & Ryan, 2009). Same-sex parents may refer to their partners as "friends" or "housemates" or present themselves as single parents. At the same time, *not* disclosing exacts a high price because they must always be on their guard and cannot engage openly with teachers and other parents. Casper and Schultz (1999) vividly describe how painful and complicated these decisions are. Using numerous examples, the authors illustrate the many factors that parents need to consider such as their goals for their children, the attitudes of other parents, the comfort level of the teachers, and the support of the school administration.

These dilemmas are not unique to the United States. Lee (2010) describes how the lesbian mothers she interviewed in New Zealand felt torn between wanting to be open and visible with teachers and other parents, yet fearing discrimination if they were honest about themselves. Lesbian mothers in Australia (Skattebol & Ferfolja, 2007) echoed these sentiments as they talked about vacillating between "playing it straight" or "coming out" (p. 13). Parents in both studies noted that, although they knew that they themselves could cope with discrimination, they dreaded the idea that their children would be teased and bullied because of their parents' sexual orientation. At the same time, all of the mothers agreed that they wanted to prepare their children to withstand the inevitable discrimination they would face as children being raised by lesbian mothers. They felt that being open and positive about being lesbians, socializing with other GBLT families, and talking about diverse families would strengthen their children and help them withstand any attacks. In a study done in the United States, lesbian parents echoed these views and strategies (Litovich & Langhout, 2004). They also made a point of reassuring their children that homophobic remarks targeted the family's demographic, not the child her- or himself. While they encouraged their children to be assertive, they also told them that they did not have to take on the burden of defending all lesbian families.

Because disclosures about sexual orientation are so sensitive, and their ramifications vary across individuals and situations, parents should always have control over what and how information is shared. Teachers, even when they are supportive or are themselves GBLT, must be careful not to push parents to disclose information prematurely (Kroeger, 2001). Above all, these discussions with parents must be treated with absolute confidentiality (Andrew et al., 2001).

Overcoming Anxieties About Discussing Sexual Orientation and Identity

Understandably many teachers are wary of challenging the heteronormative assumptions that prevail in most communities. In their interviews with Casper and Schultz (1999), teachers often disclosed that they worried about encouraging children to talk about GBLT individuals and issues because they feared the reactions of parents or school administrators. Teachers were concerned about possible sanctions, isolation, and job loss. Given the vitriolic response to even token efforts to incorporate these issues into classrooms, these concerns were justified.

Not surprisingly, lesbian and gay parents often express frustration about teachers' discomfort and avoidance (Kroeger, 2006; Skattebol & Ferfolja, 2007). Lee and Duncan (2008) point out that many teachers do not recognize that "heterosexual families receive constant affirmation through language, literature, and images" (p. 25) and do not consider what it is like to be a gay or lesbian couple with a child at their center. Often parents themselves have to educate the teachers, which is also problematic (Brown et al., 2009). A gay adoptive parent described the tension between "enlightening the school (teachers and administrators) about gay issues without embarrassing our kids" (p. 240).

In their study Casper and Schultz (1999) also observed that teachers' discomfort affected how they responded to children's questions about sexual orientation. They urge that teachers work closely with colleagues and parents to gain information and alleviate these anxieties. The account that I summarize below may be useful to teachers who are struggling with how to work with GBLT parents and their children. This teacher goes from feeling uncomfortable and avoidant to finding ways to support children from diverse families and to challenge homophobic stereotypes.

Souto-Manning and Hermann-Wilmarth (2008) wrote an inspiring and detailed description of how Souto-Manning changed her views about raising GBLT issues. Initially, she was apprehensive when she learned that Jackson, one of her 1st-grade students, was being raised by his lesbian mother and her same-sex partner. Souto-Manning felt betrayed because nothing in her teacher education program had prepared her to deal with sexual diversity. "I felt incompetent and untrained . . . I was paralyzed" (p. 269).

However, after observing Jackson's isolation and the teasing from the other children, she knew that she had to act. After many conversations with Jackson's mother she decided to introduce the children to books that represented diverse families. As she read and discussed the books with the children, she learned that some held negative views about same-sex partners and realized that she needed to challenge those prejudices just as she would any other ones. By emphasizing the diversity of families, she was able to include all the children in the conversations as many types of households were represented in the class, including those with grandparents, divorced parents, blended families, and single parents. In their discussions, the children and Souto-Manning concluded that there was no such thing as a typical family and that everyone needs to be respectful about all families, including those with same-sex parents.

As she had initially feared, some parents complained about these discussions. However, because she had become more knowledgeable and confident, Souto-Manning was able to demonstrate the purpose of the conversations by showing them the books and explaining the value of learning about multicultural contemporary families. Souto-Manning and Hermann-Wilmarth (2008) conclude that challenges and conflicts "help us to envision new possibilities for our traditionally marginalized students" (p. 278).

As illustrated above, teachers have good reason to worry that talking about sexual identities and orientation will lead to conflicts with colleagues and parents. However, there are often allies among colleagues and parents (see Kroeger, 2006, summarized in Supplemental Resource 7.2 for Chapter 7, at www.tcpress.com). Teachers can identify and work closely with individuals who are supportive and develop ways to approach those who are resistant. Because these issues are controversial, Blaise and Taylor (2012) advise teachers to stay in close communication with families about classroom discussions and children's questions and concerns. When appropriate, teachers might share with parents how they themselves have worked through their own discomfort. Parents often appreciate "a teacher's honest reflection on what can sometimes be a difficult but important discussion" (p. 96).

Many teachers are also afraid to raise these issues because they assume that discussing same-sex parents means that they will have to talk about sexual practices. However, just as conversations about heterosexual parents do not include this information, there is no reason to bring it up. Another challenge is finding relevant materials. Homophobic attacks in the press have made many authors and publishers shy away from any suggestion of same-sex relationships or nonheterosexual behavior in children's books (Lester, 2007). Fortunately, there are some excellent sources; several are included in the list of "Suggested Books for Children" at the Supplemental Materials at www.tcpress.com, Free Downloads.

Despite the many challenges, teachers need to become comfortable talking about GBLT issues and challenging related inequities. Suppressing or avoiding questions tacitly affirms children's heteronormative assumptions and stereotypes. Silence may also exacerbate the discomfort of children from diverse families who often face conflicts in loyalties similar to those of children who are crossing racial, cultural, and class boundaries between home and school.

CHILDREN'S UNDERSTANDING
OF SEXUAL ORIENTATION AND IDENTITY

As discussed above, many people are vehemently opposed to any mention of GBLT individuals and issues in schools. This situation makes it virtually impossible to conduct formal studies about young children's understanding of sexual orientation and attitudes toward homosexuality and heterosexuality. However, as discussed at length in the previous sections, young children are immersed in heteronormative values and enthusiastically enact them in early childhood classrooms.

Casper and Schultz (1999) did one of the very few studies on children's ideas about sexual orientation. They conducted extensive observations in early childhood classrooms that contained a number of children from families with same-sex parents. Their findings may not generalize to more closed, heterosexist environments, but they do give us an idea of the questions and concerns children would express if they were encouraged to do so.

Most of the children's questions and comments were about whether one needed to have had both a mother and a father to be born and who could make up a family. In their play the children often argued over who was the mommy or the daddy and whether or not there could be two (or more) mommies or daddies. Preschoolers still have a fairly flexible idea of family membership, but they quickly learn from parents, teachers, older peers, and the media that all families have one mommy and one daddy (which of course eliminates lots of families). Lee (2010) noted a similar pattern in her interviews; very young children of lesbian mothers are likely to be open about their family composition, but as they get older and are exposed to more heteronormative and homophobic views, they become more reticent. Litoviceh and Langhout (2004) interviewed children and their lesbian parents and found a similar pattern. One 16-year-old recalled,

> Well, when I was in preschool, I wasn't faced with any homophobia . . . I was very proud [of her two moms] at that point . . . in first grade and for the first time . . . I experienced homophobia . . . two boys [teased her saying], "did half of you come out of one mom and the other mom the other half?" . . . there was a lot of homophobia around fourth and fifth grade . . . people started saying, "that's so gay" or "you're gay." (pp. 424–425)

Casper and Schultz (1999) noted that children were most likely to bring up questions about family composition and reproduction when they had ample time to develop their fantasies and when they had toys that gave them the latitude to play out different family constellations (e.g., multiple adult puppets or dolls). Books and pictures that portrayed a range of families including those with two mothers and two fathers also stimulated their questions and comments. Under these conditions, children as young as kindergartners demonstrated a fairly sophisticated understanding of gay and lesbian relationships and other family constellations that differed from the "typical" heterosexual nuclear family. (To learn how older children understand and discuss sexual orientation, see Chasnoff & Cohen's [1996] videotape *It's Elementary: Talking About Gay Issues in School*.)

LEARNING AND CHALLENGING WHAT CHILDREN KNOW, THINK, AND FEEL ABOUT GENDER AND SEXUAL ORIENTATION

To support children constructing equitable and open gender-related concepts and attitudes, teachers need to learn what children already know and feel about different family constellations, gender roles, and sexual identities. As discussed in earlier sections, children are usually very forthright about their views on gender and reveal their feelings in their selection and rejection of playmates and dramatic play roles. However, teachers often overlook power dynamics between boys and girls or heteronormative expectations underlying their play because they are the "norm."

As pointed out earlier, children enjoy "performing gender" (Boldt, 2011) and trying to suppress these expressions or insist that children change their behavior and playmates is probably futile. Instead you can ask questions, challenge children's statements, point out inequities when one group excludes or dominates the other, and encourage children who resist gender roles and restrictions to speak out. Stories, photographs, skits, puppet shows, and other media can be used to to instigate conversations and to present alternative views. The following suggestions are geared toward identifying covert as well as overt heteronormative dynamics and using children's responses to start conversations and to challenge these "norms."

1. Observe children's play groups for gender divisions. Where and when are they most gender-segregated? least segregated? What happens when you merge centers, relocate gender-typed materials (e.g., put trucks in the role play corner), or create mixed-sex groups? Which children accept/resist these arrangements? What do they say and do? Follow up with conversations to explore how the children felt about these changes. Encourage children to talk about why they are drawn to certain activities and resistant to joining others. Use their responses to develop strategies to help them to become more flexible in their choices of activities and friends.

2. What power differentials do you notice in the classroom? Are some boys intimidating the girls? or vice versa? Or is power fairly balanced among the groups? Do some individual children exert more power than others? What contributes to that dynamic (e.g., gender, personality)? Encourage children to notice and discuss exclusionary or dominating situations and identify when and where in the classroom these most often occur. Tell or read stories about similar dynamics and see what children have to say. Talk with them about what procedures or rules would make the classroom more fair and comfortable for everyone.

3. Show children photographs of people who represent different ages and genders and ask them whom they would go to for help? to play a ball game? to get food? Depending on their answers, you can encourage them to consider a wider range of possibilities by presenting additional information that challenges gender stereotypes (e.g., "I know you said that you would not invite this girl to play ball with you, but what if she likes to play ball and is really good at throwing?").

4. Using the same photographs, ask children which of the people portrayed might be in the same family or household? Arrange the photographs to make families with many constellations, or set up a few "families" in the doll house, including single parents and same-sex parents. Listen to children's questions and comments, and try to hear their underlying assumptions about gender, sexual orientation, and family composition. Encourage them to talk about who can

be in a family and to play out different scenarios with the dolls. Explore their reasons for rejecting or accepting different family groups. Follow up with stories about diverse families and encourage them to rethink their ideas.

5. When children are enacting roles or playing with puppets and dolls, what roles do children assign to each other or to male and female figures? How flexible are they? In particular, what assumptions are expressed in their enactment of family roles—both in terms of composition of families and the gender roles within them? What happens when two girls or two boys want to play the parents? How do the gender roles reflect heteronormative assumptions (e.g., girls talking about making dinner or being beautiful, boys ordering the girls around or insisting on "driving the car," a boy and girl having a pseudo romance or being teased for being "in love")? Ask children about the roles they choose or are assigned and how they feel about them. "Wonder along" with children about what it means to be "in love" or get married. Use stories and images of all kinds to present counter-stereotyped possibilities and alternative ways of interacting and see how children respond.

6. Show children photographs of men, women, girls, and boys in both stereotyped and counter-stereotyped activities and explore their responses. What do they notice about the person in the photograph? Ask them to tell stories about the people depicted and use those to raise alternative scenarios/stories.

7. Listen to children's insults to see if they reflect negative assumptions related to gender (e.g., boys derisively calling each other "girl" or "woman") or sexual orientation (e.g., the derogatory use of the term "gay"). Ask them what these terms mean and, depending on their responses, point out how they are hurtful and based on misinformation. Encourage them to say what they really mean (e.g., "I am mad at you").

In terms of planning curriculum, emphasizing the diversity of families is an excellent starting place (Lee, 2010; Lester, 2007). This topic interests children and is inclusive since all children live with people who, regardless of the situation or the individuals involved, function as a family. This approach also is a vehicle for showing how many dimensions of difference (e.g., race, gender, culture, age, family constellations) overlap and interact in all people's lives. As Souto-Manning learned, reading children books that illustrate many types of families can break the silence and open up conversations in which teachers and children can explore and rethink heteronormative assumptions.

Families and family connections are not frozen in time, rather they evolve as babies are born, young children are adopted, foster children move

to new families, grandparents die, parents get divorced or married, step-sib-
lings and parents enter or leave. All children experience stress when families
change, but this perspective is particularly critical for children living in unstable situations such as foster care. Already they probably are experiencing the
loss and grief of many disruptions and may feel further marginalized when
they are surrounded by stories and images that portray all (other) families
are stable and happy "forever families." The fact that families change should
be reflected in stories and discussions about families and may require some
modifications in time-honored activities as described in the next paragraph.

Many early childhood programs introduce the idea of family diversity with family-made books or posters that show different aspects of their
lives such as household members, favorite foods, activities, and rituals (see
Chapter 3). In keeping with the concern about misrepresenting families as
completely stable, Skattebol and Ferfolja (2007) note that one disadvantage
of this approach is that the books and posters are one-time representations
and may overemphasize who is in the family at a particular moment and
de-emphasize how family groups and connections change over time and
across situations (e.g., a child may spend a vacation with an aunt and cousin, a grandparent may move in for a while, a mother may have to tempo-
rarily relocate for work, a father may be incarcerated for a period of time).
The authors suggest that family posters and books be continually updated
and emphasize what families do with different members and friends rather
than focusing on family membership per se. The modification has many
advantages: it is more inclusive and honest; it keeps families engaged in the
process and enhances communication among children and parents; and the
updates help to maintain children's interest and keep the posters and books
from becoming "stale."

Almost all materials and activities can be used to encourage children to
explore a wide variety of roles and to recognize and challenge gender stereotypes and heteronormative assumptions. Blaise and Taylor (2012) suggest one possibility to encourage children to re-think gender-typed clothing
and roles. First, the children are asked to sort clothing in the dramatic play
area into 3 piles: 1 for girls, 1 for boys and girls, and 1 for boys. Then the
teachers encourage children to express and rethink their assumptions and
to try wearing types of clothing other than those they usually choose. To
further embolden children to experiment with dressing up, Dykstra (2005)
suggests posting photographs that feature individuals in a variety of roles
that challenge common expectations (e.g., female construction workers,
male dancers, drag queens and kings). To challenge beliefs that gender is a
binary concept and that boys/men and girls/women are mutually exclusive
groups, Dykstra suggests introducing a doll with no visible gender cues.
Give the doll a gender neutral name and avoid using pronouns. See what
assumptions or questions children express. How do they respond when you
dress the doll in masculine clothing and then shift to feminine clothing?

Recently I visited a child-care center and saw a wonderful example of teachers supporting children to challenge and expand gender roles and sexual identities. In one preschool classroom (mostly 4-year-olds) the teachers had been using books and images to encourage children to think and talk about diverse families, and in the process children had become interested in weddings. That morning two girls had decided to get married. The teachers helped them with some of the logistics (e.g., getting needed materials and equipment) but made sure that the girls remained "in charge" of the project. The girls recruited other classmates to join in the planning and production of the wedding. By the time I observed late in the day, the girls had orchestrated a masterful rendition of a wedding, with all the other children participating as musicians, attendants, or audience. After the first wedding, several other children, sometimes in pairs and other times in larger groups, "got married" in smaller, less elaborate ceremonies. This event illustrates how teachers can lay the groundwork for children to do their own explorations and to construct their ideas and concepts. What was particularly striking was how much fun everyone had; although the underlying issues are serious and complex, the children enjoyed the freedom of "playing" with the concepts of "marriage" and "weddings." (For an example of the challenges and successes of implementing a schoolwide curriculum supporting sexual equalities, see Supplemental Resource 7.3 for Chapter 7, at www.tcpress.com)

The following story describes how one teacher took the risk of confronting homophobic views expressed in his classroom and engaged children and parents in challenging these views.

Paul, a Chinese American 2nd-grade teacher in a racially and economically mixed public school, was distressed to hear his children use the word *gay* for anything that they thought was negative (e.g., "Those pants are so gay, why'd you buy them?" "I hate this project, it's sooo gay!"). He suspected that some of them did not even know what the word meant, but realized that prevalent homophobic attitudes were becoming part of their worldviews.

Given the sensitivity of the issues, he knew it was critical to communicate with the parents before talking with the children. From his earlier conversations with parents, he predicted that some parents would be supportive, and that others would be vehemently opposed. He wrote a carefully worded letter, telling the parents what he had heard the children say and pointing out that they were learning to be prejudiced. He realized that some of the parents who might be the most resistant had themselves suffered from discrimination. Thus he explicitly pointed out the connection between prejudice against gay and lesbian people and biases related to race, ethnicity, gender, social class, and disabilities. He then invited the parents to a meeting to discuss this problem and explore possible solutions. Many parents were upset, and there were many tensions between those who supported and those who opposed talking about sexual orientation. Paul opened the meeting by reading Martin Niemoeller's famous statement about the German's failure to speak out against the Nazis (Jewish Virtual Library, 2014):

> First they came for the Communists, but I was not a Communist so I did not speak out. Then they came for the Socialists and the Trade Unionists, but I was neither, so I did not speak out. Then they came for the Jews, but I was not a Jew so I did not speak out. And when they came for me, there was no one left to speak out for me.

As he slowly read, the parents were quiet and thoughtful. Paul then started the discussion by having each person state her or his responses to the reading and feelings about exploring the topic of sexual orientation with the children. There was no discussion until everyone had spoken. Then Paul explained his concerns and talked about possible classroom strategies for addressing them. At that point the discussion opened up. It was often heated, but it was also productive, and by the end, the parents agreed on some guidelines and strategies that they were all more or less comfortable with. They also formed a small committee made up of parents with different views to work more closely with Paul as he implemented the strategies.

After more planning and several discussions with the committee, Paul then introduced the topic to the children by telling them that he had often heard them use the word *gay* and asking them what they meant by it. As he had suspected, a number of them had only a vague idea of what it meant. However, others did know, and some embellished their responses with derogatory terms such as *faggot* and *dyke*. Using photographs and children's books, Paul talked about sexual orientation in terms of families with same-sex parents (he had agreed with the parents not to discuss sexual practices, bisexuality, or transgendered people with the children). He then organized several activities about name calling including ones in which children talked about names that they had been called and how they felt.

Over the next several weeks Paul invited several gay and lesbian people to visit the classroom to talk about their lives and to share their work with the children (e.g., a gay coach showed the children some new basketball moves; a lesbian chef did a cooking project) so that children could see that gay and lesbian people had lives, jobs, and children like other adults they knew. Each visit also included a discussion about discrimination that the guest experienced and how derogatory terms hurt them. After each visit, Paul sent a newsletter home that included the children's descriptions of the visit and some of the comments that children had made during the discussion. After the first couple of visits, Paul began to invite parents to come to meet the guests and listen to the discussion. He was thrilled when one of the parents who had been most opposed showed up for one of the visits. She sat and listened and later in a subdued voice thanked him.

Paul was never sure to what extent he had changed parents' thinking, but the children in his class no longer used the word *gay* pejoratively (at least not in his hearing), and he sometimes heard them on the playground telling children in other classes not to use the term. His biggest surprise came several months after the original parent meeting. A mother who had been very quiet during all of the discussions told him that she was lesbian and that for the first time she felt comfortable disclosing that fact to her child's teacher.

NOTE

Intersex refers to anyone with genital anomalies, some evident at birth and others manifesting later in life. According to the Intersex Society of North America (ISNA), about 1 in 1,500–2,000 babies are born with clear anomalies, but 1 in 100 individuals have bodies that vary from standard male or female characteristics (Intersex Society of North America, 2008).

CHAPTER 8

The Context of Abilities and Disabilities

REFLECTIONS ON ABILITIES AND DISABILITIES

In response to the Part II introduction question "Who am I?" did you include whether or not you had a disability? Because "ableness" is another social "norm" in our culture, most people without identified disabilities rarely include that information in their list. However, *all* of us have a range of abilities and disabilities, some more visible in specific cultures and circumstances than others. It is important to recognize this continuum and avoid making a sharp distinction between "abled" and "disabled" people. As with the other attributes discussed so far (race, economic class, culture, gender, and sexual identity and orientation), this division is, in part, socially constructed and far more fluid and complex than commonly acknowledged. To understand how your own abilities and disabilities have affected your life, you can ask yourself:

- What activities, tasks, and situations make me feel confident? uncomfortable or incompetent?
- What skills have been hard for me to learn? When I have had to struggle to learn something, how have I felt about myself? about people who grasped it more easily than I did? What skills have I mastered easily? How do I regard those individuals who have difficulty in those areas?
- How have my strengths and limitations affected my schooling? job choices? recreational activities? social life?

The following comments and questions are directed primarily to readers who do not identify themselves as "disabled." However, even those who have a "disabilty" may harbor misconceptions about other types of impairments and find it useful to go through these exercises. I should also confess at this point that, for lack of better terminology, I refer to "children/

individuals with/without disabilities" throughout this chapter. As explained in Chapter 1, a few decades ago we used the term "differently abled," which reflects my view that we all have a range of abilities. However, many people found the term too cumbersome and "politically correct," and it has fallen out of use. So, reluctantly, I use the binary terms of *ability/disability* and *abled/disabled* and urge readers to interpret them as movable points on many continua.

Many people have strong emotional reactions when they see others with visible disabilities; they may feel fear, pity, or revulsion (Palmer, 2001). Teachers need to recognize and, in many cases, rethink their responses and assumptions in order to create inclusive classrooms where children of all abilities are equal members.

To begin that process, consider the fact that most individuals go through life being judged for what they *can* do, whereas people with identified disabilities are usually seen through a lens of what they *cannot* do. Moreover, people often assume that impairment in one area means that other functions are also affected (e.g., a person who is deaf is also socially isolated).

To explore your emotional reactions and assumptions related to disabilities, ask yourself the following questions:

- How do I react when I meet an adult or child with a disability? Do I feel pity? respect? curiosity? Am I horrified? relieved that I am not that person? Am I afraid that the same thing might happen to me or a member of my family? Since anyone can become "disabled" in a moment (e.g., car accident, bad fall), seeing someone with a disability often evokes this fear.
- What assumptions about the person's capabilities do I make on the basis of the disability? Are they warranted or not?
- Do I find myself wanting to help or protect the person? Do I wait for him or her to ask for assistance? Or do I look away and hope that I will not have to help?
- How would I react if I learned that my new doctor was in a wheelchair? my child's new teacher was blind? my next door neighbor had been in a psychiatric hospital? the applicant for the school administrative assistant position had severe facial scarring from burns?

As you consider these situations, note your initial reactions, and then try to shift your focus away from what the individuals *cannot* do to what they *can* do. For example, a teacher who is blind may not be able to watch children with his eyes but may be sensitive to the emotional subtleties in children's voices that a sighted teacher might miss. Also, children in his class may have opportunities to learn nuances of sound, touch, smell, and taste that they might not otherwise experience.

GROWING UP IN AN "ABLED" WORLD

How people define and respond to abilities and disabilities is, to a large extent, culturally and economically determined. For example, in a society where livelihoods and social prestige depend on cooperating with other group members, a person lacking social skills may be judged as more "disabled" than someone who cannot read. In our society where logical and analytical thinking is valued, people who "hear voices" are labeled as emotionally disturbed; in a more spiritual and mystical society these same people might be regarded as seers blessed by divine wisdom (Fadiman, 1997). In short, the same characteristic might be seen as a disability in one environment and as an asset in another. Educational programs for children with disabilities also reflect cultural values. For example, the common goal of self-sufficiency is an expression of our society's high regard for living independently. This aspiration may contradict expectations of families who assume that their children with disabilities will be cared for by the extended family for the rest of their lives (Harry, 1998).

Influences on Perceptions of Disability

In most Western countries disabilities are viewed from a medical or deficit model. Typically, physicians or psychologists diagnose disabilities and then prescribe pharmaceutical, surgical, curricular, and behavioral remedies in order to correct or compensate for specific impairments. Children are often defined by their disability, and the medical and educational professionals, empowered by their expertise, usually make treatment and placement decisions; children, especially if they are young, and their parents usually have little say (Zaretsky, 2005).

In contrast to the medical emphasis on "fixing" impairments or individuals, the social–relational model views disabilities as an interaction between individual abilities and structural factors in the environment (Nind, Flewitt & Payler, 2010). Although the limitations imposed by disabilities often require targeted interventions we must also consider how some social and physical environments are "disabling" and how to change them to be more "abling." Ironically, just as I started work on this chapter, I fell while out walking and broke my wrist. Although I would never equate my injury with a lifelong limitation or condition, this event gave me some immediate insights into how physical and social environments can "able" or "disable" a person. Almost immediately, my physical world became divided into one-handed or two-handed tasks, tools, and routines. Likewise, I noticed how some people's reactions—for example, being overly solicitous or begrudging with their assistance, telling me horrible stories about wrist fractures that never healed—made me feel discouraged and helpless. Other responses—matter-of-factly providing a needed hand, tool, or ride; sharing a laugh while tying my shoes—made me feel hopeful and competent and helped me to adapt to my single-handed state. This experience made me very conscious of how we all need to pay attention to the details of the social and physical environments when anyone is dealing with either a temporary or long-term limitation or "disability."

Societal inequities also play a role in how people with disabilities are viewed and treated. Racial prejudice, economic disadvantage, cultural discontinuities between schools and families, and assumptions about gender roles often contribute to academic and social difficulties that result in diagnoses of disability (Franklin, 1992; Odom, Peck, et al., 1996).

Moreover, future prospects of children with disabilities are affected by the affluence of their families. Parents with more money and skills to advocate for their children (as described in Chapter 5) are more likely to get optimal equipment and services for their children than are those who are poor, new to this country, and/or intimidated by school personnel (Hanson, 2002).

In many countries, including the United States, the approach to educating children with disabilities has changed dramatically over the past 40 years. Whereas in the past they were often hidden away in special programs or kept at home, we now strive to educate them in the "least restricted environment" and ensure that "all children, no matter how diverse their needs, should expect to be served in the regular education setting that they would attend at any specific age" (Sheridan, Foley, & Radlinski, 1995, p. 42). With the passage of the Americans with Disabilities Act in 1990, people with disabilities began to participate in educational institutions, workplaces, and a wide range of organizations. Yet fully integrating into the society continues to be a challenge. The general public still tends to see children and adults with disabilities as second-class citizens, burdens, objects of pity, and incapable of making positive contributions. In 2008 the Disability Rights Education & Defense Fund recognized that the media often embraces "negative and inaccurate beliefs" about people with disabilities (para. 2). In response the Fund started a Media and Disability program to push the media to counteract demeaning images and stereotypes and to become an ally "in changing perceptions, eliminating discrimination, and raising public awareness" (para. 3).

Inclusion in Educational Settings

Efforts to include children with disabilities in regular classrooms (formerly referred to as "mainstreaming") have followed a number of different models, such as "pull-out" programs, in which children leave their regular classrooms for special academic help. Alternatively, specialists and/or aides come into the regular classroom and work with the students there (Devore & Russell, 2007; Mogharreban & Bruns, 2009; see Odom, Buysse,

& Soukakou, 2011, for reviews of types of inclusion practices and how they are implemented and evaluated).

Often children with severe disabilities are able to function in regular classrooms with one-on-one assistance. However, too much adult help may lead classmates to believe that the child is not a competent potential playmate (Connors & Stalker, 2007) and undermine the child's possible social connections (Diamond & Huang, 2005; Harper & McCluskey, 2003; Kishida & Kemp, 2009; Nind et al., 2010; Walker & Berthelsen, 2008).

Despite the challenges, there are many advantages for including children with disabilities in a regular classroom full-time. Specialists and teachers working together in the same classroom have the potential to develop a team-teaching model that blends "the rich knowledge traditions of regular and special education . . . [and] address[es] issues of disability as well as cultural and linguistic differences among [the] children" (Zaretsky, 2005, p. 76).

Authentic inclusion, however, is more than simply placing children in regular classrooms and scheduling specialists. Thornton and Underwood (2013) critically note that the way inclusion is usually described and practiced "suggests the existence of a core social group in which children [with disabilities] are to be included" (p. 60), almost as unwelcome guests. Like Nind et al. (2010), Thornton and Underwood (2013) see disability "as a form of oppression produced through the interplay of the individual and her or his social environment" (p. 62). They point out that there is a difference between including a child in a classroom and practicing inclusion. The former implies placing children in a classroom and expecting them to conform to existing routines and expectations. The latter means providing necessary supports and adaptations and directly challenging discriminatory attitudes toward individuals with identified disabilities. At its best, "inclusion provides all children with a model for the world as a place of acceptance and ability, where every member of the group has much to offer and much to learn" (Parlakian, 2012, p. 71).

Despite worldwide support for inclusive education, as attested by many UNESCO position papers and guidelines published over the past 2 decades (e.g., UNESCO Bangkok, 2009), inclusion remains an elusive goal, especially in early childhood education (Odom et al., 2011). Several studies have shown that teachers often support the idea of inclusion but are reluctant to have children with particular diagnoses or challenging behavior patterns in their classrooms (Huang & Diamond, 2009; Killoran, Tymon, & Frempong, 2007; Yang & Rusli, 2012). Extensive field work in successful inclusive classrooms is critical to preparing teachers to work with children with a range of abilities. These experiences prompt preservice teachers to rethink their views about disabilities and gain confidence that they can teach in an inclusive classroom (Voss & Bufkin, 2011). Without multiple opportunities to identify and challenge assumptions about children with disabilities, teachers are vulnerable to seeing children with disabilities as objects of pity (Clark, 1997) and being overly protective and intrusively helpful.

Similar to teachers, parents may support the concept of inclusion but then have concerns when it involves their own children (Diamond, Hestenes, & O'Connor, 1994). Those with "typical" children may worry that their children will be shortchanged because teachers are spending so much time with children with identified disabilities. Parents of children with disabilities sometimes express fears that their children and they themselves will be socially isolated or that their children will not get needed services in a regular classroom. As these concerns demonstrate, authentic inclusion requires that the parents of all children in a classroom be involved so that inclusion is a community effort, not simply the domain of special education experts. (For an example of how teachers and parents can collaborate to develop inclusion plans, see Supplemental Resource 8.1 for Chapter 8, at www.tcpress.com).

Practicing authentic inclusion requires a multifaceted approach including close and respectful coordination among children, parents, teachers, and specialists; careful scheduling of transportation, tutoring, and medications; and creative adaptations of curriculum, classroom routines, and the physical environment. Moreover, it means challenging assumptions and stereotypes about disabilities and creating classrooms of acceptance and ability, where every member is honored as a learner and a teacher (Parlakian, 2012). A full consideration of all of these aspects is beyond the scope of this book. Fortunately a number of resources describe excellent strategies and examples of successful inclusive classrooms (see, e.g., Diamond & Stacey, 2000; Feuerstein, Falik, Feuerstein, & Bohács, 2013; Kemple, 2004; Kostelnik, Onaga, Rohde, & Whiren, 2002; Odom, 2002; Perez, 2013; Recchia & Lee, 2013; Sheridan et al., 1995). In this chapter, I will focus on two aspects that are most germane to multicultural education: the social participation of children with identified disabilities and the need to recognize and challenge children's ideas and feelings about individuals with different abilities.

SOCIAL PARTICIPATION OF CHILDREN WITH DISABILITIES

Despite the widely accepted goal of inclusion, numerous studies show that children with identified disabilities are often socially and academically isolated from their peers (e.g., Guralnick, Hammond, Connor, & Neville, 2006; Guralnick, Neville, Hammond, & Connor, 2007; Kishida & Kemp, 2009; Odom, Zercher, Li, Marquart, Sandall, & Brown, 2006; Walker & Berthelsen, 2007, 2008). In the United States and many other countries, the emphasis on individual achievement, competition, and high-stakes testing often undermines authentic inclusion because children at an early age learn to judge themselves and others by what they can do and what they know.

I vividly recall how, when my son Daniel walked through the door of his kindergarten on the first day of school, he was greeted by a child saying, "I can count up to 100, can you?"

Facilitating social participation in preschools is a little easier than it is in elementary schools because teachers are less bound by mandated curricula. Also preschoolers are rarely divided into "ability" groups that highlight skill differences. Because young children vary widely in their development, those with disabilities may not appear to be that different from their peers, and teachers are accustomed to adjusting activities to meet a broad range of skill levels. Moreover, the array of options in most preschool classrooms allows children who have difficulty with one type of learning situation to join classmates at other activities that play to their strengths.

Studying Social Participation

Odom and his colleagues did an extensive study of children's social inclusion in 16 preschool programs (Odom, Zercher, Li, et al., 2006; Odom, Zercher, Marquart, et al., 2002). They found that across all of them about one-third of the children with disabilities were rejected and one-third were well-liked by their peers. The latter group tended to be easy going and affectionate, socially and communicatively skilled, emotionally responsive and positive, and willing to follow classroom routines and rules. Those disliked by their peers were aggressive, disruptive, withdrawn, and lacking in communication skills (i.e., had speech/language limitations) and often engaged in conflicts with peers and adults (Odom, Zercher, Marquart, et al., 2002; Odom, Zercher, Li, et al., 2006). Interestingly, these behaviors are similar to those found in general populations of accepted and rejected children (Ramsey, 1991a). When asked how they feel about their classmates with disabilities, young children often say that they dislike them because they are disruptive and/or aggressive (Nabors & Keyes, 1995). Not surprisingly, teachers also express more wariness about children who are disruptive (Huang & Diamond, 2009), which may also affect children's views. Parents, especially if they do not understand the nature of the disability, may encourage their children to stay away from impulsive and/or aggressive peers (Han, Ostrosky, & Diamond, 2006).

Even children with only mild delays and no emotional and behavioral problems often socially lag behind their peers. Guralnick and colleagues observed that, after attending an inclusive preschool program for 2 years, children with mild delays gained skills in initiating social contacts and engaging in positive interactions, including conversations with peers (Guralnick, Hammond, et al., 2006; Guralnick, Nevill, et al., 2007). However, they did not learn how to sustain interactive play, nor did they develop reciprocal friendships with peers. Despite these limitations, Guralnick and colleagues point out that children are still learning how to interact with peers and building skills that may eventually enable them to form reciprocal relationships (Guralnick, Nevill, et al., 2007).

Interestingly, children with disabilities do not always "see" their rejection by peers, often telling teachers and interviewers that they have more friends than is evident from their classmates' comments about them (Helper, 1994). However, they also may be learning not to be too hopeful about their prospects for social participation. In a series of interviews with children with and without physical disabilities, children with disabilities expressed low expectations of social success (Trepanier-Street, Hong, Silverman, Keefer, & Morris, 2011).

The social impact of an identified disability is often exacerbated by gender, race, culture, and economic class. For example, girls with learning disabilities often have the lowest status in classrooms (Helper, 1994; Juvonen & Bear, 1992), perhaps because peers expect girls to be more, rather than less, academically competent. In some classrooms, the isolation of children with disabilities may be worsened if they are racially or culturally a minority in that setting. The absence of a shared language inevitably limits communication among teachers, parents, and children and may undermine efforts to form close partnerships to provide optimal support (Hanson, Gutierrez, Morgan, Brennan, & Zercher, 1997).

Social isolation, however, is not inevitable. Recall that Odom and his colleagues found that one-third of the children with disabilities were accepted by their peers (Odom, Zercher, Marquart, et al., 2002; Odom, Zercher, Li, et al., 2006). Even children who are quite distant from the social mainstream may have one friend who serves as a social buffer and provides companionship (Juvonen & Bear, 1992). In one inclusion program in Australia, children with disabilities had fewer reciprocal friendships, but their social activity profiles and levels of peer acceptance were similar to those of their classmates (Walker & Berthelsen, 2007).

Social acceptance may vary by the situation and the nature of disability. For example, children are more likely to reject peers with orthopedic limitations as partners for physical activities (Diamond & Hong, 2010; Diamond & Tu, 2009). On the other hand, children who cannot hear can still engage in these activities and can use sign language, which their classmates often enjoy learning (Swadener & Johnson, 1989). These differential responses on the part of children suggest that they are aware of what circumstances and activities are more or less disabling for their peers. All children can participate in discussions about how to make the classroom accessible to everyone by changing procedures, providing different tools, or rearranging physical spaces. (For more detailed accounts of research and approaches to support inclusion, see Supplemental Resource 8.2 for Chapter 8, at www.tcpress.com).

Facilitating Social Inclusion

Observations of how some children with disabilities struggle to initiate and sustain interactions and peer relationships highlight the cognitive and emotional complexity of the required social skills (Walker & Berthelsen, 2007). Supporting the social participation of children with severe disabilities requires a great deal of dedication, observation, planning, and flexibility by adults. A number of studies and reviews have identified specific ways that teachers and parents, working with children, can create equitable and fair environments where all children are welcomed and empowered (e.g., Batchelor & Taylor, 2005; Connors & Stalker, 2007; Diamond & Stacey, 2000; Kostelnik et al., 2002; Odom, 2002; Odom, Peck, et al., 1996; Parlakian, 2012; Sheridan et al., 1995; Swadener & Johnson, 1989; Walker & Berthelsen, 2007, 2008). Their main points are summarized below:

1. Everyone—children, teachers, and parents—should view children with disabilities as full members of the group and support them to be an integral part of all activities. They should also challenge the dichotomy of abilities and disabilities by seeing them as a continuum, and recognizing that everyone has a range of capacities and limitations. All aspects of the environment should be designed to be "abling" so that every child can participate as fully as possible. Medications and therapies should be administered in a matter-of-fact unobtrusive way.

2. With particularly challenging children and situations, administrators and colleagues must support teachers (e.g., classroom aids, training, access to consultants) so that they understand the issues and develop strategies that enable them to enjoy their interactions with all the children, nurture positive peer interactions and relationships, and remain optimistic that everyone will be part of the classroom community.

3. Images and examples of people with disabilities engaging in a wide range of activities (e.g., work, sports, politics, parenting) should be provided. Adults can read and tell stories about people with identified disabilities who have had interesting and fulfilling lives. Themes of equity and justice can be incorporated by teaching children about disability rights activists and having children "meet" some activists either in person or through Skype or Facetime. Parents and community people with disabilities can visit the classroom to talk about their lives and how they compensate for their limitations, stressing all the things they *can* do and the skills they have developed because of their disability (e.g., navigating by touch and sound). They also might speak about times that they

have been mistreated because of their disability and how they advocate for disability rights.

4. Parents, teachers, and specialists should collaborate to facilitate social participation of all children both inside and outside of the classroom (e.g., playdates, swimming lessons, library story hours). Parents of children with disabilities should talk with other parents honestly about their child's limitations and capabilities. Then they can work together to find solutions to logistical and social and emotional barriers to getting children together outside of school.

5. When children are struggling to become part of the social mainstream, adults can facilitate social interactions in a number of ways, including (but not limited to) the following:

   a. Closely observing the social contacts of children with disabilities and noting how often and with whom they are interacting; assessing the quality of the interactions to identify those that are positive and egalitarian and those in which classmates are overtly or covertly patronizing, bullying, rejecting, or ignoring a classmate with disabilities.

   b. Identifying children's social strengths and challenges and scaffolding them to build on existing skills (e.g., setting up activities that play to a child's strengths; placing the target child with classmates who are receptive and flexible and most likely to support his or her efforts to interact; subtly providing modeling, coaching, and physical help as needed without intruding on the activity).

   c. Challenging assumptions about what children cannot do by drawing attention to their skills and accomplishments (in a casual, matter-of-fact way).

   d. Providing activities to foster all children's social skills and positive peer relations (e.g., stories, skits, and coaching to encourage children to empathize with others, to see their perspectives, and to regulate their own emotions).

   e. Setting up activities where children can interact or collaborate at different levels (e.g., working side by side as well as directly interacting) and with different levels and types of skills.

   f. Providing enough academic and physical support so that children are not floundering and getting frustrated—without being overbearing.

   g. Encouraging all children to learn about disabilities and associated equipment and, when possible, participate in exercises and other therapies.

   h. Monitoring frequency and length of adult-child interactions and stepping back as much as possible to allow more space for peer interactions.

i. Observing all aspects of the physical and social environment to identify and address ways that the classroom might be a physically or socially "disabling" environment for some children; monitoring the ever-changing social dynamics of the classroom and adapting strategies accordingly.

Working with children of all abilities requires continually questioning goals and assumptions. For example, enthusiasm for social inclusion should not lead to the one-way assimilation that has been experienced by many marginalized groups. Besides providing activities to facilitate connections between peers with and without disabilities, programs should also include opportunities for children with disabilities to form friendships with each other and to enjoy being a member of those groups as well (Harry, Park, & Day, 1998).

As educators and citizens, we need to continually and critically reflect on how an overemphasis on individual performance and competition hurts children of all abilities and undermines efforts to create accepting and re-spectful communities. Finally, we have to challenge demeaning stereotypes of people with disabilities and the very notion that the world is divided into people with and without disabilities.

CHILDREN'S KNOWLEDGE AND FEELINGS
RELATED TO ABILITIES AND DISABILITIES

Knowing how children think and feel about abilities and disabilities can help teachers recognize and address children's concerns and questions, chal-lenge misinformation, and create a more genuinely inclusive classroom en-vironment. All children, those with and without identified disabilities, are "active meaning-makers" (Nind et al., 2010, p. 656), constructing their concepts of disabilities as they encounter a range of people, environments, and media images.

Many studies in the past 3 decades have contributed to knowledge about children's awareness and attitudes related to disabilities. However, most of this work has used materials and questions that assume that a dis-ability is an individual characteristic, rather than examining the interplay between individuals and different environments. Thus there are some major gaps in understanding.

Children's awareness and understanding varies across type of disability (Diamond & Hestenes, 1996; Diamond & Hong, 2010; Diamond & Tu, 2009; Dyson, 2005). Many notice orthopedic disabilities first, because of the visibility of the associated equipment, such as crutches or wheelchairs. They are least aware of cognitive or psychological disabilities. This vari-ability is not surprising because children often interpret disabilities on the basis of their own experience (Diamond & Innes, 2001). For example, they can compare blindness with not being able to see in a dark room, but they are usually less conscious about how their cognitions and emotions function and therefore have difficulty understanding these types of disabilities (Gasser, Malti, & Buholzer, 2014; Nabors & Keyes, 1995).

Many children have misconceptions about the causes of disabilities. They often explain disabilities by the equipment that children use (Diamond & Innes, 2001) (e.g., "He can't walk because he has a wheelchair"). Alternatively, they assume that disabilities are related to immaturity (e.g., "She hasn't learned to talk yet.") or some kind of illness, injury, or other trauma (e.g., "He had a really bad earache and now can't hear.") (Diamond & Hestenes, 1996; Diamond & Huang, 2005).

Children's attitudes toward people with disabilities are inconsistent and shift during their preschool and elementary school years. Preschoolers often state that they could be friends with peers with disabilities (Diamond & Hestenes, 1996). However, there is often a gap between these assertions and actually forming friendships (Dyson, 2005). Moreover, as they get older, children tend to develop more biases against persons with disabilities (DeGrella & Green, 1984; J. F. Goodman, 1989). In elementary school children become concerned about how their skills compare with others' and judge others accordingly. In a series of interviews with 5-8-year-olds with and without disabilities, Trepanier-Street et al. (2011) found that children without disabilities underestimated the academic and physical competence of their classmates with disabilities, which, in turn, may make them less desirable work and play partners. In contrast, children with disabilities often overestimate their skills and assumed that they were comparable to those of their peers (Connors & Stalker, 2007).

As they get older, children are more likely to reject peers who are labeled and are treated in ways that make them stand out (Milich, McAnnich, & Harris, 1992). During elementary school, academic work becomes increasingly test-driven and challenging, and children with certain disabilities have a harder time "keeping up" with their peers. As interactions between children with and without disabilities decline, they have less common ground on which to build friendships, so that the children with disabilities may become increasingly isolated. Moreover, during the elementary school years, mutual friendships between peers with and without disabilities tend to shift to lopsided caretaking relationships. Often, friends of children with disabilities are pushed into that role by teachers and peers who rely on them to communicate with and accompany children with disabilities (Dyson, 2005; Salisbury & Palombar, 1998).

Children's also attitudes vary across type of disability. As mentioned before, children are most likely to reject their peers with emotional and cognitive disabilities. When children are emotionally volatile and act unpredictably, their peers learn to distrust and avoid them. Likewise, impulsive actions are often interpreted as misbehavior (Kostelnik et al., 2002). Children are more accepting of peers who have disabilities that are clearly no fault of their own (e.g., blindness) but reject peers whom they perceive as being responsible for their disability (e.g., obesity; poor impulse control) (Diamond & Innes, 2001).

Despite these challenges, many studies show that children with disabilities thrive both socially and academically in inclusive settings (see Diamond & Innes, 2001; Odom, 2002). Moreover, children without disabilities also benefit; they become more sensitive to other people, more accepting of differences, and more likely to hold positive views of peers with disabilities (Diamond, Hestenes, Carpenter, & Innes, 1997; Favazza & Odom, 1997). Often they develop more confidence and skills by supporting peers with disabilities (Batchelor & Taylor, 2005). However, teachers need to be sure that children without disabilities do not treat their peers with disabilities as helpless and that they are doing things *with* them rather than *for* them (Salisbury & Palombar, 1998). "If children are continually prompted to yield to . . . [or help] people with disabilities, they might develop feelings of pity toward individuals with special needs, rather than developing coequal relationships" (Han et al., 2006, p. 7). Likewise, encouraging "typically developing children to be proud of themselves for being nice and playing with children with disabilities [can lead to] unbalanced relationships" (p. 6). A much more productive approach is to ensure that children learn accurate information about the nature and parameters of specific disabilities and be able to distinguish respectful and appropriate support from intrusive or demeaning services. Finally, teachers should use every opportunity to foster common interests between children with and without disabilities, to highlight the strengths of children with disabilities and, when appropriate, to encourage them to take leadership roles (Han et al., 2006; Kostelnik et al., 2002; Palmer, 2001).

LEARNING AND CHALLENGING WHAT CHILDREN KNOW, THINK, AND FEEL ABOUT ABILITIES AND DISABILITIES

Classrooms where some children have obvious disabilities provide opportunities to observe how children with and without impairments interact, and conversations about disabilities may occur spontaneously. In other cases, when disabilities are less visible, children may not be consciously aware of them, although they may react to behaviors that make them uncomfortable. The following activities are some of the many ways that you might learn what individual children are thinking and feeling and challenge their misperceptions:

1. Make available stories, dolls, puppets, and pictures that depict people with different types of disabilities and use them to start

conversations to see what children notice and what they think and feel. Encourage them to express their ideas about the causes and effects of particular disabilities. If they mention demeaning views and stereotypes, read stories or show images that challenge those misperceptions (e.g., skiers who are blind, basketball players who are in wheelchairs, construction workers who are also amputees). Listen to their reactions and facilitate conversations in which they can explore and construct new and more accurate concepts about disabilities.

2. Put these dolls and puppets out in the classroom and see how the children play with them—what roles they assign and the stories they create. If the figures with disabilities are ignored or relegated to passive roles, you might enter into the play briefly and assign more active roles to them and see what the children say or do.

3. Use sign language in storytelling and singing, and see how children respond. Teach them how to use some sign language and emphasize that, like any skill, it takes practice. For children who can read, do similar activities with Braille. Use these activities to emphasize the skills, strength, and determination that are involved in compensating for various limitations. Encourage children to see these abilities and adaptations as intriguing and admirable (e.g., the fluid and intricate motions used in sign language, the intriguing patterns of Braille, the quick turns and stops and "tricks" that some people can do in their wheelchairs).

4. Develop a series of activities in which children briefly experience the effects of different disabilities (e.g., using crutches, being blindfolded or wearing opaque glasses, wearing thick gloves or elastic bands around their fingers). As they try to do different tasks with these simulated limitations, listen to their questions and assumptions and help them empathize with (not pity) people with these impairments. Sometimes these simulations make children anxious, and they may exaggerate the helplessness of people with specific disabilities or enact negative stereotypes of them (Palmer, 2001). To counteract this tendency, encourage children to describe what they had to do or learn in order to manage during the experience of not being able to walk, see, or move their fingers. Have them consider how people who have these impairments experience the environment and what physical changes and types of social support would be helpful.

5. Listen carefully for children using disability-related insults such as "retard" or dismissing peers because they are "stupid" or "can't do anything." When you hear these types of statements, talk with the children and find out what they are really trying to say, why they chose these particular words, and if they understand what

they mean. Use stories, skits, and puppet shows to illustrate how insulting others is hurtful and does not resolve anything, whereas telling someone why you are angry can be constructive.

As you observe children with and without disabilities interacting with each other and engage children in conversations, you may identify problematic social dynamics and hear comments and questions about disabilities that reflect commonly held fears and stereotypes. You can encourage children to see that abilities and disabilities are fluid continua rather than defining characteristics and that everyone feels more or less confident in different situations. This awareness may help children feel less anxious about their own abilities and more accepting of those with identified disabilities.

As discussed earlier in this chapter, children who have emotional and/or behavioral problems are most likely to be rejected by their peers and thwart efforts to practice authentic inclusion. For this reason, I am using the following story to illustrate the complexity of these challenges and how teachers can collaborate with each other, parents, and children and work on multiple levels to create a truly inclusive classroom.

Michelle (African American) and Tara (European American) were teachers in a racially mixed, lower-middle-class preschool. They were frustrated by the constant conflicts between Bobby (Asian American), who had been diagnosed with ADHD, and his classmates. Bobby was bright and could be a lot of fun, but frequently he rushed into play spaces, destroying everything in his path. When he was frustrated, he would strike out either with words or fists. Not surprisingly, the other children had started to avoid him, and the teachers frequently overheard comments about how "bad" Bobby was. Some children had made comments that suggested that they were beginning to associate Bobby's race with his behavior. A couple of parents had reported that their children were scared of Bobby, and they urged the teachers to "make him behave."

Michelle and Tara decided to first have some informal conversations with Bobby to find out what he was feeling. He refused to sit down and talk, but in a few short exchanges on the playground, the teachers did learn that Bobby thought that the other kids were "mean" and never let him play with them or use certain toys. He also said that he hated school, especially circle time, and that he only liked outside time because then he could run.

Michelle and Tara then took turns watching Bobby and his interactions with both teachers and peers to get a better idea of what was happening. After a couple of days they noticed that they themselves often publicly reprimanded Bobby and that rarely did they or anyone else in the classroom say anything positive to him. As they watched, it also became clear that many of the conflicts occurred when Bobby was trying to integrate himself into a play group. They also noted, as Bobby had said, that he was much happier and more socially involved on the playground.

They discussed their observations with Bobby's parents, who were very concerned and willing to help, as they were hoping to avoid using medication at this point. Together, the teachers and parents decided on the following plan, which would be followed at school and, as much as possible, at home:

1. Engage in positive interactions with Bobby.
2. Limit the number of reprimands and, unless it was an emergency, avoid making them in public.
3. Help Bobby learn how to regulate his emotions and calm himself down (e.g., taking a few deep breaths, humming a song, looking at a couple of favorite books).
4. As unobtrusively as possible, coach him on social skills, such as how to recognize what another child is feeling and how to respond appropriately, how to enter groups of children, and how to ask for toys and materials.
5. Subtly intervene when necessary to prevent or mitigate conflicts.
6. Work with all of the children to help them see how everyone has trouble sometimes and help them be more patient and less judgmental when someone makes them angry.
7. Look at the physical environment with an eye to making adaptations to reduce Bobby's frustrations (e.g., making an area bigger or smaller, reducing the amount of stimulation).
8. Increase the time that Bobby is outside and physically active (e.g., he helps put away toys after the other children go inside).

They talked to Bobby, and together they implemented this plan. There were several rocky moments, but Tara and Michelle learned to use the environment and quiet coaching to support Bobby to enter and sustain peer interactions and avoid conflicts. They monitored themselves and each other closely and retrained themselves to stop making public reprimands. Most significantly, as they made a point to have positive contacts with Bobby, they found that they started enjoying their times with him; the other children, noticing the fun, were often eager to join them. For a few activities each week, they partnered Bobby with one or two children who were patient and calm and not bothered by his constant chatter and motion. As he became more skilled and confident in his peer interactions, Bobby was less anxious and able to stay with a group for longer periods of time. Although he was still emotionally volatile, he was able to calm himself down on occasion or would at least let a teacher take him to a quiet area where he could look at books and escape the frustrating situation.

The teachers continued conversations with the parents of the other children in the class and explored with them their fears and their perceptions of their children as fragile and in need of protection. The teachers also held a parent meeting and had all the parents talk about the strengths and vulnerabilities of their children. This honest exchange helped everyone to see that all children have "abilities" and "disabilities" and that everyone needed to make an emotional as well as physical space for all children to be included. They made a point of pairing Bobby's parents up with other families whose children played well with Bobby and encouraged parents to consider playdates.

Bobby still had many conflicts, and his reputation did not die easily. Some of the children continued to talk about how "bad" he was and avoided or teased him. Michelle and Tara talked to them and challenged them to rethink their assumptions about Bobby. The teachers also read some books to the children and performed a few puppet shows that (often humorously) focused on how everyone does things that annoy others and how silly we are when we judge people by only one thing they do. They made sure that their examples would not single out Bobby but would encourage children to think a moment before making assumptions about anyone. Bobby continued to be a challenging child in the classroom, but the teachers felt that at least they had interrupted and maybe even reversed Bobby's slide into social isolation, as well as making steps toward creating a more authentically inclusive classroom.

Conclusion

As I conclude this fourth edition of *Teaching and Learning in a Diverse World*, I have been reflecting on the 3 decades that have passed since I wrote the first edition and have been imagining what might lie ahead. I see much to celebrate, yet much to do. We have elected the first African American president of the United States, and increasing numbers of people of color occupy powerful political and business positions. Women, too, have made many gains in education, politics, and careers. Slowly and with much struggle, GBLT individuals and groups have won some legal rights, and, in many communities, they are increasingly visible and accepted. With the implementation of the Americans with Disabilities Act and the growth of assistive technology, individuals with disabilities have more access to education, jobs, politics, and sports. In many places, environmental degradation has been halted and even reversed. Rivers that were once toxic are now open for swimming and fishing; abandoned industrial areas are now parks and community gardens.

At the same time, the challenges are daunting. All over the world, ethnic, religious, political, and economic conflicts are devastating many countries and disrupting national and international relationships. At home, the shrill diatribes that pass for political discourse attest to the increasing political and economic polarization, rising intolerance, and the further marginalizing of disadvantaged groups, particularly immigrants and poor people. Climate change is affecting everyone around the world, but economic interests continue to block any meaningful attempts to control the practices (e.g., use of fossil fuels) that are causing it. The future of our planet is in serious jeopardy, and the effects of climate change are falling hardest on poor families and countries. Economies all over the world are increasingly strained and inequitable. In the United States the growing economic gaps are consigning ever greater numbers of poor children to devastated schools and desolate neighborhoods. In sharp contrast, the wealthiest individuals are amassing more resources, gaining more control of the economy, and using these means to exert more political power.

With all of these tensions, education at all levels in the United States and in many other countries is under enormous pressure. Many of the current "reforms" are leading to increased marginalization and disparities.

As schools become increasingly diverse, narrowly defined curricula and accountability testing make it more difficult for teachers to accommodate divergent needs and to address complex issues. Cuts in educational funding and the privatization of large sectors of public schools have eroded the ideal of equal access to education.

Yet, as I visit schools and talk to veteran teachers and those just entering the field, I see many creative and bold initiatives to make schools inclusive and to imagine egalitarian and sustainable ways of living. While intolerance and violence sadly seem to be endemic to the human race, so are compassion, generosity, and resilience. In many classrooms, teachers, children, and families are exploring difficult and complex issues and seeing new possibilities and becoming agents of change. I have compiled many of the examples of the wonderful work that I have seen into a story, "A Day at Wilson Street School" (see Supplemental Resource C.1, for Conclusion, at www.tcpress.com).

We, as multicultural early childhood educators, face many challenges, but we are strong, dedicated, resilient, and creative and will continue to forge ahead, finding ways through and around whatever obstacles lie in our paths. Over the past several decades I have come to appreciate that genuine social change is incremental rather than sweeping or dramatic. It is also a collaborative process, and everyone can contribute, from a child who asks penetrating questions, to teachers who adapt their curriculum, to families and schools who join together to protest local injustices. This book is just one part of this collective effort, and I hope that it will encourage teachers, parents, and, most of all, children to sow and nurture the seeds for social justice in early childhood classrooms.

References

Aboud, F. E., & Amato, M. (2001). Developmental and socialization influences on intergroup bias. In R. Brown & S. L. Gaerther (Eds.), *Blackwell handbook of social psychology: Intergroup processes* (pp. 65–85). Malden, MA: Blackwell.

Adair, J., & Tobin, J. (2008). Listening to the voices of immigrant parents. In C. Genishi & L. Goodwin (Eds.), *Diversities in early childhood education: Rethinking and doing* (pp. 137–150). New York, NY: Routledge.

Addy, S., Engelhardt, W., & Skinner, C. (2013). Basic facts about low-income children: Children under 18 years, 2011. In *National Center for Children in Poverty, Columbia University*. Retrieved from www.nccp.org/publications/pub_1074.html

Aina, O. E., & Cameron, P. A. (2011). Why does gender matter? Counteracting stereotypes with young children. *Dimensions of Early Childhood, 39*(3), 11–19.

Alejandro-Wright, M. N. (1985). The child's conception of racial classification: A socio-cognitive developmental model. In M. B. Spencer, G. K. Brookins, & W. R. Allen (Eds.), *Beginnings: The social and affective development of Black children* (pp. 185–200). Hillsdale, NJ: Lawrence Erlbaum.

Allen, P. G. (1992). *The sacred hoop: Recovering the feminine in American Indian traditions.* Boston, MA: Beacon Press.

Allport, G. W. (1954). *The nature of prejudice.* Reading, MA: Addison-Wesley.

Amanti, C. (2005). Beyond a beads and feathers approach. In N. González, L. C. Moll, & C. Amanti (Eds.), *Funds of knowledge: Theorizing practices in households, communities, and classrooms* (pp. 131–141). New York, NY: Routledge.

Andrew, Y., Baird, J., Benjamin, R., Dean, S., Holmes, R., MacNaughton, G., . . . Payne, C. (2001). Mother Goose meets Mardi Gras: Lesbian and gay issues in early childhood. In E. Dau (Ed.), *The anti-bias approach in early childhood* (2nd ed., pp. 63–81). Frenchs Forest, New South Wales, Australia: Pearson Education Australia.

Atkinson, S. (2009). Adults constructing the young child, "race," and racism. In G. MacNaughton & K. Davis (Eds.), *"Race" and early childhood education: An international approach to identity, politics, and pedagogy* (pp. 139–153). New York, NY: Palgrave MacMillan.

Ayvazian, A. (1997). Barriers to effective mentoring across racial lines. *Multicultural Education, 4*(4), 13–17.

Banaji, M. R., Baron, A. S., Dunham, Y., & Olson, K. (2008). The development of intergroup social cognition: Early emergence, implicit nature, and sensitivity to group status. In S. R. Levy & M. Killen (Eds.), *Intergroup attitudes and relations in childhood through adulthood* (pp. 197–236). Oxford, United Kingdom: Oxford University Press.

Banks, J. A. (1997). *Educating citizens in a multicultural society.* New York, NY: Teachers College Press.

Banks, J. A. (1999). *Introduction to multicultural education* (2nd ed.). Boston, MA: Allyn & Bacon.

Barbero, Adriana (Producer). (2008). *Consuming kids: The commercialization of childhood* (DVD). Northampton, MA: Media Education Foundation. Available from www.mediaed.org/cgi-bin/commerce.cgi?preadd=action&key=134#filmmaker-about

Bardhan-Quallen, S. (2012). *The Pirate Princess* (J. McElmurry, Illus.). New York, NY: Harper Collins.

Barraza, L., & Robottom, I. (2008). Gaining representations of children's and adults' constructions of sustainability issues. *International Journal of Environmental and Science Education, 3*(4), 179–191.

Barraza, L., & Walford, R. A. (2002). Environmental education: A comparison between English and Mexican school children. *Environmental Education Research, 8*(2), 171–186. doi:10.1080/13504620220128239

Barrett, J. R., & Roediger, D. (2002). How White people became white. In P. S. Rothenberg (Ed.), *White privilege: Essential readings on the other side of racism* (pp. 29–34). New York, NY: Worth.

Batchelor, D., & Taylor, H. (2005). Social inclusion—the next step: User-friendly strategies to promote social interaction and peer acceptance of children with disabilities. *Australian Journal of Early Childhood, 30*(4), 10–18.

Bem, S. L. (1981). Gender schema theory: A cognitive account of sex typing. *Psychological Review, 88,* 354–364.

Bem, S. L. (1983). Gender schema theory and its implications for child development: Raising gender-aschematic children in a gender-schematic society. *Journal of Women in Culture and Society, 8*(4), 597–616.

Benn, J. (2004). Consumer education between "consumership" and citizenship: Experiences from studies of young people. *International Journal of Consumer Studies, 28*(2), 108–116.

Bergerson, A. A. (2003). Critical race theory and White racism: is there room for White scholars in fighting racism in education? *Qualitative Studies in Education, 16*(1), 51–63. doi:10.1080/0951839032000033527

Bhana, D. (2007). "Emma and Dave sitting on a tree, K I S S I N G": Boys, girls and the "heterosexual matrix" in a South African primary school. *International Journal of Equity and Innovation in Early Childhood, 5*(2), 84–96.

Bigler, R. S. (1995). The role of classification skill in moderating environmental influences on children's gender stereotyping: A study of the functional use of gender in the classroom. *Child Development, 66,* 1072–1087.

Bigler, R. S. (1997). Conceptual and methodological issues in the measurement of children's sex-typing. *Psychology of Women Quarterly, 21,* 53–69.

Bigler, R. S., & Liben, L. S. (2007). Developmental intergroup theory: Explaining and reducing children's social stereotyping and prejudice. *Current Directions in Psychological Science, 16,* 162–166.

Blaise, M. (2005). *Playing it straight: Uncovering gender discourses in the early childhood classroom.* New York, NY: Routledge.

Blaise, M. (2010). Kiss and tell: Gendered narratives and childhood sexuality. *Australasian Journal of Early Childhood, 35*(1), 1–9.

Blaise, M., & Taylor, A. (2012). Using queer theory to rethink gender equity in early childhood education. *Young Children, 67*(1), 88–96, 98.

Blanchard, P. B., & Buchanan, T. K. (2011). Environmental stewardship in early childhood. *Childhood Education, 87*(4), 232–238.

Boho, A. (2011). Income inequality in the United States: Some facts. Retrieved from https://andrewboho.wordpress.com/2011/10/11/income-inequality-in-the-united-states-some-facts/#more-147

Boldt, G. M. (2011). One hundred hotdogs, or performing gender in the elementary classroom. In T. Jacobson (Ed.), *Perspectives on gender in early childhood* (pp. 77–93). St. Paul, MN: Redleaf Press.

Boutte, G. S. (2000). Multiculturalism: Moral and educational implications. *Dimensions of Early Childhood Education, 28*(3), 9–16.

Boutte, G., López-Robertson, J., & Powers-Costello, E. (2011). Moving beyond colorblindness in early childhood classrooms. *Early Childhood Education Journal, 39*(5), 335–342. doi:10.1007/s10643-011-0457-x

Bowers, C. A. (2001). *Educating for eco-justice and community.* Athens, GA: University of Georgia Press.

Bowman, B. T., & Stott, F. M. (1994). Understanding development in a cultural context. In B. L. Mallory & R. S. New (Eds.), *Diversity and developmentally appropriate practices: Challenges for early childhood education* (pp. 119–133). New York, NY: Teachers College Press.

Boyer, W. (2013). Getting back to the woods: Familial perspectives on culture and preschoolers' acquisition of self-regulation and emotion regulation. *Early Childhood Education Journal, 41*(2), 153–159. doi:10.1007/s10643-012-0536-7

Bronfenbrenner, U. (1979). *The ecology of human development.* Cambridge, MA: Harvard University Press.

Bronfenbrenner, U. (1986). Ecology of the family as context for human development. *Developmental Psychology, 22,* 723–742.

Bronfenbrenner, U., & Morris, P. A. (1998). The ecology of developmental process. In W. Damon (Series Ed.) & R. M. Lerner (Vol. Ed.), *Handbook of child psychology: Theoretical models of human development* (5th ed., Vol. 1, pp. 993–1028). Hoboken, NJ: Wileys.

Brown, S., Smalling, S., Groza, V., & Ryan, S. (2009). The experiences of gay men and lesbians in becoming and being adoptive parents. *Adoption Quarterly, 12*(3 & 4), 229–246. doi:10.1080/10926750903313294

Bullard, R. D. (2005). *The quest for environmental justice: Human rights and the politics of pollution.* San Francisco, CA: Sierra Club Books.

Bullard, R. D. (2014, January 1). Make 2014 the year of environmental justice executive order. In *OpEdNews.com.* Retrieved from www.opednews.com/articles/Make-2014-the-Year-of-Envi-by-Robert-Bullard-Climate_Environmental-Racism_Environmentalism_Environmentalist-140101-428.html

Cadwell, L. B. (2003). *Bringing learning to life: The Reggio approach to early childhood education.* New York, NY: Teachers College Press.

Campaign for a Commercial-Free Childhood, Alliance for Childhood, & Teachers Resisting Unhealthy Children's Entertainment (2012). *Facing the screen dilemma: Young children, technology and early education.* Boston, MA: Campaign for a Commercial-Free Childhood. Retrieved from www.truceteachers.org/docs/facing_the_screen_dilemma.pdf

Cannella, G. S. (1997). *Deconstructing early childhood: Social justice and revolution.* New York, NY: Peter Lang.

Carroll, G. (1998). Mundane extreme environmental stress and African American families: A case for recognizing different realities. *Journal of Comparative Family Studies, 29*(2), 271–284.

Casper, B., & Schultz, S. B. (1999). *Gay parents, straight schools: Building communication and trust.* New York, NY: Teachers College Press.

Castelli, L., Carraro, L., Tomelleri, S., & Amari, A. (2007). White children's alignment to the perceived racial attitudes of the parents: Closer to the mother than the father. *British Journal of Developmental Psychology, 25,* 353–357. doi:10.1348/026151006X159851

Castelli, L., Zogmaister, C., & Tomelleri, S. (2009). The transmission of racial attitudes within the family. *Developmental Psychology, 45*(2), 586–591. doi: 10.1037.a0014619

Center for a New American Dream. (n.d.). *Kids unbranded: Tips for parenting in a commercial culture.* Retrieved from http://act.newdream.org/page/s/kids-unbranded

Center on Race, Poverty, and the Environment. (2011). Climate justice: Addressing the disproportionate impact of climate change on low-income communities and communities of color. Retrieved from http://www.crpe-ej.org/crpe/index.php/campaigns/climate-justice

Chafel, J. A. (1997). Children's views of poverty: A review of research and implications for teaching. *The Educational Forum, 61,* 360–371.

Chang, H. N., Muckelroy, A., Pulido-Tobiassen, D., & Dowell, C. (2000). Redefining child care and early education in a diverse society: Dialogue and reflection. In L. D. Soto (Ed.), *The politics of early childhood* (pp. 142–164). New York, NY: Peter Lang.

Chasnoff, D., & Cohen, H. (1996). *It's elementary: Talking about gay issues in school* [Videotape]. Available from San Francisco, CA: Women's Educational Media.

Chawla, L., & Cushing, D. (2007). Education for strategic environmental behavior. *Environmental Education Research, 13*(4), 437–452. doi:10.1080/13504620701581539

Clark, K. B., & Clark, M. P. (1947). Racial identification and preference in Negro children. In T. M. Newcomb & E. L. Hartley (Eds.), *Readings in social psychology* (pp. 169–178). New York, NY: Holt, Rinehart & Winston.

Clark, M. D. (1997). Teacher response to learning disability: A test of attributional principles. *Journal of Learning Disabilities, 30*(1), 69–79.

Cleovoulou, Y., McCollam, H., Ellis, E., Commeford, L., Moore, I., Chern, A., & Pelletier, J. (2013). Using photographic picture books to better understand young children's ideas of belonging: A study of early literacy strategies and social inclusion. *Canadian Children, 38*(1), 11–20.

Coles, R. (1996). *The moral life of children.* Boston, MA: Atlantic Monthly Press.

Coles, R. (2010). *The story of Ruby Bridges* (Special anniversary ed., G. Ford, Illus.) New York: NY: Scholastic.

Conflict Solutions Center. (2009). Retributive vs. Restorative Justice [Table]. Retrieved from www.cscsb.org/restorative_justice/retribution _vs _restoration. html

Connors, C., & Stalker, K. (2007). Children's experiences of disability: Pointers to a social model of childhood disability. *Disability and Society, 22*(1), 19–33.

Corenblum, B., & Annis, R. C. (1993). Development of racial identity in minority and majority children: An affect discrepancy model. *Canadian Journal of Behavioural Science, 25*(4), 499–521.

Corsaro, W. A. (2003). *We're friends, right? Inside kids' culture.* Washington, DC: Joseph Henry Press.

Cottle, T. J. (1974). *Black children, White dreams.* New York, NY: Dell.

Crawford, J. (1999). *Bilingual education: History, politics, theory, and practice* (4th ed.). Los Angeles, CA: Bilingual Education Services.

Cristol, D., & Gimbert, B. (2008). Racial perceptions of young children: A review of literature post-1999. *Early Childhood Educational Journal, 36,* 201–207. doi:10.1007/s10643-008-0251-6

Cross, W. E. (1985). Black identity: Rediscovering the distinction between personal identity and reference group orientation. In M. B. Spencer, G. K. Brookins, & W. R. Allen (Eds.), *Beginnings: The social and affective development of Black children* (pp. 155–171). Hillsdale, NJ: Lawrence Erlbaum.

Cross, W. E. (1987). A two-factor theory of Black identity: Implications for the study of identity development in minority children. In J. Phinney & M. J. Rotheram (Eds.), *Children's ethnic socialization* (pp. 117–133). Beverly Hills, CA: Sage.

Cross, W. E. (1991). *Shades of black.* Philadelphia, PA: Temple University Press.

Crystal, D. S., Killen, M., & Ruck, M. (2008). It is who you know that counts: Intergroup contact and judgments about race-based exclusion. *British Journal of Developmental Psychology, 26,* 51–70. doi:10.1348/026151007X198910

Csikszentmihalyi, M. (1999). If we are so rich, why aren't we happy? *American Psychologist, 54,* 821–827.

Cullen, F., & Sandy, L. (2009). Lesbian Cinderella and other stories: Telling tales and researching sexualities equalities in primary school. *Sex Education, 9*(2), 141–154. doi:10.1080/14681810902829513

Cunningham, S. J., & Macrae, C. N. (2011). The colour of gender stereotyping. *British Journal of Psychology, 102,* 598–614. doi:10.1111/j.2044-8295.2011.02023.x

Damon, W. (1980). Patterns of change in children's social reasoning: A two-year longitudinal study. *Child Development, 51,* 1010–1017.

Darder, A. (1991). *Culture and power in the classroom: A critical foundation for bicultural education.* New York, NY: Bergin & Garvey.

Davis, J. (2009). Revealing the research "hole" of early childhood education for sustainability: A preliminary survey of the literature. *Environmental Education Research, 15*(2), 227–241.

De Brunhoff, J. (1984). *The story of Barbar.* New York, NY: Random House.

DeGaetano, Y., Williams, L. R., & Volk, D. (1998). *Kaleidoscope: A multicultural approach for the primary school classroom.* Columbus, OH: Merrill (Prentice Hall).

DeGrella, L. H., & Green, V. P. (1984). Young children's attitudes toward orthopedic and sensory disabilities. *Education of the Visually Handicapped, 16*(1), 3–11.

Delgado-Gaiten, C., & Trueba, H. (1991). *Crossing cultural borders*. New York, NY: Falmer Press.

DeLone, R. H. (1979). *Small futures*. New York, NY: Harcourt Brace Jovanovich.

Derman-Sparks, L., & Edwards, J. O. (2010). *Anti-bias education for young children and ourselves*. Washington, DC: National Association for the Education of Young Children.

Derman-Sparks, L., & Phillips, C. B. (1997). *Teaching/learning anti-racism: A developmental approach*. New York, NY: Teachers College Press.

Derman-Sparks, L., & Ramsey, P. G. (2011). *What if all the kids are White?: Anti-bias multicultural education with young children and their families* (2nd ed.). New York, NY: Teachers College Press.

Devine, P. G., Plant, E. A., & Buswell, B. N. (2000). Breaking the prejudice habit: Progress and obstacles. In S. Okamp (Ed.), *Reducing prejudice and discrimination* (pp. 185–208). Mahwah, NJ: Lawrence Erlbaum.

DeVore, S., & Russell, K. (2007). Early childhood education and care for children with disabilities: Facilitating inclusive practice. *Early Childhood Education Journal, 35*(2), 189–198.

Dewar, B. A., Servos, J. E., Bosacki, S. L., & Coplan, R. (2013). Early childhood educators' reflections on teaching practices: The role of gender and culture. *Reflective Practice, 14*(3), 381–391. doi:10.1080/14623943.2013.767234

Diamond, K. E., & Hestenes, L. L. (1996). Preschool children's conceptions of disabilities: The salience of disability in children's ideas about others. *Topics in Early Childhood Special Education, 16*, 458–475.

Diamond, K. E., Hestenes, L. L., Carpenter, E. S., & Innes, F. K. (1997). Relationships between enrollment in an inclusive class and preschool children's ideas about people with disabilities. *Topics in Early Childhood Special Education, 17*(4), 520–536.

Diamond, K. E., Hestenes, L. L., & O'Connor, C. E. (1994). Integrating young children with disabilities in preschool: Problems and promise. *Young Children, 49*(2), 69–75.

Diamond, K. E., & Hong, S. (2010). Young children's decisions to include peers with physical disabilities in play. *Journal of Early Intervention, 32*(3), 163–177.

Diamond, K. E., & Huang, H. (2005). Preschoolers' ideas about disabilities. *Infants and Young Children, 18*, 37–46.

Diamond, K. E., & Innes, F. K. (2001). The origins of young children's attitudes toward peers with disabilities. In M. J. Guralnick (Ed.), *Early childhood inclusion: Focus on change*. Baltimore, MD: Brookes.

Diamond, K. E., & Stacey, S. (2000). The other children at preschool: Experiences of typically developing children in inclusive programs. *Young Exceptional Children Monograph Series No. 2: Natural Environments and Inclusion*, 59–68.

Diamond, K. E., & Tu, H. (2009). Relations between classroom context, physical disability, and preschool children's inclusion decisions. *Journal of Applied Developmental Psychology, 30*, 75–81.

DiAngelo, R., & Sensoy, Ö. (2010). "OK, I get it! Now tell me how to do it!": Why we can't just tell you how to do critical multicultural education. *Multicultural Perspectives, 12*(2), 97–102. doi:10.1080/15210960.2010.481199

Diesendruck, G., & Markson, L. (2011). Children's assumption of the conventionality of culture. *Child Development Perspectives, 5*(3), 189–195. doi:10.1111/j.1750-8606.2010.00156.x

Dovidio, J. F., Kawakami, K., & Gaertner, S. L. (2000). Reducing contemporary prejudice: Combating explicit and implicit bias at the individual and intergroup level. In S. Okamp (Ed.), *Reducing prejudice and discrimination* (pp. 137–163). Mahwah, NJ: Lawrence Erlbaum.

Doyle, A. (1982). Friends, acquaintances, and strangers. In K. H. Rubin & H. S. Ross (Eds.), *Peer relationships and social skills in childhood* (pp. 229–252). New York, NY: Springer.

Doyle, A., & Aboud, F. E. (1993). Social and cognitive determinants of prejudice in children. In K. A. McLeod (Ed.), *Multicultural education: The state of the art* (pp. 28–33). Toronto, Canada: University of Toronto Press.

Dressner, M., & Gill, M. (1994). Environmental education at summer nature camp. *Journal of Environmental Education, 25*(3), 35–41.

Duhn, I. (2012). Making "place" for ecological sustainability in early childhood education. *Environmental Education Research, 18*(1), 19–29. doi:10.1080/13 504622.2011.572162

Dykstra, L. A. (2005). Trans-friendly preschool. *Journal of Gay & Lesbian Issues in Education, 3*(1), 7–13. doi:10.1300/J3767v03n01_03

Dyson, L. L. (2005). Kindergarten children's understanding of and attitudes toward people with disabilities. *Topics in Early Childhood Special Education, 25*(2), 95–105.

Earick, M. E. (2009). *Racially equitable teaching: Beyond the whiteness of professional development for early childhood educators.* New York, NY: Peter Lang.

Earick, M. E. (2010). The power of play and language on early childhood racial identity in three U.S. schools. *Diaspora, Indigenous, and Minority Education, 4,* 131–145. doi:10.1080/15595691993635955

Ehrensaft, D. (2009). One pill makes you boy, one pill makes you girl. *International Journal of Applied Psychoanalytic Studies, 6*(1), 12–24. doi:10.1002/aps.185

Elliott, S. (2010, March/April). Essential, not optional: Education for sustainability in early childhood centres. *Exchange* (ChildCareExchange.com), *192,* 34–37.

Enesco, I., Lago, O., Rodríguez, P., & Guerrero, S. (2011). "We are the good guys but they are not bad." In-group positivity and cognitive performance in preschoolers. *British Journal of Developmental Psychology, 29,* 593–611. doi:10.1348/026151010X524896

Ergazaki, M., & Andriotou, E. (2010). From "forest fires" and "hunting" to disturbing "habitats" and "food chains": Do young children come up with any ecological interpretations of human interventions within a forest? *Research in Science Education, 40,* 187–201.

Ernest, J. M., Causey, C., Newton, A. B., Sharkins, K., Summerlin, J., & Albaiz, N. (2014). Extending the global dialogue about media, technology, screen time, and young children. *Childhood Education, 90*(3), 182–191.

Ernst, J., & Tornabene, L. (2012). Preservice early childhood educators' perceptions of outdoor settings as learning environments. *Environmental Education Research, 18*(5), 643–664. doi:10.1080/13504622.2011.640749

Fadiman, A. (1997). *The spirit catches you and you fall down.* New York, NY: Farrar, Straus, & Giroux.

Farrell, W. C., & Olson, J. (1982, April). *Kenneth Clark revisited: Racial identification in light-skinned and dark-skinned Black children.* Paper presented at the annual meeting of the American Educational Research Association, New York, NY.

Farver, J. M., Kim, Y. K., & Lee, Y. (1995). Cultural differences in Korean- and Anglo-American preschoolers' social interaction and play behaviors. *Child Development, 66,* 1088–1099.

Farver, J. M., & Shin, Y. L. (1997). Social pretend play in Korean- and Anglo-American preschoolers. *Child Development, 68*(3), 544–556.

Farver, J. M., Welles-Nystrom, B., Frosch, D. L., Wimbarti, S., & Hoppe-Graff, S. (1997). Toy stories: Aggression in children's narratives in the United States, Sweden, Germany, and Indonesia. *Journal of Cross-Cultural Psychology, 28*(4), 393–420.

Favazza, P., & Odom, S. L. (1997). Promoting positive attitudes of kindergarten-age children toward people with disabilities. *Exceptional Children, 63,* 405–418.

Feuerstein, R., Falik, L. H., Feuerstein, R. S., & Bohács, K. (2013). *A think-aloud and talk-aloud approach to building language: Overcoming disability, delay, and deficiency.* New York, NY: Teachers College Press.

Finkelstein, N. W., & Haskins, R. (1983). Kindergarten children prefer same-color peers. *Child Development, 54,* 502–508.

Fishbein, H. D., & Imai, S. (1993). Preschoolers select playmates on the basis of gender and race. *Journal of Applied Developmental Psychology, 14,* 303–316.

Fox, D. J., & Jordan, V. B. (1973). Racial preference and identification of Black, American Chinese, and White children. *Genetic Psychology Monographs, 88,* 229–286.

Franklin, K. L., & McGirr, N. (Eds.). (1995). *Out of the dump: Writings and photographs by children from Guatemala.* New York, NY: Lothrop, Lee, & Shepard.

Franklin, M. E. (1992). Culturally sensitive instructional practices for African-American learners with disabilities. *Exceptional Children, 59*(2), 115–122.

Freeman, N. K. (2007). Preschoolers' perceptions of gender appropriate toys and their parents' beliefs about genderized behaviors: Miscommunication, mixed messages, or hidden truths? *Early Childhood Education Journal, 34*(5), 357–366. doi:10.1007/s10643-006-123-x

Fulmer, C. L. (2010). Unpacking evidence of gender bias. *Journal of Women in Education Leadership, 8*(2), 81–97.

Gandini, L., Hill, L. T., Cadwell, L. B., & Schwall, C. (2005). *In the spirit of the studio: Learning from the Atelier of Reggio Emilia.* New York, NY: Teachers College Press.

Garcia, R. L. (1990). *Teaching in a pluralistic society: Concepts, models, and strategies* (2nd ed.). New York, NY: HarperCollins.

García Coll, C., Lamberty, G., Jenkins, R., McAdoo, H. P., Crnic, K., Wasik, B. H., & Vázquez García, H. (1996). An integrative model for the study of developmental competencies in minority children. *Child Development, 67,* 1891–1914.

Gasser, L., Malti, T., & Buholzer, A. (2014). Swiss children's moral and psychological judgments about inclusion and exclusion of children with disabilities. *Child Development, 85*(2), 532–548. doi:10.1111/cdev.12124

Gay, G. (1995). Mirror images on common issues: Parallels between multicultural education and critical pedagogy. In C. E. Sleeter & P. L. McLaren (Eds.),

Multicultural education, critical pedagogy, and the politics of difference (pp. 155–189). Albany: State University of New York Press.

Gay, G. (2000). *Culturally responsive teaching: Theory, research & practice.* New York, NY: Teachers College Press.

Gollnick, D. M., & Chinn, P. C. (1998). *Multicultural education in a pluralistic society* (5th ed.). Columbus, OH: Merrill.

González, N., Moll, L. C., & Amanti, C. (Eds.). (2005). *Funds of knowledge: Theorizing practices in households, communities, and classrooms.* Mahwah, NJ: Lawrence Erlbaum.

Gonzalez-Mena, J. (1992). Taking a culturally sensitive approach in infant–toddler programs. *Young Children, 47*(2), 4–9.

Gonzalez-Ramos, G., Zayas, L. H., & Cohen, E. V. (1998). Child-rearing values of low-income, urban Puerto Rican Mothers of preschool children. *Professional Psychology: Research and Practice, 29*(4), 377–382.

Goodman, J. F. (1989). Does retardation mean dumb? Children's perceptions of the nature, cause, and course of mental retardation. *The Journal of Special Education, 23*(3), 313–329.

Goodman, M. (1952). *Race awareness in young children.* Cambridge, MA: Addison-Wesley.

Grace, C. (1998). Mundane extreme environmental stress and African American families: A case for recognizing different realities. *Journal of Comparative Family Studies, 2* (2), 271–284.

Grace, R., & Trudgett, M. (2012). It's not rocket science: The perspectives of Indigenous early childhood workers on supporting the engagement of Indigenous families in early childhood settings. *Australasian Journal of Early Childhood, 37*(2), 10–18.

Gregg, K., Rugg, M., & Stoneman, Z. (2012). Building on the hopes and dreams of Latino families with young children: Findings from family member focus groups. *Early Childhood Education Journal, 40*(2), 87–96. doi:10.1007/s10643-011-0498-1

Grieshaber, S., & Cannella, G. S. (2001). *Embracing identities in early childhood education: Diversity and possibilities.* New York, NY: Teachers College Press.

Grodzińska-Jurczak, M., Stępska, A., & Nieszporek, K. (2006). Perception of environmental problems among pre-school children in Poland. *International Research in Geographical and Environmental Education, 15*(1), 62–76.

Guo, K., & Dalli, C. (2012). Negotiating and creating intercultural relations: Chinese immigrant children in New Zealand early childhood education centres. *Australasian Journal of Early Childhood, 37*(3), 129–136.

Guralnick, M. J., Hammond, M. A., Connor, R. T., & Neville, B. (2006). Stability, change, and correlates of the peer relationships of young children with mild developmental delays. *Child Development, 77*(2), 312–324.

Guralnick, M. J., Neville, B., Hammond, M., & Connor, R. (2007). The friendships of young children with developmental delays: A longitudinal analysis. *Journal of Applied Developmental Psychology, 28*, 64–79.

Hallinan, M. T., & Teixeira, R. A. (1987). Opportunities and constraints: Black–White differences in the formation of interracial friendships. *Child Development, 58*, 1358–1371.

Han, J., Ostrosky, M. M., & Diamond, K. E. (2006). Children's attitudes toward peers with disabilities: Supporting positive attitude development. *Young Exceptional Children, 10*(1), 2–11.

Hanson, M. J. (2002). Cultural and linguistic diversity: Influences on preschool inclusion. In S. L. Odom (Ed.), *Widening the circle: Including children with disabilities in preschool programs* (pp. 137–153). New York, NY: Teachers College Press.

Hanson, M. J., Gutierrez, S., Morgan, M., Brennan, E. L., & Zercher, C. (1997). Language, culture, and disability: Interacting influences on preschool inclusion. *Topics in Early Childhood Special Education, 17*(3), 307–336.

Hare, J., & Anderson, J. (2010). Transitions to early childhood education and care for indigenous children and families in Canada: Historical and social realities. *Australasian Journal of Early Childhood, 35*(2), 19–27.

Harper, L. V., & McCluskey, K. S. (2003). Teacher–child and child–child interactions in inclusive preschool settings: Do adults inhibit peer interactions? *Early Childhood Research Quarterly, 18*(2), 163–184.

Harry, B. (1998). Parental visions of "una vida normal/a normal life:" Cultural variations on a theme. In L. H. Meyer, H.-S. Park, M. Grenot-Scheyer, I. S. Schwarz, & B. Harry (Eds.), *Making friends: The influences of culture and development* (pp. 47–62). Baltimore, MD: Brookes.

Harry, B., Park, H.-S., & Day, M. (1998). Friendships of many kinds: Valuing the choice of children and youth with disabilities. In L. H. Meyer, H.-S. Park, M. Grenot-Scheyer, I. S. Schwarz, & B. Harry, (Eds.), *Making friends: The influences of culture and development* (pp. 393–402). Baltimore, MD: Brookes.

Hayes, C., & Juárez, B. G. (2009). You showed your Whiteness: You don't get a "good" White people's medal. *International Journal of Qualitative Studies in Education, 22*(6), 729–744. doi:10.1080/09518390903333921

Haymes, S. N. (1995). *Race, culture, and the city: A pedagogy for Black urban struggle.* Albany: State University of New York Press.

Helm, J. H., & Beneke, S. (Eds.). (2003). *The power of projects: Meeting contemporary challenges in early childhood classrooms—strategies and solutions.* New York, NY: Teachers College Press.

Helms, J. E. (1990). Toward a model of white racial identity development. In J. E. Helms (Ed.), *Black and White racial identity: Theory, research, and practice,* (pp. 49–66). New York, NY: Greenwood Press.

Helper, J. B. (1994). Mainstreaming children with learning disabilities: Have we improved their social environments? *Social Work in Education, 16*(3), 143–154.

Hensley, M. (2005). Empowering parents of multicultural backgrounds. In N. González, L. C. Moll, & C. Amanti (Eds.), *Funds of knowledge: Theorizing practices in households, communities, and classrooms* (pp. 143–151). Mahwah, NJ: Lawrence Erlbaum.

Hinds, J., & Sparks, P. (2008). Engaging with the natural environment: The role of affective connection and identity. *Journal of Environmental Psychology, 28*(2), 109–120. doi:10.1016/j.jenvp.2007.11.001

Hirschfield, L. A. (1995). Do children have a theory of race? *Cognition, 54,* 209–252.

Hoffman, M. (2000). *Empathy and moral development: Implications for caring and justice.* Cambridge, United Kingdom: Cambridge University Press.

Holmes, R. (1995). *How young children perceive race*. New York, NY: Sage.

Howard, G. R. (1999). *We can't teach what we don't know*. New York, NY: Teachers College Press.

Howes, C., & Ritchie, S. (2002). *A matter of trust: Connecting teachers and learners in early childhood classrooms*. New York, NY: Teachers College Press.

Huang, H., & Diamond, K. E. (2009). Early childhood teachers' ideas about including children with disabilities in programmes designed for typically developing children. *International Journal of Disability, Development and Education, 56*(2), 169–182.

Husband, T., Jr. (2010). He's too young to learn about that stuff: Anti-racist pedagogy and early childhood social studies. *Social Studies Research and Practice, 5*(2), 61–75.

Husband, T., Jr. (2012). "I don't see color": Challenging assumptions about discussing race with young children. *Early Childhood Education Journal, 39,* 365–371. doi:10.1007/s10643-011-0458-9

Huston, A. C. (1991). Children in poverty: Developmental and policy issues. In A. C. Huston (Ed.), *Children in poverty: Child development and public policy* (pp. 1–22). Cambridge, United Kingdom: Cambridge University Press.

Hyun, E. (2005). How is your children's intellectual culture of perceiving nature different from adults? *Environmental Education Research, 11*(2), 199–214.

Inequality.org. (2014). Racial inequality. Retrieved July 4, 2014, from inequality.org/racial-inequality/#sthash.s4Hy16JN.dpuf

Intersex Society of North America (ISNA). (2008). How common is intersex? Retrieved November 30, 2013, from www.isna.org/faq/frequency

Irving, D. (2014). *Waking up White*. Chicago, IL: Elephant Room Press.

Janmohamed, Z. (2010). Queering early childhood studies: Challenging the discourse of developmentally appropriate practice. *Alberta Journal of Educational Research, 56*(3), 304–318.

Jewish Virtual Library. (2014.). Martin Niemoeller. Retrieved from www.jewishvirtuallibrary.org/jsource/biography/niemoeller.html

Johnson, D. W., & Johnson, R. T. (2000). The three Cs of reducing prejudice and discrimination. In S. Okamp (Ed.), *Reducing prejudice and discrimination* (pp. 239–268). Mahwah, NJ: Lawrence Erlbaum.

Jordan, P. E., & Hernandez-Reif, M. (2009). Re-examination of young children's racial attitudes and skin tone preferences. *Journal of Black Psychology, 35*(3), 388–403.

Juvonen, J., & Bear, G. (1992). Social adjustment of children with and without learning disabilities in integrated classrooms. *Journal of Educational Psychology, 84,* 322–330.

Kahriman-Öztürk, D., Olgan, R., & Güler, T. (2012, Autumn). Preschool children's ideas on sustainable development: How preschool children perceive three pillars of sustainability with the [*sic*] regard to 7R. *Educational Sciences: Theory and Practice,* 2987–2995.

Kang, B., & Ramsey, P. G. (1993, April). *The effects of gender, race, and social class differences on children's friendships*. Paper presented at the annual meeting of the American Educational Research Association, Atlanta, GA.

Katz, P. A. (1976). The acquisition of racial attitudes in children. In P. A. Katz (Ed.), *Towards the elimination of racism* (pp. 125–154). New York, NY: Pergamon.

Katz, P. A. (1982). Development of children's racial awareness and intergroup attitudes. In L. G. Katz (Ed.), *Current topics in early childhood education* (pp. 17–54). Norwood, NJ: Ablex.

Katz, P. A. (2003). Racists or tolerant multiculturalists? How do they begin? *American Psychologist, 58*(11), 897–909.

Katz, P. A., & Kofkin, J. A. (1997). Race, gender, and young children. In S. Luthar, J. Burack, D. Cicchetti, & J. Weisz (Eds.), *Developmental perspectives on risk and pathology* (pp. 51–74). New York, NY: Cambridge University Press.

Kemple, K. M. (2004). *Let's be friends: Peer competence and social inclusion in early childhood classrooms.* New York, NY: Teachers College Press.

Kendall, F. (1996). *Diversity in the classroom: New approaches to the education of young children* (2nd ed.). New York, NY: Teachers College Press.

Kennedy, E., Cameron, R. J., & Greene, J. (2012). Transitions in the early years: Educational and child psychologists working to reduce the impact of school culture shock. *The British Psychological Society, 29*(1), 19–31.

Kich, G. K. (1992). The developmental process of asserting a biracial, bicultural identity. In M. P. P. Root (Ed.), *Racially mixed people in America* (pp. 304–317). Newbury Park, CA: Sage.

Killoran, I., Tymon, D., & Frempong, G. (2007). Disabilities and inclusive practices within Toronto preschools. *International Journal of Inclusive Education, 11*(1), 81–95.

Kincheloe, J. L. (1993). *Toward a critical politics of teacher thinking: Mapping the postmodern.* Westport, CT: Bergin & Garvey.

Kishida, Y., & Kemp, C. (2009). The engagement and interaction of children with autism spectrum disorder in segregated and inclusive early childhood center-based settings. *Topics in Early Childhood Special Education, 29*(2), 105–118.

Kivel, P. (2002). *Uprooting racism: How White people can work for racial justice.* Gabriola Island, BC, Canada: New Society Publishers.

Kline, S. (1993). *Out of the garden: Toys and children's culture in the age of TV marketing.* London, United Kingdom: Verso.

Kobayashi-Winata, H., & Power, T. G. (1989). Child rearing and compliance: Japanese and American families in Houston. *Journal of Cross-Cultural Psychology, 20*(4), 333–356.

Kostelnik, M. J., Onaga, E., Rohde, B., & Whiren, A. (2002). *Children with special needs: Lessons for early childhood professionals.* New York, NY: Teachers College Press.

Kowalski, K. (2003). The emergence of ethnic and racial attitudes in preschool-aged children. *The Journal of School Psychology, 143*(6), 677–690.

Kozleski, E. B., & Jackson, L. (1993). Taylor's story: Full inclusion in her neighborhood elementary school. *Exceptionality, 4*(3), 153–175.

Kozol, J. (1991). *Savage inequalities.* New York, NY: Crown.

Kroeger, J. (2001). A reconstructed tale of inclusion for a lesbian family in an early childhood classroom. In S. Grieshaber & G. S. Cannella (Eds.), *Embracing identities in early childhood education: Diversity and possibilities* (pp. 73–86). New York, NY: Teachers College Press.

Kroeger, J. (2006). Stretching performances in education: The impact of gay parenting and activism on identity and school change. *Journal of Educational Change, 7*, 319–337. doi:10.1007/s10833-006-9000-z

Kroll, L. R. (2013). Early childhood teacher preparation: Essential aspects for the achievement of social justice. *Journal of Early Childhood Education, 34*, 63–72. doi:10.1080/10901027.2013.758538

Krugman, P. (2014, May). Now that's rich. *New York Times*, A25.

Ladson-Billings, G. (1998). Just what is critical race theory and what's it doing in a nice field like education? *International Journal of Qualitative Studies in Education, 11*(1), 7–24. doi:10.1080/095183998236863

Lalley, J. (2008). Activism brings us power: An interview with Hilda Magaña. In A. Pelo (Ed.), *Rethinking early childhood education* (pp. 183–196). Milwaukee, WI: Rethinking Schools.

Lam, V., Guerrero, S., Damree, N., & Enesco, I. (2011). Young children's racial awareness and affect and their perceptions about mothers' racial affect in a multiracial context. *British Journal of Developmental Psychology, 29*, 842–864. doi:10.1348/2044-835X.00213

Lambert, W. E., & Klineberg, O. (1967). *Children's views of foreign peoples*. New York, NY: Appleton-Century-Crofts.

Lareau, A. (2011). *Unequal childhoods: Class, race, and family life* (2nd ed.). Berkeley: University of California Press.

Leahy, R. (1983). The development of the conception of social class. In R. Leahy (Ed.), *The child's construction of inequality* (pp. 79–107). New York, NY: Academic Press.

Leahy, R. (1990). The development of concepts of economic and social inequality. *New Directions for Child Development, 46*, 107–120.

Lebra, T. S. (1994). Mother and child in Japanese socialization: A Japan–U.S. comparison. In P. M. Greenfield & R. R. Cocking (Eds.), *Cross-cultural roots of minority child development* (pp. 259–274). Hillsdale, NJ: Lawrence Erlbaum.

Lee, D. (2010). Gay mothers and early childhood education: Standing tall. *Australasian Journal of Early Childhood, 35*(1), 16–23.

Lee, D., & Duncan, J. (2008). On our best behavior: Lesbian-parented families in early childhood education. *Early Childhood Folio, 12*, 22–26.

Lester, N. A. (2007). (Un)Happily ever after: Fairy tale morals, moralities, and heterosexism in children's texts. *Journal of Gay & Lesbian Issues in Education, 4*(2), 55–74. doi:10.1300/J367v04n02_05

Lev, A. I. (2010). How queer!—The development of gender identity and sexual orientation in LGBTQ-headed families. *Family Processes, 49*(3), 268–290.

Levine, J. (1994, March/April). White like me: When privilege is written on your skin. *Ms.*, 22–24.

Lewis, E., Mansfield, C. F., & Baudains, C. (2010). Going on a turtle egg hunt and other adventures: Education for sustainability in early childhood. *Australasian Journal of Early Childhood, 35*(4), 95–100.

Li, G. (2008). Parenting practices and schooling: The way class works for new immigrant groups. In L. Weiss (Ed.), *The way class works: Readings on school, family, and the economy* (pp. 149–166). New York, NY: Routledge.

Liben, L. S., & Bigler, R. S. (2002). The developmental course of gender differentiation: Conceptualizing, measuring, and evaluating constructs and pathways. *Monographs of the Society for Research in Child Development, 67*(2, Serial No. 269).

Lin, Q. (2005). Multicultural visions in early reading classrooms: Implications for early childhood teacher educators. *Journal of Early Childhood Teacher Education, 25,* 237–245.

Litovich, M., & Langhout, R. D. (2004). Framing heterosexism in lesbian families: A preliminary examination of resilient coping. *Journal of Community & Applied Social Psychology, 14,* 411–435. doi:10.1002/casp.780

LoBue, V., & DeLoache, J. S. (2011). Pretty in pink: The early development of gender-stereotyped colour preferences. *British Journal of Developmental Psychology, 29,* 656–667. doi:10.1111/j.2044-835x.2011.02027.x

Longstreet, W. S. (1978). *Aspects of ethnicity.* New York, NY: Teachers College Press.

Louv, R. (2008). *Last child in the woods: Saving our children from nature-deficit disorder.* Chapel Hill, NC: Algonquin Books of Chapel Hill.

Luhby, T. (2013, February 27). Wealth inequality between Blacks and Whites worsens. *CNN Money.* Retrieved from money.cnn.com/2013/02/27/news/economy/wealth-whites-blacks/index.html

Luthar, S. S., & Becker, B. E. (2002). Privileged but pressured? A study of affluent youth. *Child Development, 73*(5), 1593–1610.

MacNaughton, G. (2000). *Rethinking gender in early childhood education.* London, United Kingdom: Sage. Retrieved from dx.doi.org/10.4135/9781446222355

MacNaughton, G., & Davis, K. (Eds.). (2009). *"Race" and early childhood education: An international approach to identity, politics, and pedagogy.* New York, NY: Palgrave MacMillan.

MacNaughton, G., Davis, K., & Smith, K. (2009). Exploring "race-identities" with young children: Making politics visible. In G. MacNaughton & K. Davis (Eds.), *"Race" and early childhood education: An international approach to identity, politics, and pedagogy* (pp. 31–47). New York, NY: Palgrave MacMillan.

Mahalingam, R. (2007). Essentialism, power, and the representation of social categories: A folk sociology perspective. *Human Development, 50,* 300–319. doi:10.1159/000109832

Mapp, K. L. (2002, April). *Having their say: Parents describe how and why they are involved in their children's education.* Paper presented at the annual meeting of the American Educational Research Association, New Orleans, LA.

Martin, C. L., & Halverson, C. (1981). A schematic processing model of sex typing and stereotyping in children. *Child Development, 52,* 1119–1134.

Martin, C. L., & Ruble, D. (2004). Children's search for gender cues: Cognitive perspectives on gender development. *Current Directions in Psychological Science, 13*(2), 67–70.

Martínez-Lozano, V., Sánchez-Medina, J. A., & Goudena, P. P. (2011, September 9). A cross-cultural study of observed conflicts betw184een young children. *Journal of Cross-Cultural Psychology, 42*(6), pp. 895–907. (Original version published online September 9, 2010 1–13. doi:10.1177/0022022110381361)

McAdoo, H. P. (1993). *Family ethnicity: Strength in diversity.* Beverly Hills, CA: Sage.

McGinnis, H., Smith, S. L., Ryan, S. D., & Howard, J. A. (2009). *Beyond culture camp: Promoting healthy identity formation in adoption.* New York, NY: Evan B. Donaldson Adoption Institute. Retrieved from adoptioninstitute.org/publications/beyond-culture-camp-promoting-healthy-identity-formation-in-adoption

McHenry, J., & Buerk, K. (2008). Infants and toddlers meet the natural world. *Young Children, 63*(1), 40–41.

McIntosh, P. (1995). White privilege and male privilege: A personal account of coming to see correspondences through work in women's studies. In M. L. Anderson & P. H. Collins (Eds.), *Race, class, and gender: An anthology* (pp. 76–87). Belmont, CA: Wadsworth.

McLaren, P. (1994). White terror and oppositional agency: Towards a critical multiculturalism. In D. T. Goldbert (Ed.), *Multiculturalism: A critical reader* (pp. 45–74). Cambridge, MA: Blackwell.

McLoyd, V. C. (1998). Socioeconomic disadvantage and child development. *American Psychologist, 53*, 185–204.

McLoyd V. C., & Ceballo, R. (1998). Conceptualizing and assessing the economic context: Issues in the study of race and child development. In V. C. McLoyd & L. Steinberg (Eds.), *Studying minority adolescents: Conceptual, methodological, and theoretical issues* (pp. 251–278). Mahwah, NJ: Lawrence Erlbaum.

Mednick, L. G., & Ramsey, P. G. (2008). Peers, power and privilege: The social world of a second grade. *Rethinking Schools, 23*, 27–31.

Menchu, R. (1983). *I, Rigoberta Menchu: An Indian woman in Guatemala.* London, United Kingdom: Verso.

Milich, R., McAnnich, C. B., & Harris, M. J. (1992). Effects of stigmatizing information on children's peer relations: Believing is seeing. *School Psychology Review, 21*(3), 400–409.

Milton, B., Cleveland, E., & Bennett-Gates, D. (1995). Changing perceptions of nature, self, and others: A report on a park/school program. *Journal of Environmental Education, 26*(3), 32–39.

Minami, M., & Ovando, C. J. (1995). Language issues in multicultural contexts. In J. A. Banks & C. A. M. Banks (Eds.), *Handbook of research on multicultural education* (pp. 427–444). New York, NY: Macmillan.

Minority children [Special issue]. (1990, April). *Child Development, 61*(2), 263–589.

Mogharreban, C. C., & Bruns, D. A. (2009). Moving to inclusive pre-kindergarten classrooms: Lessons from the field. *Early Childhood Education Journal, 36*(5), 407–414.

Moll, L. C., Amanti, C., Neff, D., & González, N. (1992). Funds of knowledge for teaching: Using a qualitative approach to connect homes and classrooms. *Theory Into Practice, 31*(2), 132–141.

Molnar, J. M., Rath, W. R., & Klein, T. P. (1990). Constantly compromised: The impact of homelessness on children. *Journal of Social Issues, 46*, 109–124.

Moran, C. E., & Hakuta, K. (1995). Bilingual education: Broadening research perspectives. In J. A. Banks & C. A. M. Banks (Eds.), *Handbook of research on multicultural education* (pp. 445–462). New York, NY: Macmillan.

Moule, J. (2012). British Columbia's full day of kindergarten program guide: A critical race analysis. *Canadian Children, 37*(1), 12–20.

Nabors, L., & Keyes, L. (1995). Preschoolers' reasons for accepting peers with and without disabilities. *Journal of Developmental and Physical Disabilities, 7*(4), 335–355.

Nagel, N., & Wells, J. (2009). Honoring family and culture: Learning from New Zealand. *Young Children, 64*(5), 40–44.

Naimark, H. (1983). *Children's understanding of social class differences.* Paper presented at the biennial meeting of the Society for Research in Child Development, Detroit, MI.

Nelson, M. K., & Schutz, R. (2007). Day care differences and the reproduction of social class. *Journal of Contemporary Ethnography, 36*(3), 281–317. doi:10.1177/0891241606293137

Newman, M. A., Liss, M. B., & Sherman, F. (1983). Ethnic awareness in children: Not a unitary concept. *The Journal of Genetic Psychology, 143,* 103–112.

Newman, R. (2014, June 24). For most families, wealth has vanished. *Daily Ticker.* Retrieved from finance.yahoo.com/blogs/daily-ticker/for-most-families-wealth-has-vanished-172130204.html

Nieto, S., & Bode, P. (2012). *Affirming diversity: The sociopolitical context of multicultural education* (6th ed.). Boston, MA: Pearson Education.

Nightingale, C. H. (1993). *On the edge: A history of poor Black children and their American dreams.* New York, NY: Basic Books.

Niles, M., Byers, L., & Krueger, E. (2007). Best practice and evidence-based research in indigenous early childhood intervention programs. *Canadian Journal of Native Education, 30*(1), 108–125.

Nimmo, J., & Hallett, B. (2008, January). Childhood in the garden: A place to encounter natural and social diversity. *Young Children, 63*(1), 32–38.

Nind, M., Flewitt, R., & Payler, J. (2010). The social experience of early childhood for children with learning disabilities: Inclusion, competence and agency. *British Journal of Sociology of Education, 31*(6), 653–670.

Noddings, N. (1992). *The challenge to care in schools: An alternative approach to education.* New York, NY: Teachers College Press.

Noddings, N. (2002). *Educating moral people: A caring alternative to character education.* New York, NY: Teachers College Press.

Nxumalo, F., Pacini-Ketchabaw, V., & Rowan, M. (2011). Lunch time at the child care center: Neoliberal assemblages in early childhood education. *Pedagogický Časopis, 2*(2), 195–223.

O'Brien, A. S. (2012). *A path of stars.* Watertown, MA: Charlesbridge.

Odom, S. L. (2002). *Widening the circle: Including children with disabilities in preschool programs.* New York, NY: Teachers College Press.

Odom, S. L., Buysse, V., & Soukakou, E. (2011). Inclusion for young children with disabilities: A quarter century of research perspectives. *Journal of Early Intervention, 33*(4), 344–356.

Odom, S. L., Peck, C. A., Hanson, M., Beckman, P. J., Kaiser, A. P., Lieber, J., . . . Schwartz, I. S. (1996). Inclusion at the preschool level: An ecological systems analysis. *Social Policy Report of the Society for Research in Child Development, 10*(2 & 3), 18–30.

Odom, S. L., Zercher, C., Li, S., Marquart, J. M., Sandall, S., & Brown, W. H. (2006). Social acceptance and rejection of preschool children with disabilities: A mixed-method analysis. *Journal of Educational Psychology, 98*(4), 807.

Odom, S. L., Zercher, C., Marquart, J., Li, S., Sandall, S. R., & Wolfberg, P. (2002). Social relationships of children with disabilities and their peers in inclusive classrooms. In S. L. Odom (Ed.), *Widening the circle: Including children with disabilities in preschool programs* (pp. 61–80). New York, NY: Teachers College Press.

Oliveira-Formosinho, J., & Araújo, S. B. (2011). Early education for diversity: Start-ing from birth. *European Early Childhood Education Research Journal, 19*(2), 223–235.

Orellana, M. F. (1994). Appropriating the voice of the superheroes: Three preschool-ers' bilingual language uses in play. *Early Childhood Research Quarterly, 9,* 171–193.

Orlick, T. (1982). *The second cooperative sports and games book: Over 200 brand-new cooperative games for kids and adults and both.* Ann Arbor, MI: North American Students of Cooperation.

Orlick, T. (2006). *Cooperative games and sports: Joyful activities for everyone.* New York, NY: Pantheon Books.

Palmer, A. (2001). Responding to special needs. In E. Dau (Ed.), *The anti-bias ap-proach in early childhood* (2nd ed., pp. 83–94). Frenchs Forest, New South Wales, Australia: Pearson Education Australia.

Palmer, J., & Suggate, J. (1996). Environmental cognition: Early ideas and miscon-ceptions at the ages of four and six. *Environmental Education Research, 2*(3), 301–329. doi:10.1080/1350462960020304

Pang, V. O. (2001). *Multicultural education: A caring-centered, reflective approach.* Boston, MA: McGraw Hill.

Pang, V. O. (2005). *Multicultural education: A caring-centered, reflective approach* (2nd ed.). New York, NY: McGraw Hill Higher Education.

Parlakian, R. (2012). Inclusion in infant/toddler child development settings: More than just including. *Young Children, 67*(4), 66–71.

Patterson, M. M., & Bigler, R. S. (2006). Preschool children's attention to environ-mental messages about groups: Social categorization and the origins of inter-group bias. *Child Development, 77,* 847–860.

Pelo, A. (2008a). A pedagogy for ecology. In A. Pelo (Ed.), *Rethinking early child-hood education* (pp. 123–130). Milwaukee, WI: Rethinking Schools.

Pelo, A. (2008b). Introduction: Embracing social justice in early childhood educa-tion. In A. Pelo (Ed.), *Rethinking early childhood education* (pp. ix–xiii). Mil-waukee, WI: Rethinking Schools.

Pelo, A. (2013). *The goodness of rain: Developing an ecological identity in young children.* Redmond, WA: Exchange Press.

Perez, K. D. (2013). *The new inclusion: Differentiated strategies to engage ALL students.* New York, NY: Teachers College Press.

Perkins, D. M., & Mebert, C. J. (2005). Efficacy of multicultural education for preschool children: A domain-specific approach. *Journal of Cross-Cultural Psy-chology, 36*(4), 497–512. doi:10.1177/0022022105275964

Peters, M. F. (1985). Racial socialization of young Black children. In H. P. McAdoo & J. L. McAdoo (Eds.), *Black children: Social, educational, and parental envi-ronment* (pp. 159–173). Newbury Park, CA: Sage.

Phelan, P., & Davidson, A. L. (1993). *Renegotiating cultural diversity in American schools.* New York, NY: Teachers College Press.

Piaget, J. (1951). *The child's conception of the world.* New York, NY: Humanities Press.

Piaget, J., & Inhelder, B. (1968). *The psychology of the child.* New York, NY: Basic Books.

Piaget, J., & Weil, A. M. (1951). The development in children of the idea of the homeland and of relations to other countries. *International Social Science Journal, 3,* 561–578.

Polakow, V. (1993). *Lives on the edge.* Chicago, IL: University of Chicago Press.

Porter, J. D. (1971). *Black child, White child: The development of racial attitudes.* Cambridge, MA: Harvard University Press.

Preston, J., Cottrell, M., Pelletier, T., & Pearce, J. (2011). Aboriginal early childhood education in Canada: Issues of context. *Journal of Early Childhood Research, 10*(1), 3–18.

Quintana, S. M., & McKown, C. (2008). Introduction: Race, racism, and the developing child. In S. M. Quintana & C. McKown (Eds.), *Handbook of race, racism, and the developing child* (pp. 1–15). Hoboken, NJ: Wiley.

Raabe, T., & Beelmann, A. (2011). Development of ethnic, racial, and national prejudice in childhood and adolescence: A multinational meta-analysis of age differences. *Child Development, 82,* 1715–1737.

Radke, M., & Trager, H. G. (1950). Children's perceptions of the social roles of Negroes and Whites. *Journal of Psychology, 29,* 3–33.

Ramirez, D. A. (1996). Multiracial identity in a color-conscious world. In M. Root (Ed.), *The multiracial experience: Racial borders as the new frontier* (pp. 49–62). Thousand Oaks, CA: Sage.

Ramsey, P. G. (1982, August). *Racial differences in children's contacts and comments about others.* Paper presented at the annual meeting of the American Psychological Association, Washington, DC.

Ramsey, P. G. (1983, April). *Young children's responses to racial differences: Sociocultural perspectives.* Paper presented at the biennial meeting of the Society for Research in Child Development, Detroit, MI.

Ramsey, P. G. (1986). Possession disputes in preschool classrooms. *Child Study Journal, 16,* 173–181.

Ramsey, P. G. (1987). Young children's thinking about ethnic differences. In J. Phinney & M. Rotheram (Eds.), *Children's ethnic socialization: Pluralism and development* (pp. 56–72). Beverly Hills, CA: Sage.

Ramsey, P. G. (1991b). The salience of race in young children growing up in an all-White community. *Journal of Educational Psychology, 83,* 28–34.

Ramsey, P. G. (1991c). Young children's awareness and understanding of social class differences. *Journal of Genetic Psychology, 152,* 71–82.

Ramsey, P. G. (1995). Changing social dynamics of early childhood classrooms. *Child Development, 66,* 764–773.

Ramsey, P. G., & Mika, K. (2011). Identity of transracial adoptees: Outsiders looking in? *Anales de Psicologia, 27*(2), 611–624.

Ramsey, P. G., & Myers, L. C. (1990). Salience of race in young children's cognitive, affective and behavioral responses to social environments. *Journal of Applied Developmental Psychology, 11,* 49–67.

Ramsey, P. G., & Williams, L. R. (with Vold, E. B.). (2003). *Multicultural education: A Source book* (2nd ed.). New York, NY: RoutledgeFalmer.

Recchia, S. L., & Lee, Y-J. (2013). *Inclusion in the early childhood classroom: What makes a difference?* New York, NY: Teachers College Press.

Riojas-Cortez, M. (2001). Preschoolers' funds of knowledge displayed through sociodramatic play episodes in a bilingual classroom. *Early Childhood Education Journal, 29*(1), 35–40.

Ritchie, J. (2001). Reflections on collectivism in early childhood teaching in Aotearoa/ New Zealand. In S. Grieshaber & G. S. Cannella (Eds.), *Embracing identities in early childhood education: Diversity and possibilities* (pp. 133–147). New York, NY: Teachers College Press.

Ritchie, J. (2012). Titiro whakamuri, hoki whakamua: Respectful integration of Maori perspectives within early childhood environmental education. *Canadian Journal of Environmental Education, 17,* 62–79.

Robinson, K. (2005). Doing anti-homophobia and anti-heterosexism in early childhood education: Moving beyond the immobilising impacts of "risks," "fears," and "silences." Can we afford not to? *Contemporary Issues in Early Childhood, 6*(2), 175–188.

Rodriguez, R. (1981). *Hunger of memory: The education of Richard Rodriguez.* Boston, MA: Godine.

Roediger, D. (2005). *Working toward whiteness: How America's immigrants became White.* New York, NY: Basic Books.

Roopnarine, J. L., Lasker, J., Sacks, M., & Stores, M. (1998). The cultural contexts of children's play. In O. Saracho & B. Spodek (Eds.), *Play in early childhood* (pp. 194–219). Albany: State University of New York Press.

Root, M. P. P. (Ed.). (1992). *Racially mixed people in America.* Newbury Park, CA: Sage.

Rosenow, N. (2008). Learning to love the Earth . . . and each other. *Young Children, 63*(1),10–14.

Rowan, M.C. (2010). Disrupting colonial power through literacy: A story about creating Inuttitut-language children's books. In V. Pacini-Ketchabaw (Ed.), *Flows, rhythms, and intensities of early childhood curriculum* (pp. 155–175). New York, NY: Peter Lang.

Running-Grass. (1994). Towards a multicultural environmental education. *Multicultural Education, 2(1),* 4–6.

Rutland, A., Cameron, L., Bennett, L., & Ferrell, J. (2005). Interracial contact and racial constancy: A multi-site study of racial intergroup bias in 3–5 year old Anglo–British children. *Applied Developmental Psychology, 26,* 699–713. doi:10.1016/j.appdev.2005.08.005

Ryan, S., Ochsner, M., & Genishi, C. (2001). Miss Nelson is missing: Teacher sightings in research on teaching. In S. Grieshaber & G. Cannella (Eds.), *Shifting identities in early childhood education: Expanding possibilities for thought and action* (pp. 45–59). New York, NY: Teachers College Press.

Sadker, M., & Sadker, D. (1995). *Failing at fairness: How our schools cheat girls.* New York, NY: Simon & Schuster.

Sadker, D., Zittleman, K., Earley, P., McCormick, T., Strawn, C., & Preston, J. (2007). The treatment of gender equity in teacher education. In S. S. Klein (Ed.), *Handbook for achieving gender equity through education* (pp. 131–149). Mahwah, NJ: Lawrence Erlbaum.

Salisbury, C. L., & Palombar, M. M. (1998). Friends and acquaintances: Evolving relationships in an inclusive elementary school. In L. H. Meyer, H.-S. Park, M. Grenot-Scheyer, I. S. Schwarz, & B. Harry (Eds.), *Making friends: The influences of culture and development* (pp. 81–104). Baltimore, MD: Brookes.

Saltmarsh, S. (2009). Becoming economic subjects: Agency, consumption and popular culture in early childhood. *Discourse: Studies in the Cultural Politics of Education, 30*(1), 47–59. doi:10.1080/01596300802643082

Satterlee, D. J., & Cormons, G. D. (2008). Sparking interest in nature—family style. *Young Children, 63*(1), 16–20.

Schaffer, M., & Sinicrope, P. (1983, June). *Promoting the growth of moral judgment: An inservice teacher training model.* Paper presented at the annual meeting of the Jean Piaget Society, Philadelphia, PA.

Scholl, L. (2002, April). *Hybridity in (multicultural) education.* Paper presented at the annual meeting of the American Educational Research Association, New Orleans, LA.

Schoorman, D. (2011). Reconceptualizing teacher education as a social justice undertaking: Underscoring the urgency for critical multiculturalism in early childhood education. *Childhood Education, 87*(5), 341–344.

Schor, J. (2004). *Born to buy: The commercialized child and the new consumer culture.* New York, NY: Scribner.

Schussler, D. L., Stooksberry, L. M., & Bercaw, L. A. (2010). Understanding teacher candidates' dispositions: Reflecting to build self-awareness. *Journal of Teacher Education, 61*(4), 350–363.

Schwartz, N. D. (2014, February 2). The middle class is steadily eroding. Just ask the business world. *New York Times, 163*(56401). Retrieved from www.nytimes.com/2014/02/03/business/the-middle-class-is-steadily-eroding-just-ask-the-business-world.html

Seele, C. (2012). Ethnicity and early childhood: An ethnographic approach to children's ethnifying practices in peer interactions at preschool. *International Journal of Early Childhood, 44*(3), 307–325. doi:10.1007/s13158-012-0070-1

Segura-Mora, A. (1999). What color is beautiful? *NEA Today, 18*(2), 7.

Shah, A. (2010, November 21). Children as consumers. *Global Issues.* Retrieved from www.globalissues.org/article/237/children-as-consumers

Sheridan, M. K., Foley, G. M., & Radlinski, S. H. (1995). *Using the supportive play model: Individualized intervention in early childhood practice.* New York, NY: Teachers College Press.

Silin, J. G. (1995). *Sex, death, and the education of children: Our passion for ignorance in the age of AIDS.* New York, NY: Teachers College Press.

Silverstein, S. (1964). *The giving tree.* New York, NY: Harper & Row.

Simmons, D. A. (1994). Urban children's preferences for nature: Lessons for environmental education. *Children's Environments, 11*(3), 194–203.

Singleton, L. C., & Asher, S. R. (1977). Peer preferences and social interaction among third-grade children in an integrated school district. *Journal of Educational Psychology, 69,* 330–336.

Skattebol, J. (2003). Dark, dark and darker: Negotiations of identity in an early childhood setting. *Contemporary Issues in Early Childhood, 4,* 149–166.

Skattebol, J., & Ferfolja, T. (2007). Voices from an enclave: Lesbian mothers' experiences of child care. *Australian Journal of Early Education, 32*(1), 10–18.

Skelton, R., & Miller, V. (2006). *The environmental justice movement.* New York, NY: Natural Resources Defense Council.

Skott-Myhre, K. (2012). Nomadic youth care. *International Journal of Child Youth and Family Studies, 3*(2 & 3), 300–315.

Slavin, R. E. (1995). Cooperative learning and intergroup relations. In J. A. Banks & C. A. M. Banks (Eds.), *Handbook of research on multicultural education* (pp. 628–634). New York, NY: Macmillan.

Sleeter, C. E. (1994). White racism. *Multicultural Education, 1*(5–8), 39.

Sleeter, C. E., & Grant, C. A. (1988). *Making choices for multicultural education: Five approaches to race, class, and gender.* New York, NY: Macmillan.

Smith, S. (2010, August 30). Tobacco signs still target city's poorer areas. *Boston Globe.* Retrieved from www.boston.com/news/health/articles/2010/08/30/to-bacco_signs_still_target_citys_poorer_areas/

Smith, S. C. (2012). Cultural relay in early childhood education: Methods of teaching school behavior to low-income children. *Urban Review, 44,* 571–588. doi:10.1007/s11256-012-0205-6

Souto-Manning, M. (2007). Acting out and talking back: Negotiating discourses in American early educational settings. *Early Child Development and Care, 179*(8), 1083–1094.

Souto-Manning, M., & Hermann-Wilmarth, J. (2008). Teacher inquiries into gay and lesbian families in early childhood classrooms. *Journal of Early Childhood Research, 6*(3), 263–280. doi:10.1177/1476718X08094450

Souto-Manning, M., & Price-Dennis, D. (2012). Critically redefining and repositioning media texts in early childhood teacher education: What if? And why? *Journal of Early Childhood Teacher Education, 33,* 304–321. doi:10.1080/10 901027.2012.732669

Souto-Manning, M., & Swick, K. (2006, October). Teachers' beliefs about parent and family involvement: Rethinking our family involvement paradigm. *Early Childhood Education Journal, 34*(2), 187–193

Spencer, M. B., Brookins, G. K., & Allen, W. R. (1985). *Beginnings: The social and affective development of Black children.* Hillsdale, NJ: Lawrence Erlbaum.

Spencer, M. B., & Markstrom-Adams, C. (1990). Identity processes among racial and ethnic minority children in America. *Child Development, 61,* 290–310.

Starhawk. (1988). *Truth or dare: Encounters with power, authority and mystery.* San Francisco, CA: HarperSanFrancisco.

Stipek, D. J., & Ryan, R. H. (1997). Economically disadvantaged preschoolers: Ready to learn but further to go. *Developmental Psychology, 33*(4), 711–723.

Stott, F., & Bowman, B. (1996). Child development knowledge: A slippery base for practice. *Early Childhood Research Quarterly, 11,* 169–183.

Stronge, J. H. (Ed.). (1992). *Educating homeless children and adolescents: Evaluating policy and practice.* Newbury Park, CA: Sage.

Sutfin, E. L., Fulcher, M., Bowles, R. P., & Patterson, C. J. (2008). How lesbian and heterosexual parents convey attitudes about gender to their children: The role of gendered environments. *Sex Roles, 58,* 501–513. doi:10.1007/s11199-007-9368-0

Swadener, E. B., & Johnson, J. E. (1989). Play in diverse social contexts: Parent and teacher roles. In M. N. Bloch & A. D. Pellegrini (Eds.), *The ecological context of children's play* (pp. 214–244). Norwood, NJ: Ablex.

Tajfel, H. (1973). The roots of prejudice: Cognitive aspects. In P. Watson (Ed.), *Psychology and race* (pp. 76–95). Chicago, IL: Aldine.

Tatum, B. D. (1992). Talking about race, learning about racism: The application of racial identity development theory in the classroom. *Harvard Educational Review, 62*(1), 1–24.

Tatum, B. D. (1997). *"Why are all the Black kids sitting together in the cafeteria?" and other conversations about race.* New York, NY: Basic Books.

Tenery, M. F. (2005). La Visita. In N. González, L. C. Moll, & C. Amanti (Eds.), *Funds of knowledge: Theorizing practices in households, communities, and classrooms* (pp. 119–130). Mahwah, NJ: Lawrence Erlbaum.

Terry, J. (2009). 50 awesome ways to use Skype in the classroom [Blog post]. *Blog at TeachingDegree.org*. Retrieved July 28, 2014, from www.teachingdegree.org/2009/06/30/50-awesome-ways-to-use-skype-in-the-classroom

Tharp, R. G. (1989). Psychological variables and constants: Effects on teaching and learning in schools. *American Psychologist, 44,* 349–359.

Tharp, R. G., & Gallimore, R. (1988). *Rousing minds to life: Teaching, learning, and schooling in social context.* Cambridge, United Kingdom: Cambridge University Press.

Theokas, C. (1991). *Modifying sex-typed behavior and contact patterns in a kindergarten classroom with an outer space intervention curriculum* (Unpublished master's thesis). Mount Holyoke College, South Hadley, MA.

Thompson, A. (1998). Not the color purple: Black feminist lessons for educational caring. *Harvard Educational Review, 68*(4), 522–554.

Thorne, B. (1986). Girls and boys together . . . but mostly apart: Gender arrangements in elementary schools. In W. W. Hartup & Z. Rubin (Eds.), *Relationships and development* (pp. 167–184). Hillsdale, NJ: Lawrence Erlbaum.

Thornton, C., & Underwood, K. (2013). Conceptualisations of disability and inclusion: Perspectives of educators of young children. *Early Years, 33*(1), 59–73.

Tobin, J. J., & Kurban, F. (2010). Preschool practitioners' and immigrant parents' beliefs about academics and play in the early childhood educational curriculum in five countries. *Orbis Scholae, 4*(2), 75–87.

Tobin, J. J., Wu, D. Y., & Davidson, D. H. (1989). *Preschool in three cultures: Japan, China, and the United States.* New Haven, CT: Yale University Press.

Trautner, H. M., Ruble, D. N., Cyphers, L., Kirsten, B., Behrendt, R., & Hartmann, P. (2005). Rigidity and flexibility of gender stereotypes in childhood: Developmental or differential? *Infant and Child Development, 14,* 365–381.

Trenka, J. J., Oparah, J. C., & Shin, S. Y. (Eds.). (2006). *Outsiders within: Writing on transracial adoption.* Cambridge, MA: South End Press.

Trepanier-Street, M., Hong, S., Silverman, K., Keefer, L. R., & Morris, T. L. (2011). Young children with and without disabilities: Perceptions of peers with physical disabilities. *International Journal of Early Childhood Special Education, 3*(2), 117–128.

Tropp, L., & Prenovost, M. (2008). The role of intergroup contact in predicting children's inter-ethnic attitudes: Evidence from meta-analytic and field studies. In S. R. Levy & M. Killen (Eds.), *Intergroup attitudes and relations in childhood through adulthood* (pp. 236–248). Oxford, United Kingdom: Oxford University Press.

Tudge, J. (2008). *The everyday life of young children.* New York, NY: Cambridge University Press.

Tudge, J., Odero, D., Piccinini, C., Doucet, F., Sperb, T., & Lopes, R. (2006). A window into different cultural worlds: Young children's everyday activities in the United States, Brazil, and Kenya. *Child Development, 77*(5), 1446–1469.

UNESCO Bangkok. (2009). *Towards inclusive education for children with disabilities: A guideline.* Bangkok, Thailand: UNESCO Bangkok.

Urberg, K. A., & Kaplan, M. G. (1989). An observational study of race-, age-, and sex-heterogeneous interaction in preschoolers. *Journal of Applied Developmental Psychology, 10,* 299–311.

Valdés, G. (1996). *Con respeto: Bridging the distances between culturally diverse families and schools.* New York, NY: Teachers College Press.

Van Ausdale, D., & Feagin, J. R. (2001). *The first R: How children learn race and racism.* Lanham, MD: Rowman & Littlefield.

Vorrasi, J. A., & Gabarino, J. (2000). Poverty and youth violence: Not all risk factors are created equal. In V. Polakow (Ed.), *The public assault on America's children: Poverty, violence and juvenile injustice* (pp. 59–77). New York, NY: Teachers College Press.

Voss, J. A., & Bufkin, L. J. (2011). Teaching all children: Preparing early childhood preservice teachers in inclusive settings. *Journal of Early Childhood Teacher Education, 32*(4), 338–354.

Vygotsky, L. S. (1978). *Mind in society: The development of higher psychological processes.* Cambridge, MA: Harvard University Press.

Walker, S., & Berthelsen, D. C. (2007). The social participation of young children with developmental disabilities in inclusive early childhood programs. *Electronic Journal for Inclusive Education, 2*(2).

Walker, S., & Berthelsen, D. (2008). Children with autistic spectrum disorder in early childhood education programs: A social constructivist perspective on inclusion. *International Journal of Early Childhood, 40*(1), 33–51.

Wals, A. E. J. (1994). "Nobody planted it, it just grew!" Young adolescents' perceptions and experiences of nature in the context of urban environmental education. *Children's Environments, 11*(3), 177–193.

Wardle, F. (1996). Multicultural education. In M. Root (Ed.), *The multiracial experience: Racial borders as the new frontier* (pp. 380–391). Thousand Oaks, CA: Sage.

Wells, R., & Zeece, P. D. (2007). My place in my world: Literature for place-based environmental education. *Early Childhood Education Journal, 35*(3), 285–291. doi:10.1007/s10643-007-0181-8

West, C. (1993). *Race matters.* Boston, MA: Beacon.

Whiting, B. B., & Edwards, C. P. (1988). *Children of different worlds: The formation of social behavior.* Cambridge, MA: Harvard University Press

Whiting, B. B., & Whiting, J. W. M. (1975). *Children of six cultures: A psychocultural analysis.* Cambridge, MA: Harvard University Press.

Wight, V. R., & Chau, M. (2009). Basic facts about low-income children, 2008: Children under age 6. National Center for Children in Poverty (NCCP). Retrieved from http://www.nccp.org/publications/pub_896

Williams, J. E., & Morland, J. K. (1976). *Race, color and the young child.* Chapel Hill: University of North Carolina Press.

Williams, L. R., & Norton, N. E. L. (2008). Thought-provoking moments in teaching young children: Reflections on social class, sexuality, and spirituality. In C. Genishi & A. Lin Goodwin (Eds.), *Diversities in early childhood education: Rethinking and doing* (pp. 103–118). New York, NY: Routledge.

Wilson, R. A. (1993). Educators for earth: A guide for early childhood instruction. *Journal of Environmental Education, 24*(2), 15–21.

Wilson, R. A. (1995). Nature and young children: A natural connection. *Young Children, 50*(6), 4–11.

Winter, J. (2008). *Wangari's trees of peace: A true story from Africa*. Orlando, FL: Harcourt Books.

Wise, T. (2009). *Between Barack and a hard place: Racism and White denial in the age of Obama*. San Francisco, CA: City Lights Books.

Wong-Filmore, L. (1991). When learning a second language means losing the first. *Early Childhood Research Quarterly, 6*(3), 323–346.

Wubie, B. (2005). Interconnectedness of young children's home and classroom experiences: Implications for multicultural curriculum. *Canadian Children, 30*(2), 17–22.

Yang, C., & Rusli, E. (2012). Teacher training in using effective strategies for preschool children with disabilities in inclusive classrooms. *Journal of College Teaching & Learning, 9*(1), 53.

Yolen, J. (2000). *How do dinosaurs say good night?* (M. Teague, Illus.). New York, NY: Blue Sky Press (Scholastic).

Zaretsky, L. (2005). From practice to theory: Inclusive models require inclusive theories. *American Secondary Education, 33*(3), 65–86.

Zosuls, K. M., Ruble, D. N., Tamis-LeMonda, C. S., Shrout, P. E., Bornstein, M. H., & Greulich, F. K. (2009). The acquisition of gender labels in infancy: Implications for gender-typed play. *Developmental Psychology, 45*(3), 688–701.

Index

Abilities
  children's awareness/understanding
    of, 162–168
  reflections on, 152–153. *See
    also* Disabilities
Aboud, F. E., 76, 77, 78
Accommodation, in idea construction, 24–25
Accomplishment of natural
  growth (Lareau), 88, 93
Accountability, 9
Accreditation programs, 9
Achievement gap, 94
Activism
  communications industry and, 33
  environmental, 127–128
  multicultural education as form of, xiv
  parent-teacher, 50
Activists for social change,
  children as, 58–61
Adair, J., 113
Addy, S., 87
Aina, O. E., 135, 136, 138
Albaiz, N., 31, 32
Alejandro-Wright, M. N., 74
Alienation, home–school cultural
  discontinuities and, 114
Allen, P. G., 121, 122
Allen, W. R., 22
Allport, G. W., 28
Amanti, C., 44, 94, 103, 108, 111, 115, 119
Amari, A., 78
Amato, M., 76, 78
American Dream, myth of, 85–86, 93
Anderson, J., 113, 116
Andrew, Y., 139, 142
Andriotou, E., 125
Annis, R. C., 76
Araújo, S. B., 40, 42
Asher, S. R., 78
Assimilation, in idea construction, 24–25
Assumptions. *See* Biases

Atkinson, S., 5
Attention deficit disorders, 123, 166–168
Authentic inclusion, children with
  disabilities, 156–157
Ayvazian, A., 20

Babies, self-referenced empathy and, 51–52
Baird, J., 139, 142
Banks, J. A., 6, 64
Barbero, A., 99, 100
Bardhan-Quallen, S., 35
Barraza, L., 126
Barrett, J. R., 66
Batchelor, D., 160, 164
Bear, G., 159
Becker, B. E., 98
Beckman, P. J., 155, 160
Beelman, A., 28, 77
Behrendt, R., 137
Bem, S. L., 135, 137
Benjamin, R., 139, 142
Benn, J., 99, 101
Bennett, L., 28
Bennett-Gates, D., 128
Bercaw, L. A., 18
Bergerson, A. A., 67
Berthelsen, D., 157, 160
Berthelsen, D. C., 156, 159, 160
Bhana, D., 138
Biases, 18–20
  electronic media and, 32
  environment and, 28
  gender-based, children's behavior and, 133
  in-group, 28–29
  pervasive nature of, 18
  teachers', parent perception of, 45–46
Biases, identifying and challenging,
    18–20, 29–37
  about abilities and disabilities,
    164–168
  about culture, 118–120

Biases, identifying and challenging
    (continued)
    about economic class and
        consumerism, 102–106
    about gender and sexual
        orientation, 145–151
    about natural environment, 126–131
    about racial identity, 79–83
    as lifelong process, 20
    topics and questions for, 20
Bicultural children, outcomes for, 114–115
Bigler, R. S., 27, 28, 74, 135, 136, 137, 138
Bilingual education programs, 111–112
Biographies, 36–37
Biracial individuals, racial identity
    development stages, 71–73
Bisexual youth. See GBLT youth
Blaise, M., 134, 138, 139, 143, 148
Blame, parent and teacher, 46
Blanchard, P. B., 129
Bode, P., 6, 112
Bohács, K., 157
Boho, A., 86
Boldt, G. M., 137, 145
Books, expanding children's
    awareness through, 34–37
Borderwork, gender segregation
    and, 137–138
Bornstein, M. H., 136
Bosacki, S. L., 18
Boutte, G., 29, 34, 68, 74
Boutte, G. S., 24
Bowers, C. A., 7, 98, 107, 121
Bowles, R. P., 135
Bowman, B., 24
Bowman, B. T., 22
Boyer, W., 107, 110, 112, 116
Brennan, E. L., 159
Bronfenbrenner, U., 15
    ecological systems of, 15–17
Brookins, G. K., 22
Brown, S., 141, 142
Brown, W. H., 157, 158, 159
Bruns, D. A., 155
"Bubble wrapped children," 122–123
Buchanan, T. K., 129
Buerk, K., 128
Bufkin, L. J., 156
Buholzer, A., 163
Bullard, R. D., 7
Buswell, B. N., 18
Buysse, V., 155–156
Byers, L., 113

Cadwell, L. B., 45
Cameron, L., 28
Cameron, P. A., 135, 136, 138
Cameron, R. J., 111
Campaign for a Commercial-Free
    Childhood et al., 32
Cannella, G. S., 22, 23, 24
Care, centers of, 38
Caring, 38–39
    in Black communities, 38–39
    and empathy, 51–53
    as engagement with world, 38–39
    for environment, 39
    multicultural education and, 38
Caring and critical communities,
        creating, 38–61
    among adults, 40–50
    in the classroom, 50–61
    elements of, 38
    family–school partnerships, 42–50
    staff relationships, 40–42
Carpenter, E. S., 164
Carraro, L., 78
Carroll, G., 67
Casper, B., 141, 142, 143, 144, 145
Castelli, L., 78
Categories, forming and applying, 27–29
Causey, C., 31, 32
Ceballo, R., 99
Center for a New American Dream, 100
Center on Race, Poverty, and
        the Environment, 7
Chafel, J. A., 96
Chang, H. N., 19
Chasnoff, D., 145
Chau, M., 67
Chawla, L., 123
Chern, A., 60
Child development theories and research
    critique of, 22–24
    development within context of
        social stratification, 22–23
    developmental vs. environmental
        aspects, 22
    ideas, construction of, 24–26
    trends and processes, 24–29
Childrearing
    approach in middle-class families, 91, 93
    approach in poor families, 88, 93
    cultural influences on, 110–111
Children's literature, 34–37
    author disclosures in, 35
    biographical works, 36–37

contexts portrayed in, 35
group portrayals in, 35
nonfiction works, 36
realism vs. optimism in, balance
        between, 35–36
values reflected in, 35
Chinn, P. C., 6
Clark, K. B., 75, 76
Clark, M. D., 157
Clark, M. P., 75, 76
Class meetings, for parents
activities for, suggestions, 46–47
connections between parents,
        promoting, 48–49
sense of belonging in, encouraging, 47–48
translators for, 43
Classroom
cooperative activities in, 56
creating caring and critical
        communities in, 50–61
design and furnishing of. See
        Design of classroom space
ethnolinguistic segregation in, 117
inclusion of children with
        disabilities in, 155–156
interactions incongruent with
        home cultural values, 114
power allocation within, 40
routines and rituals in, 59–60
rules and procedures in, children's
        involvement in developing, 58–59
social divisions in, strategies
        to reduce, 55–56
Cleovoulou, Y., 60
Cleveland, E., 128
Climate change, impact on
        poor communities, 7
Clinton, Bill, 7
Cohen, E. V., 110
Cohen, H., 145
Coles, R., 36, 50
Collaboration
for multicultural community creation, 39
between staff members, 40
Color
of products, gender associations
        and, 135–136
of skin. See Skin color
Color-blind/Colorblindness, 28
myth of, 73–74
pretense of, 68, 82
Commeford, L., 60
Communication skills, development of, 53

Communications industry, activism and, 33
Community, parent-teacher
        involvement/activism in, 50
Complex issues, making meaningful, 21
Concerted cultivation (Lareau), 91, 93
Conflict
children's racial identification and, 75–76
elimination of, 57
useful purpose of, 58
Conflict resolution, 56–58
Conflict Solutions Center, 57
Connor, R., 157, 158, 159
Connor, R. T., 157, 158
Connors, C., 156, 160, 163
Consumerism, 97–106
characteristics of, 98–99
children's understanding/
        experiences of, 99–106
consequences of, 99
ecocentric vs. egocentric, 101–102
refections on, 97–98
Consumption patterns, 86
Contact hypothesis, 28
Contexts
in children's literature, 35
shaping children's world views, 20–37
of social stratification, child
        development within, 22–23
Contexts of learning
abilities and disabilities, 152–168
culture and natural environment, 107–131
economic class and consumerism, 84–106
gender and heterosexuality, 132–151
race, 65–83
Continent of origin, language used for, 13
Contradictions, xiii–xiv
accepting and codifying, 5
child's world view and, 4, 21
Conversations with children, in
        multicultural teaching, 60–61
Cooperative activities/games, 56
Cooperative communities, 39–40
Cooperative living, individual
        independence vs., 23
Coplan, R., 18
Corenblum, B., 76
Cormons, G. D., 128
Corsaro, W. A., 57
Cottle, T. J., 95
Cottrell, M., 115, 116
Crawford, J., 111
Crisis frequency, economically
        disadvantaged and, 85

Cristol, D., 73, 76
Critical communities. *See* Caring
    and critical communities
Critical consciousness, development
    in adults, 18–20
Critical friends system, 41–42
Critical Race Theory (CRT), 66–67
Critical thinking
    electronic media and, 32
    and social action, 58–61
Crnic, K., 22
Cross, W. E., 70, 76
Cross-group contacts, strategies
    encouraging, 55–56
Crystal, D. S., 28
Csikszentmihalyi, M., 98, 99, 101
Cultural affiliations
    and hone–school discontinuities, 111–116
    reflections on, 109
Cultural influences
    on childrearing, 110–111
    reflections on, 107–109
Culture
    affiliations. *See* Cultural affiliations
    children's understanding of, 116–120
    influences. *See* Cultural influences
    and natural environment,
        connections with, 120–122
    romanticization of, 33
Cunningham, S. J., 135, 136, 137
Curriculum
    including family diversity/evolution
        aspects into, 147–148
    incorporating children's
        experiences into, 48–49
    scripted vs. flexible, 9
Cushing, D., 123
Cyphers, L., 137

Dalli, C., 111, 117
Damon, W., 95
Damree, N., 74, 77, 78
Darder, A., 114
Davidson, A. L., 115
Davidson, D. H., 43
Davis, J., 74, 122, 124, 127
Davis, K., 22
Day, M., 162
De Brunhoff, J., 35
Dean, S., 139, 142
Decision making
    about classroom procedures,
        methods for, 59
    within school environment, 40, 41

DeGaetano, Y., 110
DeGrella, L. H., 163
Delgado-Gaiten, C., 115
DeLoache, J. S., 136, 137
Derman-Sparks, L., 6, 19, 68, 69, 70, 76, 84
Design of classroom space
    contributing to social divisions, 55–56
    fostering peer interactions, 54
Development intergroup theory, 27–29
Developmental competencies, 23
Devine, P. G., 18
Devore, S., 155
Dewar, B. A., 18
Diamond, K. E., 156, 157, 158,
        159, 160, 162, 163, 164
DiAngelo, R., 10
Differences, exploring vs. minimizing, 28–29
Disabilities, children/people with, 6, 7
    abled persons perceptions of,
        influences of, 154–155
    in abled world, 154–155
    children's awareness/understanding
        of, 162–168
    inclusion in educational settings, 155–157
    language used for, 14, 152–153
    reflections on, 152–153
    social participation of, 157–162. *See
        also* Social inclusion/isolation
Disendruck, G., 117
Disequilibrium, in idea construction, 25–26
Distrust, home–school cultural
    discontinuities and, 114
Doucet, F., 109, 110, 116
Dovidio, J. F., 18
Dowell, C., 19
Doyle, A., 77, 117
Dressing up activities, 138, 148
Dressner, M., 128
Duhn, I., 39, 123, 128
Duncan, J., 142
Dykstra, L. A., 133, 148
Dyson, L. L., 162, 163

Earick, M. E., 29, 42, 69, 85
Earley, P., 135
Early childhood programs, 9, 23–24, 148
Ecological Oath, 131
Ecological systems, 8, 15–17, 121–122
Economic class(es), 84–97
    adult outcomes determined by, 93
    children's awareness/views about,
        94–97, 102–106
    and family life (ethnographic
        study), 87–94

gap between, 86–87, 93
  reflections on, 84–86
  teaching styles and, 93–94
Economic divisions/segregation, 96–97
Educational philosophy, home–school
  cultural discontinuity and, 114
Educational settings. *See* Schools
Educational system, inequities in, 8–9
Edwards, C. P., 110, 135
Edwards, J. O., 6, 84
Egalitarian reform, support for, 85–86
Ehrensaft, D., 134
El Centro de la Raza program, 131
Electronic media
  expanding children's awareness
    through, 31–33
  gender-specific, 136
Elementary school children, caring
  and empathy in, 52
Elliot, S., 123
Ellis, E., 60
Empathy, and caring, 51–53
Enesco, I., 74, 76, 77, 78
Engelhardt, W., 87
Environment. *See* Natural
  environment/world
Environmental degradation/destruction
  children's awareness of, 125–126
  conquering nature mentality
    and, 8, 121–122
  poor communities and, 6, 7
Environmental Justice Movement
  (EJM), 7, 131
Equal opportunity, myth of, 85–86, 93
Ergazaki, M., 125
Ernest, J. M., 31, 32
Ernst, J., 125
Essentialist thinking, 27–28
Ethnographic study, on family life
  and economic class, 87–94
Ethnolinguistic groups, in classroom, 117
Expectations, parent-teacher mismatch, 43
Exploitation, 5–7

Fadiman, A., 154
Fairness, children's views on, 95
Falik, L. H., 157
Family
  composition of, children's
    understanding of, 144–145
  and economic class, ethnographic
    study, 87–94
  information confidentiality and, 43
  loyalty to, individual independence vs., 23

and school relationship, 12. *See also*
  Parent-child relationship
Family books, as conversation catalyst, 60
Family–school partnerships, 12, 42–50. *See
  also* Parent-teacher communication
Fantasy play, 56
Farrell, W. C., 76
Farver, J. M., 110
Favazza, P., 164
Feagin, J. R., 76, 77, 79
Ferfolja, T., 142, 148
Ferrell, J., 28
Feuerstein, R., 157
Feuerstein, R. S., 157
Finkelstein, N. W., 78
Fishbein, H. D., 78
Flewitt, R., 154, 156, 162
Foley, G. M., 155, 157, 160
Fox, D. J., 78
Franklin, K. L., 36
Franklin, M. E., 155
Freeman, N. K., 135
Frempong, G., 156
Friendships, children's
  influence of race on, 78–79
  social divisions reflected in, 55
Frosch, D. L., 110
Fulcher, M., 135
Fulmer, C. L., 135
Funds of knowledge approach
  to parent-teacher communication, 43–44
  promoting connections between
    parents, 48–49

Gabarino, J., 99
Gaertner, S. L., 18
Gallimore, R., 116
Gandini, L., 45
Garcia, R. L., 107
García Coll, C., 22
Gasser, L., 163
Gay, G., 6, 38
"Gay," pejorative use of,
  confronting, 149–150
GBLT youth, 13–14, 141–144, 149–150
Gender, 5–6. *See also* Sexual identity
  children's responses to, 136–139, 145–151
  nonconforming, 134
  as social construct, 133
Gender exclusion/segregation, 137–139
Gender roles, 134–135, 148–149
  heteronormativity reinforcing, 136
Gender stereotypes, 133–136, 137
Genishi, C., 24

Gill, M., 128
Gimbert, B., 73, 76
Gollnick, D. M., 6
González, N., 44, 94, 103, 111, 115, 119
Gonzalez-Mena, J., 46
Gonzalez-Ramos, G., 110
Goodman, J. F., 163
Goodman, M., 75, 76
Goudena, P. P., 110
Grace, C., 67
Grace, R., 115, 116
Grant, C. A., 6
Great Recession of 2008,
    consequences of, 86–87
Green, V. P., 163
Greene, J., 111
Gregg, K., 43, 44
Greulich, F. K., 136
Grieshaber, S., 23, 24
Grodzińska-Jurczak, M., 125
Group attributes, 28–29, 35
Group discussions
    adult involvement in, 19–20
    turning individual questions into, 60
Groza, V., 141, 142
Guerrero, S., 74, 76, 77, 78
Güler, T., 123, 124, 125, 126
Guo, K., 111, 117
Guralnick, M. J., 157, 158, 159
Gutierrez, S., 159

Hakuta, K., 111
Hallett, B., 128
Hallinan, M. T., 78
Halverson, C., 137
Hammond, M., 157, 158, 159
Hammond, M. A., 157, 158
Han, J., 158, 164
Hanson, M., 155, 160
Hanson, M. J., 155, 159
Hare, J., 113, 116
Harper, L. V., 156
Harris, M. J., 163
Harry, B., 154, 162
Hartmann, P., 137
Haskins, R., 78
Hayes, C., 66, 70, 71
Haymes, S. N., 99
Head Start program, 93, 94, 96
Helms, J. E., 69
Helper, J. B., 159
Hensley, M., 44, 45
Hermann-Wilmarth, J., 143

Hernandez-Reif, M., 76
Hestenes, L. L., 157, 162, 163, 164
Heteronormativity
    GBLT individuals and, 141–144
    gender roles and, 134–135, 136
Heterosexual, use of term, 14
High-stakes testing, 9
Hill, L. T., 45
Hinds, J., 123
Hirschfeld, L. A., 75
Hoffman, M., 51, 53
Holmes, R., 74, 76, 78, 139, 142
Home, and school, cultural discontinuities
    between, 111–116
Home visits, parent-teacher
    communication and, 44–45
Homelessness, impact on children, 89
Homophobic views, challenging, 149–150
Homosexual (gay) youth. See GBLT youth
Hong, S., 159, 162, 163
Hoppe-Graff, S., 110
Howard, G. R., 68
Howard, J. A., 71, 72
Howes, C., 51
Huang, H., 156, 158, 163
Humanity, divisions of, 5–6
Husband, T., Jnr., 68, 73, 75
Huston, A. C., 86
Hyperconsumption. See Consumerism
Hyun, E., 124

Ideas construction, elements in, 24–26
Imai, S., 78
Immigrant children/groups, 5, 111–115
    outcomes for, 114–115
In-group bias, 28–29, 53
Inclusion, of children with disabilities, 155–
    157, 160–162. See also Social inclusion/
    isolation, of children with disabilities
Inclusion illusion, 41
Inequality.org., 67
Infants, self-referenced empathy and, 51–52
Information processing, 20–21, 26
Inhelder, B., 24
Innes, F. K., 163, 164
Intersex, defined, 151
Intersex Society of North
    America (ISNA), 151
Irving, D., 18, 44, 68

Jackson, L., 56
Janmohamed, Z., 134
Jenkins, R., 22

Jewish Virtual Library, 150
Johnson, D. W., 39, 56
Johnson, J. E., 159, 160
Johnson, R. T., 39, 56
Jordan, P. E., 76
Jordan, V. B., 78
Journals, keeping of, 18–19
Juárez, B. G., 66, 70, 71
Juvonen, J., 159

Kahriman-Öztürk, D., 123, 124, 125, 126
Kaiser, A. P., 155, 160
Kang, B., 96
Kaplan, M. G., 78
Katz, P. A., 73, 74, 75, 76, 78
Kawakami, K., 18
Keefer, L. R., 159, 163
Kemp, C., 156, 157
Kemple, K. M., 54, 56, 157
Kendall, F., 6
Kennedy, E., 111
Keyes, L., 158, 163
Kich, G. K., 72
Killen, M., 28
Killoran, I., 156
Kim, Y. K., 110
Kincheloe, J. L., 18
Kirsten, B., 137
Kishida, Y., 156, 157
Kivel, P., 68
Klein, T. P., 89
Kline, S., 100
Klineberg, O., 116
Knowledge expansion, 20–21
Kobayashi-Winata, H., 110
Kofkin, J. A., 74
Kostelnick, M. J., 157, 160, 164
Kowalski, K., 77
Kozleski, E. B., 56
Kozol, J., 68, 94
Kroeger, J., 142, 143
Kroll, L. R., 18, 24, 29
Krueger, E., 113
Krugman, P., 86
Kurban, F., 112

Ladson-Billings, G., 66, 67
Lago, O., 76, 77
Lalley, J., 50, 131
Lam, V., 74, 77, 78
Lambert, W. E., 116
Lamberty, G., 22
Langhout, R. D., 142, 145

Language
    home–school cultural
        discontinuity and, 114
    and locale, 26
    of multicultural education, 12–14
Lareau, A., 87, 88, 89, 91, 93
Lasker, J., 110
Leahy, R., 95, 96
Learning, children's, Vygotsky
        vs. Piaget on, 25
Lebra, T. S., 110
Lee, D., 141, 142, 145, 147
Lee, Y., 110
Lee, Y-J., 157
Lesbians. See GBLT youth
Lester, N. A., 136, 144, 147
Lev, A. I., 134
Levine, J., 68
Li, G., 87
Li, S., 157, 158, 159
Liben, L. S., 27, 28, 74, 135,
        136, 137
Lieber, J., 155, 160
Lin, Q., 18
Liss, M. B., 78
Literature, children's. See
        Children's literature
Litovich, M., 142, 145
LoBue, V., 136, 137
Locale, and languages, 26
Longstreet, W. S., 116
Lopes, R., 109, 110, 116
López-Robertson, J., 29, 34, 68, 74
Louv, R., 122
Luhby, T., 67
Luther, S. S., 98

MacNaughton, G., 22, 74, 138,
        139, 142
Macrae, C. N., 135, 136, 137
Mahalingham, R., 27
Mainstreaming. See Inclusion
Malti, T., 163
Maori community, 23
Mapp, K. L., 44
Marginalized groups, 14
    outcomes for children from, 114–115
    racism and, 5
Markson, L., 117
Markstrom-Adams, C., 76
Marquart, J. M., 157, 158, 159
Martin, C. L., 135, 137
Martinez-Lozano, V., 110

Materials
  expanding children's awareness
    through, 33–34
  manufactured vs.natural, 34
McAdoo, H. P., 22
McAnnich, C. B., 163
McCluskey, K. S., 156
McCollam, H., 60
McCormick, T., 135
McGinnis, H., 71, 72
McGirr, N., 35
McHenry, J., 128
McIntosh, P., 68
McKown, C., 77
McLaren, P., 68
McLoyd, V. C., 86, 99
Meaning, attaching to categories, 27–28
Mebert, C. J., 74
Media-based play, expanding children's
    awareness through, 31–32
Mednick, L. G., 79, 96
Menchu, R., 8
Meritocracy, myth of, 85–86, 93
Middle-class families
  childrearing approach in, 91, 93
  ethnographic study findings, 91–94
Mika, K., 72
Milich, R., 163
Miller, V., 7
Milton, B., 128
Minami, M., 111
Mogharreban, C. C., 155
Moll, L. C., 44, 94, 103, 111, 115, 119
Molnar, J. M., 89
Money-free gifts, ideas for, 106
Moore, I., 60
Moran, C. E., 111
Morgan, M., 159
Morland, J. K., 77
Morris, P. A., 15
Morris, T. L., 159, 163
Moule, J., 33, 109
Muckelroy, A., 19
Multicultural community, collaboration
    for creation of, 39
Multicultural education
  activist nature of, xiv
  caring and, 38
  characteristics of, 10
  continuing challenges in, 169–170
  language of, 12–14
  parent-teacher conversations about, 49
  purpose, trends, and scope of, 6–9

social justice/injustice and, 8
  working goals in, 9–11
Multicultural teaching/work
  conversations with children in, 60–61
  engaging children and adults in, 17
  risks in, 10
  terminology challenges in, 14
Multiculturalism, 8
  creating caring and critical
    communities for, 38–61
  successes in, 169
Multiracial people, racial identity
    development stages, 71–73
Myers, L. C., 74, 76, 78

Nabors, L., 158, 163
Nagel, N., 116
Naimark, H., 95
Native Americans, 13, 113–114
  connection with natural environment, 121
Natural environment/world
  adults' biophobic approach to, 124–125
  caring for, 39
  children's knowledge/views
    about, 124–131
  degradation/destruction of. See
    Environmental degradation/
    destruction
  detachment from, detrimental
    consequences of, 122–123
  fostering connections with, 128
  homocentric vs. biocentric
    views on, 121–122
  photographs of, 31
  physical settings and, 30
  reflections on culture and, 120–122
  suburban and urban children's
    views of, 125
  and sustainability, children's knowledge/
    views about, 122–126
Nature-deficit disorder, 123
Needs of others, learning to recognize, 53
Neff, D., 44
Nelson, M. K., 93
Neville, B., 157, 159
Newman, M. A., 78
Newman, R., 86
Newton, A. B., 31, 32
Nieszporek, K., 125
Nieto, S., 6, 112
Nightingale, C. H., 99
Nigrescence, stages in achieving, 70–71
Niles, M., 113

Nimmo, J., 128
Nind, M., 154, 156, 162
No Child Left Behind (NCLB) Act, 9
Noddings, N., 38
Nonfiction books, 36
Norton, N. E. L., 95, 96
Nunavik Educator's Bookmaking
    Workshop, 35
Nxumalo, F., 113

O'Brien, A. S., 35
Ochsner, M., 24
O'Connor, C. E., 157
Odero, D., 109, 110, 116
Odom, S. L., 155–156, 157,
    158, 159, 160, 164
Olgan, R., 123, 124, 125, 126
Oliviera-Formosinho, J., 40, 42
Olson, J., 76
Onaga, E., 157, 160, 164
Oparah, J. C., 72
Opportunity gap, economic class and, 94
Orellana, M. F., 117
Orlick, T., 56
Ostrosky, M. M., 158, 164
Out-group stereotyping, 28–29
Ovando, C. J., 111

Pacini-Kethcabaw, V., 113
Palmer, A., 164, 165
Palmer, J., 124
Palombar, M. M., 163, 164
Pang, V. O., 38
Parent-child relationship, 12
Parent-teacher communication, 42–50
    about attention deficit order, 166–168
    about multicultural education, 49–50
    about race/racial identity, 82–83
    about sexual orientation, 149–150
    class meetings. See Class
        meetings, for parents
    community involvement and
        activism and, 50
    impediments to, 43
    strategies encouraging, 42–45
Parent-teacher conferences, 45–46
    translators for, 43
Parents, of GBLT children
    dilemmas faced by, 141–142
    and discussion anxiety,
        overcoming, 142–144
Park, H.-S., 162
Parlakian, R., 156, 157, 160

"Passing," 72
Pathologizing people, child
    development and, 22–23
Patterson, C. J., 135
Patterson, M. M., 28
Payler, J., 154, 156, 162
Payne, C., 139, 142
Pearce, J., 115, 116
Peck, C. A., 155, 160
Peer interactions, 54–56
    design of classroom space fostering, 54
Peer relationships
    formation of, 54–55
    physical environment
        contributing to, 55–56
    same-sex, children's preference
        for, 137–139
Pelletier, J., 60
Pelletier, T., 115, 116
Pelo, A., 9, 11, 42, 123, 128
People of color. See also Skin color
    racial identity development stages, 70–71
Perez, K. D., 157
Perkins, D. M., 74
Personal inquiry/reflection, adult
    pursuit of, 18–19
Perspectives, of children, expanding, 29–37
Peters, M. F., 67
Phelan, P., 115
Phillips, C. B., 20, 69
Photographs, expanding
    awareness with, 30–31
Piaget, J., 24, 25, 116
Piccinini, C., 109, 110, 116
Plant, E. A., 18
Play, media-based, 31–32
Pollution, 7, 8
Poor communities, environmental
    problems and, 7
Poor families
    childrearing approach in, 88, 93
    ethnographic study findings,
        88–89, 92–94
Porter, J. D., 78
Poverty, children in, 87
Power, T. G., 110
Power, types and allocation of, 39–40.
    See also Status/power differentials
Powers-Costello, E., 29, 34, 68, 74
Prenovost, M., 28
Preschoolers
    approach to natural world, 124
    caring and empathy in, 52

Preschoolers *(continued)*
   with disabilities, social
      participation of, 158–160
   understanding of cultural differences, 117
Preston, J., 115, 116, 135
Price-Dennis, D., 32
Problem-solving, 11, 25
Pulido-Tobiassen, D., 19
Pull-out programs, 155–156

Questions
   individual, turning into group
      discussions, 60
   reflective. *See* Reflection/
      Reflective questions
Quiche (Mayan) Indians, 8
Quintana, S. M., 77

Raabe, T., 28, 77
Race, 5. *See also* Skin color
   children's friendship preferences
      and, 78–79
   children's response to, 73–83
   in learning context, 65–83. *See also*
      Racial identity development;
      Racism, in U.S.
   meanings of, 4–5
   reflections on, 65
Racial advantage/disadvantage, 66–68
Racial discrimination, 67
Racial divisions/groups, 5
   children's views on, 76–83
   labeling of, 13
Racial identity development
   biracial/multiracial people, 71–73
   in children, 75–76
   in people of color, 70–71
   in Whites, 69–70
Racial knowledge, of children, 74–75
Racial privilege, of Whites, 68
Racism, in U.S., 5, 66–73
   Critical Race Theory and, 66–67
   debilitating effect of, 67–68
   historical background, 66
   material impact of, 67
   persistence of, 67
Radke, M., 75
Radlinski, S. H., 155, 157, 160
Ramirez, D. A., 66
Ramsey, P. G., 8, 54, 68, 69, 70, 72, 74,
   75, 76, 77, 78, 79, 95, 96, 117, 137
Rath, W. R., 89
Reading widely, 19

Recchia, S. L., 157
Reconceptualizing early childhood
   movement, 23–24
Reflection/Reflective questions
   on abilities and disabilities, 152–153
   on consumerism, 97–98
   on cultural affiliations, 109
   on cultural influences, 107–108
   on economic class, 84–86
   on gender identification and
      roles, 132–133
   on natural environment, 120–122
   on race, 65
   on sexual identity and orientation, 97–98
Riojas-Cortez, M., 110
Risks, in multicultural teaching/work, 10
Ritchie, J., 23, 122, 128
Ritchie, S., 51
Rituals
   classroom, 59–60
   culture and, 107, 108
   family, 92–93, 108, 118
Robinson, K., 10, 138
Robottom, I., 126
Rodríguez, P., 76, 77
Rodriguez, R., 75
Roediger, D., 66
Rohde, B., 157, 160, 164
Roopnarine, J. L., 110
Root, M. P. P., 72
Rosenow, N., 125, 128
Routines, classroom, 59–60
Rowan, M., 113
Rowan, M. C., 35
Ruble, D., 135, 137
Ruble, D. N., 136, 137
Ruck, M., 28
Rugg, M., 43, 44
Rules and procedures, children's
   involvement in developing, 58–59
Running-Grass., 7
Rusli, E., 156
Russell, K., 155
Rutland, A., 28
Ryan, R. H., 94
Ryan, S., 24, 141, 142
Ryan, S. D., 71, 72

Sacks, M., 110
Sadker, D., 135
Sadker, M., 135
Saliency, of group attributes, 27, 28
Salisbury, C. L., 163, 164

Saltmarsh, S., 100
Same-sex parents, children's
    understanding of, 144–145
Sánchez-Medina, J. A., 110
Sandall, S., 157, 158, 159
Sandall, S. R., 158, 159
Saterlee, D. J., 128
Scaffolding, problem-solving levels and, 25
Schaffer, M., 57
Scholl, L., 69, 108
School readiness, 9
Schools
    centers of care in, 38
    complementary role with family, 12
    and home, cultural discontinuities
        between, 111–116
    inclusion of children with
        disabilities in, 38
Schoorman, D., 42
Schor, J., 99, 100
Schultz, S. B., 141, 142, 143, 144, 145
Schussler, D. L., 18
Schutz, R., 93
Schwall, C., 45
Schwartz, I. S., 155, 160
Schwartz, N. D., 86
Seele, C., 116, 117
Segura-Mora, A., 75
Self-referenced empathy, babies
    and infants, 51–52
Sensoy, Ö., 10
Servos, J. E., 18
Sexual identity, 5. See also Gender
    children's understanding of, 144–145
    discussion anxieties, overcoming, 142–143
    gender roles and, 138
    language used for, 13
    reflection on, 139–140
Sexual orientation, 5–6, 7
    children's understanding of, 144–151
    discussion anxieties, overcoming, 142–143
    language used for, 13–14
    reflection on, 139–140
Shah, A., 99, 100, 102
Sharkins, K., 31, 32
Sheridan, M. K., 155, 157, 160
Sherman, F., 78
Shin, S. Y., 72
Shin, Y. L., 110
Shrout, P. E., 136
Silin, J. G., 23, 25, 43
Silverman, K., 159, 163
Silverstein, S., 35

Simmons, D. A., 128
Singleton, L. C., 78
Sinicrope, P., 57
Skattebol, J., 22, 142, 148
Skelton, R., 7
Skin color
    awareness by children, 73–74
    children's identification by, 75–76
    labeling of, language used for, 13
Skinner, C., 87
Skott-Myrhe, K., 5
Slavin, R. E., 56
Sleeter, C. E., 6, 68, 69
Smalling, S., 141, 142
Smith, S., 99
Smith, S. C., 93
Smith, S. L., 71, 72
Snack time, in schools, U.S. procedure
    vs. Maori tradition, 23
Social acceptance, of children
    with disabilities in, 159
Social action, critical thinking and, 58–61
Social change
    children as activists for, 58–61
    group identities and, 6
Social class. See also Economic class(es)
    children's views on, 95, 97
Social development/process
    children's learning as, 25
    in early childhood programs, 51
Social divisions, in classroom,
    strategies to reduce, 55–56
Social goals, early childhood, 51
Social inclusion/isolation, of children
    with disabilities, 157–162
    facilitating inclusion, 160–162
    isolation, 159
Social justice/injustice, xiii
    media vs., xiii
    multiculturalism and, 8
Social media
    for parent-teacher communication,
        42–43
    potential benefits of, 32–33
Social styles/preferences, of children, 54
Socialization. See Social development/process
Society, reorientation challenges
    in, 6, xiii–xiv
Socioeconomic divisions, in U.S.
    See Economic class(es)
Soukakou, E., 155–156
Souto-Manning, M., 32, 44, 114,
    143, 147

Space
    classroom, design of. *See* Design
        of classroom space
    for conversational opportunity,
        making, 61
Sparks, P., 123
Spencer, M. B., 22, 76
Sperb, T., 109, 110, 116
Stacey, S., 157, 160
Staff relationships, 40–42
Stalker, K., 156, 160, 163
Starhawk., 39
Status/power differentials, 5, 14
    parent-teacher communication and, 43–44
    within school environment, 41
Stępska, A., 125
Stereotypes/Stereotyping
    children engaging in, 95–96
    gender, 137
    out-group, 28–29
    photographs challenging, 31
Stipek, D. J., 94
Stoneman, Z., 43, 44
Stooksberry, L. M., 18
Stores, M., 110
Stott, F., 24
Stott, F. M., 22
Strawn, C., 135
Stronge, J. H., 89
Suggate, J., 124
Summerlin, J., 31, 32
Supportive group discussions,
    guidelines for, 19–20
Sustainability, 123
    children's understanding of, 126
    fostering awareness of, 128–131
Sutfin, E. L., 135
Swadener, E. B., 159, 160
Swick, K., 44

Tajfel, H., 76
Tamis-LeMonda, C. S., 136
Tatum, B. D., 19, 66, 69, 77
Taylor, A., 134, 138, 139, 143, 148, 164
Taylor, H., 160
Teacher-child relationship, 12
Teaching styles, authoritarian
    vs.democratic, 93–94
Teixeira, R. A., 78
Tenery, M. F., 94
Terry, J., 32
Test preparation, emphasis on, 9

Tharp, R. G., 114, 116
Theokas, C., 138
Thompson, A., 38
Thorne, B., 137, 138
Thornton, C., 156
Time, linear vs. cyclical, 122
Tobin, J., 113
Tobin, J. J., 43, 112
Tomelleri, S., 78
Tornabene, L., 125
Toys, 33–34, 100–101
Traditions. *See* Rituals
Trager, H. G., 75
Transgendered people. *See* GBLT youth
Trautner, H. M., 137
Trenka, J. J., 72
Trepanier-Street, M., 159, 163
Tropp, L., 28
Trudgett, M., 115, 116
Trueba, H., 115
Tu, H., 159, 162
Tudge, J., 108, 109, 110, 116
Tymon, D., 156

Underwood, K., 156
UNESCO, 156
United States, race/racism in, 5
Upper-middle class families, ethnographic
    study findings, 91–94
Upward mobility, myth of, 85–86, 93
Urberg, K. A., 78

Valdés, G., 115
Values, reflected in children's literature, 35
Van Ausdale, D., 76, 77, 79
Vázquez García, H., 22
Volk, D., 110
Vorrasi, J. A., 99
Voss, J. A., 156
Vygotsky, L. S., 25

Walford, R. A., 126
Walker, S., 156, 157, 159, 160
Wals, A. E. J., 125
Wardle, F., 72
Wasik, B. H., 22
Weil, A. M., 116
Welles-Nystrom, B., 110
Wells, J., 116
Wells, R., 128
West, C., 99
Whiren, A., 157, 160, 164

Whites/Whiteness, 13
  racial identity development
    stages, 69–70, 76
Whiting, B. B., 110, 135
Whiting, J. W. M., 110
Wight, V. R., 67
Williams, J. E., 77
Williams, L. R., 8, 77, 95, 96, 110
Wilson, R. A., 128
Wimbarti, S., 110
Winter, J., 35
Wise, T., 67
Wolfberg, P., 158, 159
Wong-Filmore, L., 112
Working-class families, ethnographic
  study findings, 89–91, 92–94

World views, children's
  construction of, 3–4
  contexts informing, 20–37
Wu, D. Y., 43
Wubie, B., 116

Yang, C., 156

Zaretsky, L., 154, 156
Zayas, L. H., 110
Zeece, P. D., 128
Zercher, C., 157, 158, 159
Zittleman, K., 135
Zogmaister, C., 78
Zone of proximal development, 25–26
Zosuls, K. M., 136

About the Author

Patricia G. Ramsey is professor of psychology and education at Mount Holyoke College. She has studied young children's understanding of race and social class and has written several articles and books on multicultural education for young children. She is coauthor *What If All the Kids Are White? Anti-Bias Multicultural Education with Young Children and Their Families.*